The Politics of Knowledg

Revell
2018

Routledge Research in Education

For a full list of titles in this series please visit www.routledge.com

44 Citizenship, Education and Social Conflict
Israeli Political Education in Global Perspective
Edited by Hanan A. Alexander, Halleli Pinson and Yossi Yonah

45 Emerging Teachers and Globalisation
Gerry Czerniawski

46 Social Studies as New Literacies in a Global Society
Relational Cosmopolitanism in the Classroom
Mark Baildon and James S. Damico

47 Education Policy, Space and the City
Markets and the (In)visibility of Race
Kalervo N. Gulson

48 Memory and Pedagogy
Edited by Claudia Mitchell, Teresa Strong-Wilson, Kathleen Pithouse and Susann Allnutt

49 Universities and Global Diversity
Preparing Educators for Tomorrow
Edited by Beverly Lindsay and Wanda J. Blanchett

50 Equity and Excellence in Education
Towards Maximal Learning Opportunities for All Students
Edited by Kris Van den Branden, Piet Van Avermaet and Mieke Van Houtte

51 Global Pathways to Abolishing Physical Punishment
Realizing Children's Rights
Edited by Joan E. Durrant and Anne B. Smith

52 From Testing to Productive Student Learning
Implementing Formative Assessment in Confucian-Heritage Settings
David Carless

53 Changing Schools in an Era of Globalization
Edited by John C. K. Lee and Brian J. Caldwell

54 Boys and Their Schooling
The Experience of Becoming Someone Else
John Whelen

55 Education and Sustainability
Learning Across the Diaspora, Indigenous, and Minority Divide
Seonaigh MacPherson

56 International Case Studies of Dyslexia
Edited by Peggy L. Anderson and Regine Meier-Hedde

57 Schooling and the Making of Citizens in the Long Nineteenth Century
Comparative Visions
Edited by Daniel Tröhler, Thomas S. Popkewitz and David F. Labaree

58 **Islamic Education and Indoctrination**
The Case in Indonesia
Charlene Tan

59 **Beyond Binaries in Education Research**
Edited by Warren Midgley, Mark A. Tyler, Patrick Alan Danaher and Alison Mander

60 **Picturebooks, Pedagogy and Philosophy**
Joanna Haynes and Karin Murris

61 **Personal Epistemology and Teacher Education**
Edited by Jo Brownlee, Gregory Schraw and Donna Berthelsen

62 **Teacher Learning that Matters**
International Perspectives
Edited by Mary Kooy and Klaas van Veen

63 **Pedagogy of Multiliteracies**
Rewriting *Goldilocks*
Heather Lotherington

64 **Intersectionality and "Race" in Education**
Edited by Kalwant Bhopal and John Preston

65 **The Politics of Education**
Challenging Multiculturalism
Edited by Christos Kassimeris and Marios Vryonides

66 **Whiteness and Teacher Education**
Edie White

67 **Multidisciplinary Approaches to Educational Research**
Case Studies from Europe and the Developing World
Edited by Sadaf Rizvi

68 **Postcolonial Perspectives on Global Citizenship Education**
Edited by Vanessa de Oliveira Andreotti and Lynn Mario T. M. De Souza

69 **Education in the Black Diaspora**
Perspectives, Challenges, and Prospects
Edited by Kassie Freeman and Ethan Johnson

70 **Gender, Race, and the Politics of Role Modelling**
The Influence of Male Teachers
Wayne Martino and Goli Rezai-Rashti

71 **Educating for Diversity and Social Justice**
Amanda Keddie

72 **Considering Trilingual Education**
Kathryn Henn-Reinke

73 **Commitment, Character, and Citizenship**
Religious Education in Liberal Democracy
Edited by Hanan A. Alexander and Ayman K. Agbaria

74 **Adolescent Literacies in a Multicultural Context**
Edited by Alister Cumming

75 **Participation, Facilitation, and Mediation**
Children and Young People in Their Social Contexts
Edited by Claudio Baraldi and Vittorio Iervese

76 **The Politics of Knowledge in Education**
Elizabeth Rata

The Politics of Knowledge in Education

Elizabeth Rata

Routledge
Taylor & Francis Group
NEW YORK LONDON

First published 2012
by Routledge
711 Third Avenue, New York, NY 10017

Simultaneously published in the UK
by Routledge
2 Park Square, Milton Park, Abingdon, Oxon OX14 4RN

Routledge is an imprint of the Taylor & Francis Group, an informa business

First issued in paperback 2013

Library of Congress Cataloging-in-Publication Data

Rata, Elizabeth, 1952–
The politics of knowledge in education / Elizabeth Rata.
p. cm. — (Routledge research in education ; 76)
Includes bibliographical references and index.
1. Critical pedagogy. 2. Knowledge, Theory of—Political aspects. 3. Postmodernism and education. I. Title.
LC196.R38 2012
370.11'5—dc23
2011048809

ISBN13: 978-0-415-51749-2 (hbk)
ISBN13: 978-0-203-11711-8 (ebk)
ISBN13: 978-0-415-85141-1 (pbk)

Typeset in Sabon
by IBT Global.

To my sons
Maia and Te Rata

Contents

Preface

This book has been many years in the making. It explains the "emptying out" of knowledge in the school curriculum as the outcome of localised politics and argues for a re-commitment to academic knowledge. Some of the ideas first appeared in a small monograph I wrote in 2002, others have emerged through my research over the years. They have been distilled in numerous conversations with colleagues who became friends in the process. Conversations with Chris Tremewan for well over a decade have been treasured. Similarly Jonathan Friedman's encouragement since the late 1990s has enabled me to continue writing during times when it has not been easy. His ideas have been a major influence on my work. I am indebted to both.

Although my acquaintance with Michael Young is more recent, his writings have also been inspirational and his advice hugely beneficial. I am deeply grateful not only for his encouragement of my own work but for his involvement with the Knowledge and Education Research Unit (KERU), which I direct. This Unit is a hub of intellectual activity for a number of my colleagues and doctoral students. Our sessions and conversations have contributed to this book. In particular I wish to thank Megan Lourie and Graham McPhail for reading a draft and providing insightful comments and acknowledge Robert Nola's helpful advice with some of the ideas that became chapter 5. Paul Callister's research has been an invaluable source of material that I have drawn on over the years. The support of Roger Openshaw, as a research collaborator in several research projects including our two edited books, has been greatly appreciated. Likewise my colleagues in the University Reform Globalisation and Europeanisation Research Project at Aarhus, Auckland and Bristol Universities have provided valued opportunities for discussion. Correspondence with Peter Munz and Roy Nash prior to their deaths enabled me to put my ideas to the test as their challenges stimulated deeper inquiry. I was honoured by their interest in my research. The contact is sadly missed. I would also like to thank Hugh Lauder for introducing me to the writings of Imre Lakatos.

It is difficult to say precisely what ideas came from whom to find their way into my understanding. Apart from Jonathan Friedman, Michael Young, Rob Moore, Johan Muller, and Alan Macfarlane, whose intellectual influences appear throughout the book, years of reading and writing, conversation, presenting my ideas, and listening to others at conferences and seminars, combined with the influence of the colleagues I mention above, have all contributed in some way to the argument that I present here. This argument is that the commitment to academic knowledge in democratic nations has been damaged by the forces of localisation. The objective knowledge which should be taught to all students because it takes them *beyond* their experience is replaced by knowledge based *in* experience.

The book explains the causes and consequences for democracy's future. The fundamental change to the curriculum is not something that parents only should be worried about. We have allowed the importance of academic knowledge and of teachers with that knowledge to be diluted. There is a general unease about this. Parents mutter that something is seriously wrong. Media commentators regularly rage against a "lowering of standards" and point the finger of blame at a wide range of culprits. Others, such as Sebastion Faulks in his novel, *A Week in December* (2009), go straight for the jugular, saying that 'we chose to know less'. Faulks's character, Gabriel the lawyer, tells the story of what has happened to knowledge. He 'was lucky enough to be educated at a time when teachers still thought children could handle knowledge. . . . Then teachers withheld knowledge. I suppose the next lot of teachers didn't have the knowledge to withhold. Now knowledge has been abandoned as a goal. We chose to know less' (pp. 305–306).

A similar despair and incredulity at what we have done to the knowledge that empowered the fortunate generation to which I belong is the motivation for this book. However the argument must stand or fall on its own merits. It must be independent of who I am, how I feel, and what I believe. My argument must depends upon its own logic, not on how committed I am to its premise. That approach which separates the "text" from the "context", or the argument from the author, is consistent with my claim that there is knowledge that can be known objectively by people in different times and different places from the time and place of the knowledge creator. In other words—there is such a thing as universal objective knowledge. This is the knowledge of the sciences, arts, humanities, and social sciences. It is the academic knowledge that should be taught in schools to all young people. But as Gabriel the lawyer recognised, it is the knowledge that we no longer value sufficiently to ensure that it is taught to all children. What I say in several of the chapters about the inconsistency towards content knowledge in the New Zealand curriculum is also the case with other countries affected by the forces of localisation. The tendency to replace academic knowledge for the localised social knowledge of experience is also found in the curricula of England, Scotland, and South Africa.

The shift away from valuing academic knowledge has not come from nowhere. My purpose is to explain the political and economic forces behind the shift. I argue that the social knowledge of experience supports the localised politics of the disempowered worker and the de-politicised consumer in a world that has replaced the democratic commitment to decreasing inequality with a global market that creates greater inequalities.

Globalisation has trumped universalism. The subversive nature of academic knowledge is dangerous for the new conservativism of market politics because it frees people from local confines by disturbing their common-sense understanding of the world. It provides the means for doubt, criticism, and judgement—intellectual tools that change individuals and change the world. Such powerful knowledge from the arts, humanities, social science, and sciences is essential for the type of thinking needed for a re-commitment to democracy. In order to restore academic knowledge to its rightful place in the curriculum, teachers must know their subjects well and have the ability to explain concepts and principles by drawing on the best content of those subjects. This book is a contribution to restoring academic knowledge as the purpose of schooling. It is the result of many influences, but its faults are my own.

Elizabeth Rata
Auckland
September 2011

Foreword

Of the many curious political strategies in global politics early in the twenty-first century, one merits special comment: the conscious choice of a symbolic politics that hampers the advancement and progress of individuals from disadvantaged groups rather than one that will see them prosper. This symbolic politics, a politics of cultural localism, particularly as practised in New Zealand, is the central focus of this timely and forthright book.

The central tenet of culturalist politics is to insist on the 'profound difference at the Self-Other border' (see chapter 9 in this book); that is, to base the politics on the irreducibility of difference. This tenet has become commonplace in culturally sensitive policies the world over, but there have been troubling precedents. Throughout the history of Western colonialism, culturalism of a certain kind has been the politics of choice, especially for the British, who with Lord Lugard refined 'divide and rule' policies to a nicety, co-opting local elites and cultural traditions, and governing with an iron fist in a velvet glove of limited self-rule. This is one thing in a culturally homogeneous developing country, but culturalist policies in a heterogeneous modern polity create an unbridgeable gulf in the demos, between citizens who enjoy full democratic rights and subjects who are placed under the double yoke of tradition and disadvantage. Such dual systems cultivate monumental resentment and always end badly, a fate Mahmood Mamdani shows for the Hutus and the Tutsis in contemporary Rwanda, for instance.

But there is more to the story, as Elizabeth Rata shows. We are not dealing with a crude ideological ruse, which would not work for very long. To understand what is at stake, one must also confront the fatal attractions of a politics of autonomy and identity in a fragmenting world, the deep hunger for familiarity and belonging in the burgeoning networks of cosmopolitan homelessness, a politics of symbolically anchored goods that cannot be alienated.

History tends to simplify these things. Take the historically recent case of apartheid and Bantu Education in South Africa. The architect of Bantu Education, one Dr William Eiselen, was an anthropologist and linguist of African languages. Son of Berlin Missionary Society parents, Eiselen rejected scientific racism. The principal scourge of traditional communities, he thought, lay in the symbolic abrasions inflicted by 'white (Western) civilisation', and responsible rule demanded protections from them. Otherwise put, unless positive measures were taken to ring fence traditional languages, cultures, and traditions, they would succumb to the homogenising forces of modernity. The policy of Bantu Education was crafted to do just that.

This sort of argument held and holds powerful attractions not only for anthropologists such as Eiselen and Levi-Strauss, who took the same view regarding the Nambikwara of Brazil, but crucially for traditional elites as well. The main philosophical wellsprings of culturalism after Rousseau are to be found in the nineteenth-century German romantic tradition; Herder, Hammann, and Fichte are among the best known neo-Kantians who first spelt out the cultural logic of this view. But a remorseless dialectical *realpolitik* soon put paid to the lighter, sentimental side of German idealism—cultural belonging and self-determination—and it was swallowed up by a darker side, *blut und boden* racial supremacy and the death camps. Eiselen's 'positive' apartheid in similar fashion was swallowed up by Verwoerd's separate development.

A partial grasp of this dualism remains one of the better reasons for the contemporary revolt against the Enlightenment. But its simplistic Manichaeism will not do. When the light swings to the dark, as it will, it is always the disadvantaged and dispossessed that bear the brunt. Elizabeth Rata's solution, the modernist and realist one, is to provide them with the only tool that can be relied upon to provide autonomy, innovativeness and independence of thought and action—what Michael Young calls 'powerful knowledge'. Yet this is the tool which, by a cruel twist of fate, is systematically denied to the disadvantaged by the cultural politics of localism.

This denialism follows from the logic of cultural localism. If all cultures are local, and all cultures can only be inhabited and fully understood by locals, then it follows that all forms of knowledge, a sub-set of culture, are local and are similarly tethered to the concerns and interests of some locals rather than others. Since interests differ with locality, knowledges and cultures are bound to be antagonistic, and other knowledges and cultures should be resisted lest they undermine and colonise your treasured local symbolic goods. History then becomes a succession of more or less successful struggles against colonisation, and one only affirms one's place in history by taking up the struggle.

This form of struggle politics is undeniably heroic. It is also self-defeating when it takes root in the education policies of a nation. Conceptually powerful knowledge is assigned to an other local, its people and interests—usually to 'the West'—in a foundational act of self-dispossession that fatally conflates the tools of mastery with the tools of the master, powerful knowledge with the knowledge of the powerful in Michael Young's apt phrase. There is an alternative tradition of radical cultural politics, one stemming from the work of Italian Marxist Antonio Gramsci, which is strangely out of fashion today. Gramsci was acutely alive to the canny and subversive potential of local traditions and wisdom, as were Rabelais and Bakhtin before him, but he was also unusually aware of the straightjacket that local commonsense can be. Without discounting the valuable resource potential that local knowledges could provide, Gramsci also thought that to reach its true potential, local 'commonsense' should be re-fashioned into 'good sense' by means of the conceptually boosted powerful knowledges of modernity, particularly literacy, mathematics, and the sciences. The institution that should do this was the 'common school', an institution that should teach a common curriculum to all children, so that each might have access to the powerful tools of modern de-contextualised knowledge. It was for this revolutionary proposal, amongst others, that the Italian state jailed him for the rest of his short life.

Contemporary cultural politics eschews the Gramscian route because the cultural logic it follows demonises modern scientific knowledge as knowledge of the forces of colonisation, that is, as intrinsically contextual. Elizabeth Rata shows persuasively that this confuses historical origins with epistemological status. Powerful conceptual knowledge cannot be the birthright of any local people because its epistemological status stands or falls by its universality. It is only by virtue of this status that conceptual knowledge can be a tool for projecting entirely novel possibilities hitherto unthought of. And it is this capacity that cultural politics refuses for the next generation when it insists on local rather than universal knowledge in the school curriculum.

Along with the rest of the rugby-loving world, I was privileged to watch the recent rugby World Cup so successfully hosted by New Zealand. Along with millions of others, I thrilled to the grunt and grind, the dash and inventiveness, the opening and closing ceremonies that stirred the atavistic soul to a pride long pushed to the margins by the routines of daily life. Watching the fearsome haka in its intricate variations performed by the three nations, I considered and then rejected the thought that this noble ritual had been commodified and commercialised for the consumption of the jaded global television lumpen cultural proletariat. It struck me as they performed this ritual, simultaneously for the opposing 'enemy' team and for the watching world, that this was a way of announcing that this team might be participating in a global game with global rules, but they were doing it on their own terms; a claim to the universal, but on local terms. It was heroic and stirring, and it seemed to me and many of my rugby-loving countrymen that it was only just that the All Blacks lifted the Webb Ellis trophy. But the reason they won was not principally due to the haka. It was because of superior tactics, superior fitness, and a training regimen that had more to do with science than with local knowledge. This is the message this book drives home.

Johan Muller
University of Cape Town
Cape Town November 2011

1 The Politics of Knowledge

There is a type of knowledge that should be created in universities and taught in schools and to all students regardless of race, religion, and culture. That knowledge—variously known as academic, disciplinary, epistemic, erudite, scientific, esoteric, rational, abstract, and objective—is the disciplinary knowledge of the sciences, arts, humanities, and social sciences. This book is about why academic knowledge matters and why it has lost its privileged place in the social sciences and in the school curriculum. That place now goes to another type of knowledge—social knowledge. This also has a number of terms—doxa, culture, beliefs, everyday knowledge, common sense, tacit knowledge, and folk knowledge. Disciplinary knowledge and social knowledge are both important—each for its own purpose. Social knowledge comes from an individual's experience within a socio-cultural group. It is the beliefs, values, and practices that reinforce an individual's identification with the group and ensure the group's cohesion. Disciplinary knowledge, on the other hand, disturbs that commonsense understanding of the world. It provides the means for doubt, criticism, and judgement—intellectual tools that change individuals and change the world.

Modernity recognises the two types of knowledge as distinct. Social knowledge is the domain of the family, the church, the community—all the various institutions where young people are socialised. Disciplinary knowledge, on the other hand, is the knowledge produced in universities and reproduced in schools. It takes young people out of the localised world of the family and community by providing the means societies use to transcend the limits of individual experience. Leesa Wheelahan, in the tradition of Basil Bernstein, explains how esoteric knowledge enables us 'to see beyond appearances to the real nature of relations in the natural and social world. All societies need to connect the material and immaterial, the known and unknown, the thinkable and unthinkable, the here and the not here, the specific and the general, and the past, present and future' (2010a, p. 95).

Since the 1970s the demarcation between social knowledge and disciplinary knowledge has been eroded with profound consequences for education. What young people are taught in school (the curriculum) and how that knowledge is taught (pedagogy) has changed in significant ways. This book explains the politics of knowledge that have led to such changes within the classrooms of democratic nations. I trace them to a more fundamental breakdown—the breakdown of the commitment to universalism that informed the rise of democracy in the modern period. That breakdown itself is a casualty of political and economic processes that have reversed the trend towards progressive democracy for the globalised politics of the market that favour the rise of conservative, even reactionary, forces. The contraction of the world economy since the 1970s has reduced the size and power of the working class and enfeebled the progressivism of the liberal middle class. The implications for democracy are profound. Localised corporate elites—often using justifying religious, cultural, or ethnic claims—lead the shift to conservatism and increasing inequality.

The "cultural turn" in world politics—a turn away from universalism to localised forms of identity based on ethnicity, culture, and religion—characterises this era of globalisation. It affects the production and reproduction of knowledge in profound ways. The belief that there is universal knowledge which should be taught to all students—a belief with its origins in the Enlightenment—has lost its influence in the social sciences with education particularly affected by the loss of confidence in a universalist ethos. Two anti-universalist ideologies, constructivism and culturalism, have gained an influence that permeates what is taught and how it is taught. The first ideology is the belief that knowledge is "constructed" from experience and that knowledge of one's world is tied to experience of that world. This pedagogical approach has seen teachers turn from their role as the transmitters of knowledge that their pupils don't yet know to "facilitators" in constructing knowledge drawn from their pupils' experiences—the knowledge already known to those pupils.

Culturalism is the ideology of a politicised category of people classified according to a shared history and "race". The emphasis is on the group's "culture" as a political as well as a social category. A person's experience as a member of that culture is regarded as the basis of knowledge. Both constructivism and culturalism reject the main idea of modernity—the universal reasoning subject. Instead those views promote the idea of the "constructed" subject of a distinctive cultural group, each with its own common ethno-national, cultural, or religious heritage. The values and practices of the particular or localised group are considered to be essential to the group's survival and embedded into each person's social "DNA". As significant as the belief in an essential and determining "culture" is the commitment to the idea that, because each group is fundamentally different, its political interests are also different. The various forms of cultural politics—monoculturalism, bi-culturalism, and multiculturalism—all have the same premise: that politics should start by recognising society as consisting of separate cultural groups with different interests.

In the case of monoculturalism the belief is that all other groups should assimilate into, or be subject to, the society of the dominant group. Saudi Arabia is one type of this extreme monocultural political system, whereas the fascist ideologies found for example amongst extremists in the United Kingdom, the United States, and Germany are another. Monoculturalism is a commitment to the dominance of one cultural group within any given society. What may seem surprising is the closeness between monoculturalism and multiculturalism, two types of cultural politics that are usually placed in opposition to each other. Despite the proclaimed progressive nature of pluralist politics, as with biculturalism in New Zealand and multiculturalism in a number of European nations, these are also types of culturalism—both operating from the same premise as monoculturalism.

That premise contains two inter-related ideas. One is that culture determines peoples' lives, and the other is the primacy awarded to the ancestral origins of the cultural group. These beliefs ultimately sabotage the progressive ideas behind multiculturalism because it is simply not possible to build a progressive politics when the criteria for belonging to the group is fixed in the past and when the group, not the individual, is the political unit. Genetic descent produces a racial ideology and the concept of the group as the political unit has the potential to deny political rights to the most vulnerable within the unit. Group political rights, where all members are assumed to share the same political interests, ones represented by the group's leaders, are always open to authoritarianism. The leaders who represent the group, whether as the "party" or the "people" or the "patriarch", may or may not be benevolent—that is a matter of chance. In contrast, the liberal commitment to the individual as the bearer of political rights contains within it the potential for individuals to exercise authority on their own behalf.

Since the 1970s culturalism and constructivism have influenced politics in profound ways. These ideologies changed the social sciences, in particular educational studies, just as profoundly. However the confusion between "globalisation" and "universalism" meant that those changes have been misunderstood, with globalisation being seen as a type of technologically informed universalism rather than a system of global market regulation. Although technology gives the impression that the world is united as never before, globalisation is a false "universalism". It does not refer to modernity's universal reasoning subject—the revolutionary idea of the Enlightenment. Globalisation is the all-encompassing power of the market. It includes the financial markets that control peoples' lives in unseen ways and the consumerism that turns us into products of globalisation at a personal level. Jonathan Friedman (2002) refers to 'the global [as] the true reality behind the local' (p. 37), an understanding of the interaction that is captured in the concept of the "glocal" (Robertson, 1992).

With globalisation, the universalist ideal of the common humanity of individuals who share the same capacity for reason and understanding with claims for equal rights arising from the shared humanity—this Enlightenment universalism—is replaced by the logic of the global market. Equality is measured by the market with people compared in terms of their ability to produce and consume. The ideal of a shared common humanity and the importance of the moral and aesthetic dimensions of life in regulating the destructive tendencies of the economic are replaced by an emphasis on localised difference and by economic instrumentalism. Moreover the localised difference tends to contain a racialised character; one created in the past so that cultural, religious, and ethnic differences are fixed and immutable.

The Enlightenment belief in universal science and reason is dismissed by constructivists and culturalists (often the same educationalists, social scientists, and officials) as just another cultural story. Within such relativism, the demarcation between the erudite knowledge of the disciplines and the social knowledge of cultural groups could not survive. The ideas, principles, concepts, and content developed in the disciplines of the arts, sciences, social sciences, and humanities according to procedures of scrutiny and critique that justify the disciplinary content are dismissed as ideology. They are seen as the imposition of ideas by a science that serves the West and the interests of capitalist exploitation rather than a universal science with the potential to serve humanity. In addition the demarcation between social knowledge and academic knowledge is itself regarded as contributing to the split between mental and manual labour and the growing power of the professional intellectual classes (Muller, 2000). It was within this context that intellectuals rejected the commitment to a fundamental difference between objective scientific knowledge and subjective social knowledge. Instead disciplinary knowledge is understood as a view of the world framed by the experiences of the social group to which the intellectual belonged and in that group's own interests. In other words, disciplinary knowledge is to be considered as no different from social knowledge.

This book is about why this happened. "Why did the commitment to universal science and the Enlightenment's "faith in reason" give way to the pre-modern belief in a localised socio-cultural determinism? My explanation of the politics of knowledge that has seen social constructivism and culturalism become the orthodox view amongst educationalists begins with the premise that there is a difference between disciplinary knowledge and social knowledge (Rata, 2012). This demarcation is of crucial importance for knowledge production and for how that knowledge is re-contextualised to be taught in schools. By insisting on a demarcation between epistemic knowledge (science in its broadest sense as the knowledge of all the disciplines) and social knowledge (culture) and by also arguing for the universal nature of science, I do not ignore the problem this causes sociologists of knowledge.

Imre Lakatos (1980/1995) put the issue clearly in his question; 'what distinguishes knowledge from superstition, ideology or pseudo-science?' (p. 1). For educationalists a more immediate question is what happens when the demarcation is not made? What are young people taught when science is considered to be no different from the cultural and religious beliefs of any given social group? There are numerous examples of this today. In some South African schools the science of electricity is taught alongside beliefs in the gods of lightning. A similar source is given for electricity in the mythology of the "earth mother" in New Zealand. Mathematics is made cultural in the various types of ethno-maths exemplified by Maori maths and African maths. Those committed to a radical feminist epistemology teach that there are gendered "ways of thinking", while in the United States creationists claim scientific status for their religious beliefs.

The problem here is not the beliefs themselves. Beliefs have a value for those who adhere to them. The real problem is the positioning of unexamined belief alongside examined science—the juxtapositioning of ideas that are taken "on faith" and ideas that remain open to doubt and criticism. It confuses the role of knowledge in the socialisation of children into their communities with the role of knowledge at school. As Michael Young argues 'schools are places where the world is treated as an *object of thought* and not as a *place of experience*. Subjects are the tools that teachers have for helping pupils make this step from experience to what the Russian psychologist Vygotsky referred to as the "higher forms of thought"' (Young, 2010a, p. 25).

Although the conflation of scientific knowledge and social knowledge is a major issue for sociologists of knowledge, it is accompanied by another issue at least as serious. This is the accusation that universal science is merely the ideology of the dominant group. What happens when science is considered to be always ideological—always in the interests of the scientists or the society within which the scientist has status and authority? How can science retain any intellectual values if it is considered to be always and necessarily ideological? To make the claim for disinterested disciplinary knowledge, for a universal science as I do, is not to say that science is not sometimes used for ideological purposes. Nor does the claim to a universal science ignore the existence of bad or inadequate science. The racial theories used in eugenics and anthropology in the late nineteenth and early twentieth centuries were "bad science". Those theories were also science used for ideological purposes, although not always by the scientists pursuing that research.

The contemporary version of fundamental racial and cultural difference promoted by constructivists and culturalists is either inadequate science or ideology or both. According to these views, people of different ethnicities, races, religions, and cultures are also different in their understanding of the world—in their "knowledges", "ways of knowing", and "world views". This is undoubtedly true for social knowledge, but the problem arises when all knowledge is understood to be social knowledge but is then accorded scientific status. The inclusion of indigenous, ethnic, gendered, and religious "knowledges" (also referred to as epistemologies and methodologies) in a number of universities leads to this conflation of status. At that point there is no difference between science and culture, no difference between disciplinary knowledge and social knowledge, no difference between science and ideology—yet the latter has the authority of science. But it avoids the constant scrutiny to which science is subjected—a scrutiny that earns it the status of science.

In contrast to the constructivist and culturalist educator I take the position that there is a type of knowledge that is universal and different from social knowledge. However as Rob Moore (2007a) points out, finding and justifying the demarcation was and remains a contested area. For realists, science is constituted according to its own procedures, systems, principles, and codes (Kant, 1781/1993; Durkheim, 1983; Popper, 1972; Lakatos, 1980/1995; Munz, 1985; Moore and Muller, 1999; Muller, 2000; Moore and Young, 2001, 2010). As a consequence of these procedures, science has its own internal authority—the authority of systems that allow for scrutiny and criticism. Those procedures may not stop bad science from happening. Lakatos (1980/1995) reminds us that pseudoscience research programmes may be stubbornly defended within a scientific community. This is the case with research in New Zealand that uses an indigenous epistemology—not only is such research defended but it is actively promoted as a progressive research programme. Indeed if 'the number, faith and vocal energy of its supporters' (Lakatos, 1980/1995, p. 10) are the means to judge the theoretical validity of indigenous knowledges, then these culturally based knowledges would pass the science test, as would creationism with its own energetic and loud proponents.

More is required than approval, however loud and however esteemed those approving voices may be for social knowledge to pass the test of science. Disciplinary knowledge must meet the following interdependent criteria: First, the authority for producing, scrutinising, testing, and criticising knowledge claims should be independent of the cleric, the priest, the chief, the politician, the wealthy individual, and the scientist. The conditions for the critical procedures are developed over time as constitutive parts of the discipline itself. But that criteria is insufficient alone as Lakatos (1980/1995) pointed out. Scientists may stubbornly defend 'degenerating' science (p. 5).

For that reason, the second criterion is required. This is that the scientific idea must be capable of standing independently from the person who created it and from the social and historical situation within which it was created. A third criterion of disciplinary science is identified by Lakatos (1980/1995), who refers to all the research programmes that he admires as having one characteristic in common. 'They all predict novel facts, facts which have been either undreamed of, or have indeed been contradicted by previous or rival programmes' (p. 5). This suggests the Bernsteinian emphasis on the importance of disciplinary knowledge as enabling students to think the unthinkable so that they move out of their experience and inquire into the world using intellectual tools taken from the various subjects. It is this imaginative component of science that Immanuel Kant referred to as the 'third faculty' (1781/1993, p. 135).

But constructivism and culturalism are more than social knowledge claiming the status of a scientific epistemology. These ideologies serve the interests of the global market and the increasing inequalities that characterises globalisation by contributing to the process of localisation. Mythologies and beliefs gain status as the new local "knowledges" are made commensurate with science despite their status as ways of understanding the world that come from and are confined to a particular socio-cultural group. In this relativist world, not only are there a number of "ways of knowing", but one way of knowing is considered to be as valid as any other. Science and reason are stripped of their universal character to become just another socio-cultural knowledge, and, from those claiming indigenous knowledge for example, a "Western", colonising instrument of oppression. Significantly, however, these "knowledges", whether traditional or religious in character, serve a very modern purpose as the wealth-generating resource for emerging local elites and as the ideology to justify their self-professed authority.

Constructivism and culturalism oppose the very universalism that is the basis of democracy. The irony is that these ideologies are beliefs developed and supported by progressive liberal-Leftists. Yet their social justice goals are in fact subverted by the racial ideology and anti-universalism that underpin such localised ideologies. It was in that "cultural turn" that the liberal-Left abandoned the class analysis that would have shown the anti-progressive nature of localisation, revealing how localised politics supports the inequalities of globalisation. The fundamental changes to the division of labour since the 1970s have localised the working class and sections of the professional middle class. The universalism of class consciousness that characterised the way many working people identified throughout the twentieth century, one expressed in the internationalism of trade union movements, is replaced by local forms of identification. Some turn to pre-modern identities based on race, religion, and tradition in varying degrees of fundamentalism. Others find an identity in various lifestyles based on sexuality, sport, green issues, or occupation. Many have no socio-political identity except to be consumers in a rapacious global market.

This major shift by de-politicised workers from universalism to localised identities is characterised by a loss of faith in reason, science, and progress for the false security of the local. It takes the form of increasing conservatism in liberal democracies and the entrenchment of autocracies in those parts of the world that were not democratised in the nineteenth and twentieth centuries. (It is to be hoped that the Arab Spring will prove an exception to this tendency.) The process supports and justifies the increasingly unequal access to disciplinary knowledge, now valued more as economic capital and less for its political, moral, and aesthetic role in creating progressive civilisation. In the new politics of knowledge this valuable capital resource is increasingly reserved for the upper-middle class and wealthy elites, whereas working people are more likely to receive a curriculum hollowed out of the generative principles and concepts of epistemic knowledge (Young, 2010b; Wheelahan, 2010a, 2010b). Although ideologies of localisation such as cultural relativism support the unequal transfer of knowledge wealth to these groups, constructivism in education is a means by which it occurs.

Epistemic knowledge is the disciplinary subjects of the sciences, arts, and humanities, but it is much more than content alone. It is the theoretical concepts, creativity, and advanced literacies of those disciplines. It is also the scientific procedures for testing and justifying new knowledge. In the words of philosopher Mario Bunge, science is 'the search for objective if partial truths supported by empirical tests and rational discussion before and after tests (2001, p. 454). It is also the infrastructure that maintains scientific knowledge over time—the institutions and systems of those disciplines that guarantee that new knowledge is, as Jürgen Habermas says, 'procedural reason put on trial' (2001, p. 30). Those with this knowledge are hugely advantaged because conceptual knowledge enables us to create idealised models of the natural and social worlds. In thinking about a world not experienced students can imagine possibilities unrestrained by the conventions of what is known. Disciplinary knowledge is the intellectual capital of modernity. It is, or should be, the purpose of universities to produce and schools to reproduce. It is what separates the school from the home and gives schools their distinctive purpose. It is a purpose that can only be realised when, as Young (2010a, p. 25) argues, the 'curriculum exclude(s) the everyday knowledge of students'. 'That knowledge is a resource for the pedagogic work of teachers. Students do not come to school to learn what they already know'.

The conflation of disciplinary knowledge with social knowledge and the conflation of the curriculum with pedagogy occurred within the wider context of a second 'vigorous philosophic revolt of the civilized against civilization in nearly all its essentials' (Lovejoy and Boas, 1935, p. 118). (According to Lovejoy and Boas, the first revolt was that of the Cynics in reaction against the Greek Enlightenment of the fifth and early fourth centuries BC.) The second "revolt" is postmodernism (Friedman, 1994), an intellectual turn against modernism 'in nearly all its essentials' of the post-1970s' decades. Postmodern relativism and its cynicism towards "grand narratives" and the "Enlightenment subject" eroded the privileged place of scientific knowledge in education. From within the paradigm of postmodernism, constructivism and culturalism shaped the form that postmodern ideas took in the social sciences.

Postmodern social scientists rounded on what they saw as their respective disciplines' complicity in "Western ideological domination". They became less concerned with explaining the social conditions of inequality and more with political demands for society's transformation. No discipline was more exposed to self-politicisation than the sociology of education. Indeed, Karl Maton and Rob Moore (2010) describe how that sub-discipline along with 'cultural studies among other social sciences have torn themselves to pieces' (p. 10). Within the various educational sub-disciplines, the sociology of education led the attack on modernity, one supported by postmodernism's intellectual relativism. Ironically this was accomplished in the name of social justice, although the outcome was to support a return to the inequalities of the pre-modern world.

The effect of the postmodern attack on "Western" universal knowledge in education has been considerable. The idea of universal knowledge, one supported by both the Enlightenment view that knowledge is created by individuals' capacity for reason and by the Marxist view that knowledge is created within the social relations of production, was subsumed by the view that knowledge is constructed from one's experience within a localised socio-cultural group. Although some parents were suspicious of constructivism and complained of the "dumbing down" and "emptying out" of the curriculum, the enormous influence of this approach, coming as it did in the wider intellectual climate of postmodern relativism, meant that parents and teachers who spoke out against the new order were regarded as elitist traditionalists.

New curricula, new assessment schemes, and new pedagogies were introduced into schools. These were regarded as progressive—the means for greater social justice and equity. Group work overtook individual learning as the preferred pedagogy; new knowledge was made "relevant" with children sometimes studying their own societies *ad infinitum*; knowledge was co-constructed by teachers and students, and internal assessment replaced external examinations. Individual development through knowledge acquisition and the training of the mind in reason was disparagingly referred to as the "transmission model". It had, so the claims went, led to competition, inequality, and elitism. But it wasn't pedagogy—the means of teaching and learning—alone that was dammed. Curriculum knowledge was similarly accused—portrayed as something "rammed down students' throats" to be "regurgitated" in examinations that forced young people into unsociable competition. Moreover much of the knowledge was unnecessary anyway—who needed to know about grammar, Shakespeare, and physics? History too, was equally suspect when it was a story told by the victors not the vanquished. As annual intakes of teacher trainees were reminded in their first-year education course during the 1990s in the department in which I taught—history is a matter of whose "lens" is used. The lion and the antelope tell a different tale was the preferred analogy.

It was mistakenly believed that in order to build knowledge one must move from the known as it is experienced to the unknown as it is conceptualised. This is to confuse social knowledge and subject knowledge. Although the disciplinary knowledge in school subjects does have building blocks, these are not from experience—the development is from the less-advanced idea to the more-advanced idea. The relationship between these ideas and a young person's experience may or may not be useful. It may or not be relevant. Sometimes using an example from real life to illustrate a concept does offer insights into the explanatory usefulness of a concept—or it may not. Epistemic knowledge is characterised by the operation of reason and by imagination and creativity. It is not achieved by reducing ideas to how they "fit" the limited experience of the young person. While drawing parallels between the ideas in a school subject and the student's life often motivates students, that is its pedagogical usefulness. It is not about the curriculum knowledge itself.

A second mistake is the shift to a very popular approach called "metacognition". Reflecting about one's thinking is considered to provide insights into the quality of that thinking so that limitations can be identified and the "way of thinking" improved. Indeed the exercise is seen as the means to acquire critical thinking skills. This idea is behind the "it's how one thinks" mantra of the thinking skills pedagogy that has achieved huge influence in education. While such a practice may lead a child into self-critique with all its psychological paralysing potential, it is unlikely to produce the analytical skills of criticism that develop as one is faced with thinking about real ideas. One's own experiences, however insightful and interesting these are to the metacognitive thinker, are not a replacement for the type of thinking needed when acquiring the developed knowledge of the humanities, arts, and sciences.

The critics of traditional pedagogy were certainly right in opposing poor teaching practices. The disinterested teacher, stultifying facts presented without their underpinning concepts, the mindless bullying of the boring classroom—all are to be condemned. The answer to such pedagogical crimes is not however to be found in group work, metacognition, or "relevance"—indeed it is entirely possible that boredom has increased as students are faced with the mind numbing prospect of thinking about the thoughts of their own experiences—nor is it to be found in the narcissism of endless self-reflection. The answer is already known—it is in a demanding disciplinary-based curriculum that stimulates the imagination, in teachers who know and enjoy their subjects and the task of transmitting knowledge, and in a classroom where the dignity of all is respected. None of this is new. Well-educated and dedicated teachers have always taught this way.

While it is the case that constructivism and culturalism are the unquestioned and unquestionable orthodoxies in education today, there are signs of a challenge from the emerging social realism literature in the sociology of education. This book is in part inspired by that literature, in particular by the writings of Michael Young, Rob Moore, and Johan Muller. I have drawn together the social realist analysis of curriculum knowledge with other ideas that have profoundly influenced my research over the decades. A major influence is the work of anthropologist Jonathan Friedman, particularly his theory of the identity spaces that characterise contemporary global processes. Friedman (1994) theorises the resurgence of traditionalism, postmodernism, and primitivism as identity spaces challenging modern identity within the larger structural changes to the global political economy. He describes the decentring of capital, the de-hegemonisation of the West, and the reconfiguration of socio-economic classes as powerful forces that alter people's conditions of existence and the ways in which they then identify with their society.

The changes to class relations are the outcome of the 'structural shrinkage of the workforce' under the 'flexible labor regimes' of post-industrial capitalism. There is an increasing stratification between elites and the working poor as 'downward mobility and de-industrialization has been accompanied by an upward mobility in the upper echelons of society' (Friedman, 2002, pp. 40–41). The new understanding which becomes the cultural or social knowledge sees people identifying in ways that reject what they understand to be modernity's failed project. Their response to increasing, rather than the previously expected decreasing inequalities, is to turn to the romanticised identities of primitivism, traditionalism, and postmodernism, or to the instrumentalised modernity of "homo economicus". I have used Friedman's analysis of the causes of the rejection of a progressive modernity to extend the social realism theoretical framework into a political economic analysis.

I have also been influenced by Alan Macfarlane's (2002) insightful discussion of 'partial loyalty' (p. 271) as a fundamental feature of liberal contractual societies. I apply the concept to disciplinary knowledge to argue that the independence of knowledge from the scientist who produces that knowledge (one of the two essential criterion for esoteric knowledge) is grounded in processes of individualisation. Partial loyalty develops as the human being is separated from the family and the wider kin group to become individualised. A partial connection is maintained with the primary group while at the same time new connections, also requiring a similar partial loyalty, are developed with non-kin people in the wider society. The psychological and intellectual capacity to remain simultaneously attached to and separated from the primary group and to attach to other groups is a central feature of modernity. It also provides a way to theorise the agency of intellectual individualism and avoid the determinism of both Marxist orthodoxy and culturalism. Marxist theory explains the type of social relations that replace kinship in terms of the new class relations of capitalist production, whereas a liberal explanation lies with the autonomous reasoning individual able to separate from the kin-group as a result of the objectivity that characterises reasoning. Whatever those differences between the Marxist and the Enlightenment/liberal explanation what is important for my argument is an important idea shared in common. Both explanations regard the separation of the modern individual from the primary group of the domestic sphere as the requirement for universalism and for the objectivity and critical reasoning that enable both science and liberal democratic politics.

The fourth source of ideas is my own research into processes of localisation. This is the process by which social organisation changes at the local level in response to global forces. The most important changes in the last four decades are the de-politicisation of the working class; the decline of universalism; the rise of pre-modern groups based on race, religion, and tradition; and the increasing power of global elites. I have mainly used the emergence of a re-racialised Maori tribal elite in New Zealand to illustrate this process in previous writing and refer to the New Zealand case here as well.

However, none of the processes that I identify as localisation are confined to one country. Processes in the global political economy cause changes to local societies, from New Zealand to the United Kingdom, from Russia to South Africa and elsewhere. Those processes affect wealth distribution and class reconfiguration as inequality increases. Knowledge is implicated in two major ways. It was the use of critical objective knowledge that helped justify the democratic challenge to traditional political systems—systems that relied on an unquestioning adherence to cultural knowledge for their existence. This was the "tyranny of culture" that democracy overthrew. Second, scientific knowledge is a resource that is distributed unequally. This means that, given the right socio-political conditions, its use in challenging inequality is denied to those who need it most. Three interlocking strategies contribute to the growing inequality of access to knowledge. The first is the localisation of identity and the rejection of universalism. The second is the production of constructivist and culturalist ideologies that justify the localised identities. The third strategy is the recasting of universal disciplinary knowledge as "Western" cultural knowledge.

The outcome of those strategies is to limit working-class access to disciplinary knowledge while maintaining its importance to elites and the upper-middle class. A second outcome follows on and contributes to the first. Disciplinary knowledge becomes increasingly instrumentalised. Its value is more for its economic utility than its moral, political, and aesthetic dimensions. The idea of "relevance" reinforces this commitment to "useful" knowledge. As a marketable commodity, knowledge production in universities and privatised research institutes, and its reproduction in schools takes on the character of a business. As with other capital resources, those with the intellectual capital that is developed through access to the disciplines will be advantaged over those whose understanding of the world is limited by the subjective, localised nature of social knowledge.

This book is about that politics of knowledge; about which type of knowledge matters and for what purpose. I join other realists in the sociology of education, including Michael Young, Rob Moore, Roy Nash, Johan Muller, Leesa Wheelahan, John Beck, and Karl Maton, in seeking to understand what has happened to the production and reproduction of knowledge in our education systems and with what consequences. It is a disciplinary canon that draws on the work of major thinkers such as Basil Bernstein and Randall Collins, who have, as Rob Moore describes, opened up 'new avenues for the sociology of knowledge' (2007b, p. 68). My own contribution to this literature is to add to the political economy perspective. This addresses what Michael Young (2008) has identified as one of the goals of a social realist theory—'to properly reveal the manner in which external power relations might be affecting knowledge both in research and in the curriculum' (p. 31). In responding to that goal I trace what has happened to knowledge in education in the shift from the universalism of objective knowledge to the politics of localism. It is intended that the examples from New Zealand and elsewhere will show the usefulness of localisation theory in helping our understanding of the place of knowledge in education.

The book is written with a very eclectic readership in mind. There is the friend whose eight-year-old daughter came home from school declaring that once again her class was to study "our community" when she was consumed by the desire to know about the ancient Egyptians—a topic considered "not relevant". There is the teacher required to justify teaching Shakespeare to a class of sixteen-year-old Maori students in a New Zealand school following a parent's complaint about ongoing colonisation. There are my social science colleagues who, seduced by postmodernism and cowered by self-accusations of cultural insensitivity, profess progressive politics but lack the Enlightenment agent that is required for such politics. There are my teacher education students who, after years of being educated in groups and without rigorous intellectual training in the disciplines, hold firmly to the mantra that knowledge is constructed from experience within the social group and that different people have different "knowledges". And there are those in the sociology of education who reject objective inquiry for an evangelising critical pedagogy dedicated to attacking capitalism. All this is strong motivation to write the book, but that does not make the ideas themselves ideological. Their claim to a "truth" (one that is always provisional) will depend upon their explanatory value as objective sociological ideas, not on my commitment to them.

This introductory chapter concludes with a summary of the ideas presented in each chapter so the reader can see how the argument is developed. The next chapter provides a more detailed overview of the argument than what has been presented here—how the deep structural forces of class reconfiguration and the accompanying wealth redistribution have led to localised politics. The substitution of social knowledge for disciplinary knowledge in the curriculum is an expression of localisation. Young people in the lower-middle class and the working class miss out on the content, concepts, methods, processes, and symbolic literacies of disciplinary subjects in the arts, humanities, and sciences. Denied access to the means to conceptualise a different and better future, working people are effectively de-politicised. This process is part of the declining power of the working class and is traced to the deeper forces of the contemporary global economy. Caught up in and contributing to the retreat from progressive politics is the liberal-Left's failure to hold firm to the Enlightenment belief in universalism, individualisation, and objective reasoning. Instead this compromised class took the "cultural turn" which led irrevocably to localisation.

Chapter 3 continues the discussion of the political and economic forces behind localisation to explain how the attack on scientific knowledge has removed its power as the source of trust in the modern social imaginary. 'The very power of science to hold knowledge as collective property and to focus doubt on bits of currently accepted knowledge is founded upon a degree and a quality of trust which are arguably unparalleled elsewhere in our culture' (Shapin, 1994, p. 417). With the weakening of the modern imaginary in recent decades, many in the destabilised middle and working classes have turned to pre-modern imaginaries of race, religion, and tradition. The chapter explains how postmodernism provides the intellectual justification for localisation and contributes to eroding the trust that binds the modernist imaginary of democratic nations. Without that trust, liberal-democracies like New Zealand become economic units to be managed rather than social polities to be governed.

Chapter 4 traces the nature of that relationship between the type of knowledge valued and the type of authority for that knowledge. When the modernity pole is strongest, one sees the strengthening of the authority of knowledge based on its own procedures, methods, codes, and principles. In contrast when postmodernism, primitivism, and traditionalism are resurgent as in the last four decades, the source of the authority for knowledge shifts to "who knows" rather than to an authority located in the procedures of knowledge itself. The authority claimed for social knowledge serves as a political strategy in activating ethnicity and religio-culture by reinforcing pre-modern group bonds and authorising the criteria for who can belong to the group and who is an outsider. This creation of the "other", those who are "not like us", has devastating consequences in some cases. The production of a justifying social knowledge follows from re-classifying people into pre-modern, often racial, categories. Where the justifying social knowledge is included in the university, as is the case with "indigenous knowledges", the boundary between science and social knowledge is weakened. With reference to the United Kingdom, Rwanda, and New Zealand, I discuss the consequences of that weakening. This includes the growth of an Occidentalism, an anti-Westernism that contributes to the wider politics of re-racialisation and cultural closure.

Chapter 5 takes on the central question for social realists, namely: What is the difference between disciplinary knowledge and social knowledge given that both types are produced within social and historical contexts? The work of Rob Moore is used to explain the two opposing approaches to knowledge within the sociology of knowledge. For constructivists and localisation or standpoint theorists, the very location of knowledge in the social context means that knowledge cannot be objective—that it is always tied to its producer, who in turn is constructed as a member of the social group. Social realists, on the other hand, in seeking to rescue knowledge from the failed project of relativism explain how socially produced knowledge is separated from its location to exist in its own materiality—as a product. That separation occurs in the development of concepts not tied to experience and in the application of methods and procedures by which disciplinary content is tested, criticised, and judged.

The issue of the relationship between the individual and society with which I conclude chapter 5 is used as a point of entry into chapter 6. This chapter is about the link between the objectivity developed in disciplinary knowledge and required for democracy. It draws on Alan Macfarlane's ideas about 'partial loyalty' (2002, p. 271), a concept developed in the literature about the role of contractual associations and civil society in making the modern world. According to this approach, the partial loyalty of contractual social relations of trust enables the simultaneous attachment and separation towards knowledge that is required for objectivity and criticism. The rise of objective knowledge that contains criticism as a key part of its logic is intimately associated with the shift from status-based to contractual societies. This led to the individualisation of personal identity that followed from the break down of the kinship structuring principle. The politics of knowledge has two features that are essential for science and for democracy. One is the processes of objectivity, criticism, and judgement that allows for the partial loyalty of attachment and distance exercised by intellectualised individuals in the disciplinary canons and in democratic politics. The second feature is the social relations of trust that provide the context for that partial loyalty to operate—something possible within capitalism, as Voltaire observed as early as the seventeenth century. The chapter examines how objective knowledge plays a major role as an organising principle of democratic societies in the modern world.

Chapter 7 uses the story of the sociology of education in recent decades as a cautionary tale for the social sciences. Politicised during the 1970s, subverted by postmodernism from the 1980s, the sociology of education was more concerned with creating culturalism than with explaining the social phenomenon. For three decades, the discipline insisted on reducing knowledge to the standpoint of those who produce the knowledge. This was the rationale behind the outpouring of radical feminist, indigenous, ethnic, and cultural "knowledges" where 'it is not *what* has been said that matters, it is *who* has said it' (Maton, 2010, p. 54). In this way the discipline is itself an example of the collapse of disciplinary knowledge into social knowledge. However the current revival in the sociology of education with the resurgence of critical policy analysis and the social realist inquiry into knowledge production and reproduction indicates the discipline's re-vitalisation. The chapter examines the social realist claim that by bringing back knowledge into the sociology of education, social realism positions itself as a real alternative to the politicised and relativist critical sociology of education. It will do this by proposing and developing the framework for a sociology of knowledge. The example from the New Zealand curriculum in the chapter is another cautionary tale, showing as it does, what happens when constructivism is not criticised.

Chapter 8 examines the culturalist ideology that promotes a belief in the foundational status of racial/ethnic or religio-cultural groups with their distinctive "knowledges" and "ways of being". Since the 1970s beliefs in the primacy of the foundational group have informed various forms of cultural politics—from multiculturalism to biculturalism (in New Zealand), to monoculturalism. These beliefs serve to localise people by breaking down the modernist commitment to universalism. The concept of a politicised category of people classified according to their racial ancestry is common to all forms of culturalism, an ideology that has had a strong influence on the decline of epistemic knowledge in education.

Chapters 9 and 10 address the conflation of social knowledge and science by using indigenous knowledge as an example of localisation. The example shows how indigenous knowledge has acquired the status of scholarship without being subjected to the scrutiny required of science. In protecting itself from external criticism by being 'quarantined off from legitimate assessment and evaluation by others, subject only to critical comment from those within the group' (Clark, 2006, p. 171) indigenous knowledge, by being included within the university, has the best of both worlds. It claims the status of epistemic knowledge but acts as social knowledge—by being, as John Clark puts it—'quarantined from external criticism'. Yet it is that very 'external criticism' which enables the testing of truth claims, a necessary feature of science.

Knowledge within the university that is shielded from such scrutiny fails the basic test of what is science. However producers of indigenous knowledge have used two strategies to establish this form of social localised knowledge as an "episteme". The first strategy in the production of indigenous knowledge creates the episteme itself. This is "logic of the gift" or the idea of a social group with such fundamentally different social relations of production that its study requires a new epistemology to match the ontology. The second strategy concerns how the discipline is to be controlled and managed. Systems and procedures are created to frame the indigenous knowledge; to state the criteria for who and how the knowledge is created and used; for what can be said, who is authorised to speak, and the purpose for which the knowledge is developed and used.

The final chapter returns to the question asked at the beginning of the book. What should young people be taught at school? I answer that question with reference to the Future 3 curriculum model developed by Michael Young and Johan Muller (2010). The model expresses the social realist view that access to epistemic disciplinary knowledge 'must be the primary goal of schools' (Young, 2011, p. 5). That access is provided as students are taught the concepts associated with different subjects 'because it is the inter-relatedness of concepts in a subject or a discipline that distinguish them from the everyday concepts that pupils bring to school and which offer them ways of going beyond their experience' (p. 6). It is an approach to teaching that restores knowledge to its rightful place in the curriculum and the teacher to the centre of the classroom. It requires teachers who know their subjects well and who have the ability to explain conceptual knowledge by drawing on the best content found in those subjects. For this to happen, the difference between epistemic knowledge and everyday social knowledge must be restored. It is to be found in the difference between thinking conceptually and thinking from experience; in the difference between the methods and procedures by which knowledge is produced, and in the systems that decide who authorises knowledge.

In asking what should be taught at school I have asked broader questions about the prospects for liberal democratic societies held together by contract not status when the education system reinforces the latter through its adherence to culturalism and constructivism. Is the increase in inequalities, especially those along ethnic lines currently occurring in a number of liberal democracies, the likely outcome of localisation? Will greater inequalities mean the replacement of Enlightenment rationalism, secularism, and universalism with new justifying ideologies of race, religion, and culture? The book argues that this is a possibility, made more rather than less likely by limiting epistemic knowledge to privileged groups in society and denying that knowledge to those most disempowered by globalisation. However, in Jonathan Friedman's identity spaces, modernism is also one of the four possibilities available to us. The descent into primitivism, traditionalism, and postmodernism is not fixed. All social conditions can be transformed. What is required for transformation is the understanding of those conditions. This book is intended to contribute to that understanding, to respond to Immanuel Kant's potent question 'What may I hope?' (1781/1993, p. 518).

2 Localisation

Education in countries such as New Zealand, the United Kingdom, Australia, Canada, and South Africa has been influenced since the late 1970s by progressive educators' commitment to the "social construction" approach to curriculum knowledge. This commitment brings with it a focus on what children already know. Instead of the disciplinary knowledge based on universal principles and methods, the school curriculum emphasises knowledge constructed from students' experiences. The consequences of the constructivist influence are profound. Without access, or with limited access, to the concepts, methods, and literacies of disciplinary knowledge in the arts, sciences, and humanities, young people are unable to develop the conceptual tools required for advanced intellectual activity. It is not only that many young people miss out on the content of those disciplines—although that itself is a serious problem—more important, they are denied the means to acquire the principles, concepts, and processes that enable deep understanding of the natural and social worlds.

The tools of conceptual intelligence—being able to think symbolically using the advanced literacies needed to study, for example, science, music, mathematics, and literature, can only be acquired by the systematic study of those disciplines. As well as developing advanced literacy characterised by abstract objective thinking, access to disciplinary knowledge orients us to the world in a certain way. In providing the concepts and symbolic representations to think about the world not yet experienced and in most cases, never to be experienced, disciplinary knowledge gives us a way into the future. We can imagine and then create conceptual models to represent what is imagined. But that is not all. Academic knowledge *is* power in the sense of the learner's empowerment. The ability to conceptualise the world outside the confines of our own circumstances gives us authority over those circumstances. That, in turn, is the source of the control over one's destiny celebrated by John Stuart Mill in *On Liberty*. According to Mill (1859/1985), 'he who chooses his plan for himself employs all his faculties' (p. 123). These are the faculties developed in the objectivity of the scientific method that provides 'observation to see, reasoning and judgement to foresee, activity to gather materials for decision, discrimination to decide, and when he has decided, firmness and self-control to hold to his deliberate decision' (p. 123).

The ability to reason from beyond the limiting perspective of one's own experience is required both for self-governance and involvement in social governance. It is a profoundly political ability but is only developed by thinking in objective ways. This involves taking oneself out of one's experience in order to see the experience as one detached from them. It is this objectification that enables critical judgements to be made. Those who acquire disciplinary knowledge acquire at the same time that capacity to be objective and critical. It also enables us to imagine what we have not experienced. In contrast knowledge based on experience alone limits us to what we already know about an already familiar world. It confines the imagination, restricts creativity, and limits us to an unending present. It is the inward-looking positional orientation of the working class identified by Bernstein (1971) to describe those who are relatively powerless and who remain so. That orientation reinforces subjective experience, producing a circle of limited aspirations and acceptance of "this is the way things are" or "this is my lot in life". In direct opposition to the inward looking orientation that fixes a person to an endless present is modernity's celebration of the future and of progress. Kant's famous dictum captures the interconnecting links between knowledge, individual autonomy, and progressive politics and is the underpinning theme of this book. For Kant the questions we must ask are these:

> What can I know?
> What ought I to do?
> What may I hope?
> (Kant, 1781/1993, p. 518)

'What can I know?' asks about the knowledge to be acquired by asking what is not yet known. That knowledge is the foundation for the moral and political imperative of the second line: 'What ought I to do?' and for the future orientation of the third line: 'What may I hope?' The words are directed to a future not yet known but able to be conceptualised because the individual has the ability to think about the unknown and the courage to act in accordance with those thoughts. This is the rational Enlightenment subject, one labelled a "fiction" in the cynicism of postmodernism.

Expanding universal access to academic knowledge characterised national education systems in liberal-democracies, especially in the immediate pre-war and post-war decades. In New Zealand the Prime Minister and Minister of Education, Peter Fraser, declared at the 1937 New Education Fellowship Conference, a speech subsequently reported in the national newspaper, The Dominion, that 'we are trying to give equal opportunity to all and to bring a measure of culture within reach of everyone with an appreciation of literature and art, regardless of occupation. We do not aim at an educational hierarchy (*The Dominion*, 14 July 1937, p.15). However, that ambition was seriously weakened as constructivist ideas took hold in progressive educational circles. To be committed to constructivism was now seen to be radical. This was the path to social justice and equity. Liberalism was decidedly out of favour. Support for liberalism was to favour an individualism mistakenly equated with the selfish narcissism of the consumer market or, according to critical pedagogy academics, to favour a rapacious American imperialism (for example, see McLaren and Jaramillo, 2007). To be committed to the traditional disciplines was similarly unpopular, considered (by those who had benefitted most from them) as reactionary, elitist, and Western. The growth of Occidentalism during this period was to portray the West as corrupted and corrupting, and liberalism as ineffective at best and complicit in such corruption at worst. Scientific knowledge was condemned by association.

The question I ask in this chapter is what caused the change in education systems from a commitment to academic knowledge to a focus on experience? What forces for change were so strong that progressive educators became convinced that the knowledge upon which modernity is based was an insidious Western strategy for a sophisticated late twentieth-century colonisation? Better to turn against this "knowledge/power" as Foucault (2001) described it to an understanding of freedom as something local rather than universal, and cultural rather than scientific.

The forces I describe can be traced to structural changes in the political economy of global capitalism in the late twentieth century, to the contraction of the global economy and the de-hegemonisation of the West, and to the reconfiguration of socio-economic classes (Friedman, 1994, 2000). Strategies of localisation served to weaken the universalism of modern consciousness. This contributed to the declining power of working people and to the associated increase in inequality that may be seen in liberal democracies in the post-1980s era (for which liberalism itself was blamed rather than the distorted "neoliberalism" promoted by global market adherents).

Social change occurs when an elite enters into a new relationship with power (Lachmann, 2000) so it is in the contraction of the global economy and the scramble by new elites for a greater share of wealth that the change occurs to who can access knowledge and who is excluded, or whose access is limited. My own research into this phenomenon in New Zealand shows the convergence of elite emergence and localising ideology in causing social change. In that country, an ethnicised section of the new professional class has, with enormous success, promoted the idea of a Maori tribal revival as a just response to nineteenth-century colonisation. It has secured considerable public resources as a result (Rata, 2000, 2011b), despite inherent problems with the logic of "retribalisation is the answer to detribalisation" politics and the incompatibility of a re-racialising politics with democratic citizenship.

The phenomenon of corporatised elites at various stages of privatising public resources and building huge dynastic wealth can be seen in the repressive traditionalism of Tonga and Swaziland, in the oligarchies of Russia and the Middle East, and in the libertarianism of American and European financiers. Justifying ideologies, if required (sometimes repression alone is enough to secure a population's loyalty) are found in the mythologies of ethno-nationalism and religio-culturalism, often supported by revisionist histories. In the case of the American financiers, the distortion of liberalism into the extreme libertarianism of the market is sufficient justification, although underpinning that one can find the ethnic ideology of an Anglo-Saxon culturalism.

The market value of scientific knowledge is more attractive to elites than is its moral and aesthetic value to society. (Elites do ensure however that their children are roundly educated in the arts, humanities, and sciences of course, but this is more to benefit the young person's self-governance and status positioning than to enable the individual to contribute to social governance in a democratically equal society.) Two strategies affect who can access disciplinary knowledge. First, access is regulated towards the upper-middle class and elites for whom it provides a valuable capital resource. Second, the shift from disciplinary knowledge to social knowledge for other sections of society contributes to localising, and hence depoliticising, those people.

While a causal link from knowledge in universities and schools to structural forces in politics and the economy may be seen as an exaggeration, explaining epiphenomenal change in terms of deep societal structures is within the critical realist position. This is the position being reclaimed by realist sociologists of education in their efforts to rejuvenate the discipline by 'bringing knowledge back in' (Young, 2008). Their critique of social constructivism and academic relativism, one I discuss in greater depth in chapter 7, is integral to that rejuvenation. It is an approach that, according to Roy Bhaskar, 'insists upon the reality of events and discourses' but on the understanding 'that we will only be able to understand—and so change—the social world if we identify the structures at work that generate those events and discourses' (1989, p. 3).

Explaining social phenomena in terms of deep structural forces enables links and patterns to be conceptualised so that their social meaning is revealed. These are meanings that would otherwise be invisible in the mess and fluidity of social life. The empirical method of starting from the evidence, that is, of identifying social issues by starting from real people, events, phenomena, and objects, is useful but limited. (Significantly the dominance of empiricism in the evidence-based approach found in much educational research today is part of the spread of localisation strategies.) Evidence-based research doesn't tell us much about the *social meanings* of those events and processes, meanings that change over time although the actual objects may appear the same. Nor can empirical inquiry alone reveal the deep structural forces—forces that lead to changes in the meaning of social phenomena. In contrast this book is about the social meaning of events, objects, phenomena, ideas, and processes. I start with the theoretical explanation and use empirical data to illustrate the ideas. This is possible because although knowing the social meaning is a conceptual act, it also at the same time produces an object—the knowledge product. Social meanings, like the events and phenomena they apply to, are part of social reality and can be studied as conceptual objects. If examples from reality illustrate the ideas in convincing ways, the ideas themselves can claim a greater theoretical rigour.

What has caused the profound change to the social meaning of knowledge in the past four decades? For working class children those changes to how knowledge is understood means to experience a curriculum that emphasises "relevance" to their lives. For example, in New Zealand secondary schools as in the United Kingdom, young people in poor areas are more likely than those in wealthier suburbs to study applied rather than academic subjects. For racialised groups in the working class, it means relevance to daily life as well as relevance to neotraditional beliefs. For many parents the changes in education has produced bewilderment as they sense a "dumbing down" of the curriculum. But faced with assurances from educators that children learn better by constructing knowledge from their own experiences as they co-inquire with their peers and teachers, these parents are left with no alternative to social constructivism. Those parents who are not convinced send their children to the schools that reject constructivism for a renewed commitment to the disciplines. However, these are often the schools in wealthier areas and not available to working-class children. Those families are left with constructivism and without the means to resist it.

The analysis of the politics behind the change to the social meaning of knowledge contributes to the Bernsteinian task of exploring 'the relationship between the social division of labour and the symbolic division of labour' (Moore, Arnot, Beck, and Daniels, 2006, p. 1). It makes this contribution by asking what changes to deep-seated structures have caused the shift to social knowledge in education at the expense of disciplinary knowledge? That politics is revealed in two main ways: in the growing instrumentalisation of knowledge, including within the university itself as the "knowledge business" replaces the production of knowledge for the moral and aesthetic dimensions of life, as well as for the instrumental. It is also revealed in the way the traditional disciplines of the arts, sciences, and humanities are considered less relevant or even outdated, and for some re-racialised groups, oppressive and colonising. By diminishing the value of the humanities and social sciences—the intellectual means by which we can think about ourselves—an objective means of self-knowledge that draws on profound understandings of the human condition is replaced by the subjective use of metacognition or "thinking skills". This encourages a narrow form of self-reflection that, without being placed in the full context of the experiences of humanity, limits a child to the subjective world of personal emotions and experience.

The changes to the deep-seated structures that have their expression in the changes to our understanding of knowledge are revealed in the difference between twentieth-century industrial universalism and twenty-first-century post-industrial globalisation. That difference has produced new types of relationships between social groups and reconfigured socio-economic classes (Friedman, 2000). Global corporate and financial elites control the accumulation, regulation, and movement of finance—the new source of wealth in post-industrial capitalism, although a source that is ultimately non-productive. The global market is more about trading finance than producing goods. Liberal-democratic nations are less concerned with regulating and protecting their own real economies, where people actually make and consume products, and more about maintaining financial and business systems for the orderly flow of global finance. As a consequence national politics means management rather than the contestation that characterised the labour-capital political settlement of industrial capitalism according to a Marxism interpretation, or as liberals would explain it, the contesting politics of democratic civil society. The modern nation is increasingly a management unit of the global market than a political site where capital and labour meet with the status of equal political citizens to dispute their unequal economic interests.

The shift in the role of the nation from the politics of wealth distribution to the administration of wealth can be seen in the decline of class politics. Apart from the remnants of socialist parties that clung to class analysis when the main Labour political parties jettisoned class in the 1980s and 1990s, there is little organised political opposition to growing wealth inequalities in liberal democratic nations. The class that should be championing social justice for working people can no longer do so. The Left, by abandoning class for identity politics, is so deeply implicated in localising strategies that cause and justify wealth inequality that it has lost its moral compass and progressive political direction. Neither have those liberals with less of a commitment to class analysis than the Left but still deeply committed to democracy based on the universal individual, escaped the "cultural turn". As committed as the Left is to social justice, although in an understanding of equal opportunity within civil society rather than through to a fundamental economic re-structuring, such social liberals are caught in the shift of liberalism to its extreme right-wing version of "individuals without a society"—the neoliberal version envisaged by Margaret Thatcher. Just as the Left's cultural turn has helped disenfranchise the working class by removing class from its politics, so has the cultural turn taken by social liberals emasculated the liberal-democratic agent. In both interpretations the real victim is universalism.

The decreased power of working people in the shift to financial capitalism and the reversal of the twentieth-century trend towards equality exacerbated the loss of faith in universalism and progress that had already been shaken by world wars and economic depression. Despite the role of the nation-state as capitalism's regulatory unit, the liberal-democratic nation was also within the modern ethos of universalism. Citizenship is a universalist concept—oriented to a shared future not a shared past, and inclusive of all regardless of ancestry, race, and religion. But in the post-industrial world of tradable finance, the relationship between the universal and the local is very different. The market, not the modern nation and its universal citizen, is the structuring principle of that relationship. Terence Turner (2003) refers to 'capital's new project', 'neoliberalism, [as] founded upon the substitution of the market for the nation-state as the hegemonic ideological and political-economic framework for political society' (p. 62).

The world imaginary is the globalised economy not the universalised citizen. The local imaginary draws increasingly on traditional race and religious groupings where membership is fixed in the past rather than in the modern contractual nation. In periods of economic decline, as Jonathan Friedman (1994, 2000) points out, evoking tradition, or looking to the past for an imagined stability rather than enduring the anxiety of an unknown and threatening future, becomes increasingly attractive. Traditional cosmologies and their updated versions in revised histories explain the world through the eyes of a mythological and romanticised past. For those people not connected to traditional groups, the new identity is that of the depoliticised worker and the compliant consumer. For those elements of the middle class, the working class, and marginalised social groups with 'no project other than individual commodity consumption as the instrument of production of personal social identity' (Turner, 2003, p. 58), knowledge is emptied out of its moral and aesthetic dimensions. The knowledge now valued is that considered suitable for the limited role that people are to play as depoliticised instruments of the market.

Class re-configuration in the new world of post-industrial capitalism has reformed four main groups. A small globalised professional class retains the benefits of middle-class life: high salaries, reasonably secure employment, and privileged working conditions. A second and larger group includes many who moved from the working class to the middle class in the prosperous decades after World War II. This was the result of what David Cannadine (2008) describes as unprecedented government support for a national university-based intellectual class at that time. They now fill the professions of teaching, nursing, the media, computer technologies, social services, and the like. While senior managers and professionals remain in the upper-middle class, these others are increasingly de-professionalised (despite holding professional qualifications) and often face casual or insecure employment conditions.

The large working class of industrial capitalism, now a greatly reduced and casualised source of labour for the service sector, comprises the third main group. Those who became unemployed in the 1980s, when the major change to class position occurred, are in many instances, still there. A fourth group comes from here. This inter-generational underclass consists of people who move into casual work when the economy picks up, and move back to unemployment when global finance readjusts national economies downwards. The real tragedy is that this is the group where many educated young people now find themselves.

The squeezed middle and working classes have a place in the global market as non-unionised workers and non-politicised consumers. National politics offers little except promises of further belt-tightening and anxieties about their children's future. Many people, caught in the paralysis of not knowing how to understand what is happening let along what to do about it, have found security in older, seemingly more stable imaginaries of ethnicity, religion, or tradition (Friedman, 1994). Alsayyad and Castells (2002) refer to these changes as a 'decoupling between the instrumentality of the state (i.e., citizenship) and the ethnic, cultural, and historical roots of identity' (p. 3).

This major class reconfiguration is a structural cause in the shift to localised and instrumentalised knowledge. Public institutions such as education used to be sites where the working class claimed increased resources such as scientific knowledge during the modern period. Having access to this resource at school was crucial to the social advancement of many working-class children. However, the nation's shift from its role as a site of politics to a site of administration on behalf of the market has changed the purpose of education. From 'authorising, funding, and managing mass schooling as part of an endeavour to construct a unified national polity' (Ramirez and Boli, 2007, p. 200), national education systems are increasingly concerned with educating children for their place in a globalised world, as the members of localised communities and as consumers.

As class divisions change, so does the distribution of resources, including access to higher-order knowledge. While the working class is to be found in vocational higher education, that education offers the hollowed-out knowledge of the competency training approach. Leesa Wheelahan (2010a, 2010b) and John Beck (2010) argue that the atomised content and processes that train learners to reach outcomes does not provide the full depth of academic knowledge. It is not that knowledge is denied to the working and lower-middle classes, but the knowledge is limited and limiting. Wheelahan's (2010a, 2010b) study of competency-based training in Australian vocational education and training suggests that when students are denied access to structuring principles of disciplinary knowledge, the working class and other disadvantaged social groups who make up the majority of students in these courses are excluded from access to empowering knowledge. She argues that competency-based education gives 'students access to specific content' but 'not to systems of meaning in disciplinary knowledge' (2010a, p. 106). This 'reinforces class divisions through differentially distributing access to "unthinkable" knowledge' 'because unless students have access to the generative principles of disciplinary knowledge, they are not able to transcend the particular context' and develop 'the capacity to transcend the present to imagine the future' (p. 107).

Johan Muller (2000), in a similar argument to Wheelahan, draws on Antonio Gramsci's commitment to higher-order knowledge acquisition as the purpose of schools, a purpose that if enacted means that education can provide equal opportunities to the children of the working class. 'The job of the school is to "accustom [the students] to reason, to think abstractly and schematically while remaining able to plunge back from abstraction into real and immediate life, to see in each fact or datum what is general and what is particular, to distinguish the concept from the particular instance"' (Gramsci, 1986, p. 38, cited in Muller, 2001, pp. 7–8). Gramsci was critical of progressivist educators—the forerunners of constructivism, and as with Muller and today's social realists, sees the shift from academic knowledge to the knowledge of experience as leading to 'a hardening and widening of class distinctions' (p. 8). Muller's use of a significant statement from Gramsci which captures his critique of progressivism deserves to be mentioned here because it can also be applied to constructivism today. For Gramsci, 'the most paradoxical aspect of it all is that this new type of school appears and is advocated as being democratic, while in fact it is destined not merely to perpetuate social differences but to crystallise them in Chinese complexities' (Gramsci, 1986, p. 40, cited in Muller, 2001, p. 8).

Of course access to education has always been distributed unevenly across class lines, including in modern nations founded on liberal democratic principles. From the beginnings of national education systems in the nineteenth century education has served as a "sorting house" for the labour force of developing industrial economies. This is as true for the Danish system established as early as 1814 as it is for Austria (1869), New Zealand (1877), England (1881), and Prussia (1906) (Ramirez and Boli, 2007) as it is for the establishment of universal, free, and compulsory education for all children age six to fourteen in India as recently as 2009. For those European economies that industrialised early, individuals were selected for the large manual labour force in agriculture and the city factories, or the very small number of white collar jobs for those who attended secondary school, or the even smaller number of professional positions for the few who attended university. The economic realities of rural life in New Zealand until World War II decided which opportunities were available for many young people, as this description shows:

> From the age of 12, farmers' kids just disappeared from school. . . there were numerous horse-training set-ups and many of my contemporaries were at work as horse boys at 12, dozens more back on the farms working full-time unpaid to help keep the family afloat. (McKenzie, Lee, and Lee, 1996, p. 15)

But the use of national education systems to produce labour occurred within the contradictory capitalism-democracy settlement of the twentieth century. While on the one hand, education served the economy, it also served the democratic aspirations of working people. In New Zealand government efforts to expand educational opportunity in the 1930s were captured in a saying by the Prime Minister, Peter Fraser, at the time. His equality of opportunity statement echoed an ideal not confined to New Zealand.

> The Government's objective, broadly expressed, is that every person, whatever his level of academic ability, whether he be rich or poor, whether he live in town or country, has a right, as a citizen, to a free education of the kind for which he is best fitted, and to the fullest extent of his powers. (Fraser, 1939, pp. 2–3).

By the prosperous 1950s and 1960s many young New Zealanders from working-class homes went not only to secondary school but also to university. Such social mobility earned education its reputation as the path to social advancement and the means to overcome social inequalities. Many who benefited from the post-war prosperity retained socialist ideals from their working-class origins. Accustomed to progress and prosperity (but with the unwelcome memories of the 1930s' Depression experiences of their parents' generation lurking behind the heady optimism), the first mass university-educated generation moved into a position of power just at the time when the prosperity was coming to an abrupt end. Education was blamed for no longer delivering on its promises of providing equal opportunity. By the late 1970s it had played out its role in allocating places into the middle class, creating the new professional class of the post-war "baby-boomer" generation in the process. With the shift to the growing inequalities of financial capitalism, the future looked bleak for increasing numbers of school leavers. Education was implicated in the loss of faith in what had been seen as an inevitable progress towards equality.

In New Zealand, as in other liberal democracies, the solution was to be a new direction for education. The New Zealand Director-General of Education, W. L. Renwick referred explicitly to a 'transition' to a new approach, one committed to 'equity' and 'social justice'. Renwick claimed that 'times, and the tides of opinion, are changing' acknowledging that the liberal 'twin doctrines of equality of opportunity and individual need' had extended access to education but 'did not go far enough' (1986, p. 29). It is not surprising that the new professional class adopted a moral position towards equality and were prepared to use education as the means to engine the new "good" society. Gouldner refers to the 'goodness and power' character of this class (1979, p. 36). They had the power to put their ideals into practice and the moral conviction to make it happen. Not only had the shift to equity enabled Leftists in the new professional class to maintain their socialist ideals from a position of relative wealth but for a radicalised generation who wanted to socialise the world and overcome the limitations of liberalism, "equity" was more satisfying than "equality of opportunity". The political and intellectual elite of the new generation, these 'legitimate defenders of the common good' (Kellner and Berger, 1992, p. 11) were to 'do well by doing good' as Tom Lehrer mocked in *The Old Dope Peddler.*

Renwick's 1977 address to the New Zealand Royal Society's Social Science section is the clearest statement of the new professional class's challenge to the liberal philosophy that had dominated New Zealand education since 1877.

> Equality of educational opportunity will lead to inequality of educational results. But that premise, so long accepted even by those who argued from the standpoint of needs, is no longer acceptable to radical critics who now view educational needs not in terms of equality of access but equality of results. (Renwick, 1986, pp. 29–30)

In a major break with the liberal approach which stressed individual responsibility for taking up the opportunities offered by education, Renwick stated categorically that the responsibility for the inequalities suffered by member of these groups lay 'not with these disadvantaged minorities but with society itself' (1986, p. 30).

> These people are seen to be the unfortunate victims of a social system which has been shown to be selective in the distribution of public goods to groups and individuals. The public debate is no longer about equality of educational opportunity: it is about equity, that is to say, fair treatment or social justice. (p. 30)

This signalled a major shift in educational theory that I discuss in the account of the sociology of education in chapter 7. Any suggestion of individual responsibility for educational achievement was seen as "blaming the victim", an approach that became unacceptable in the education discourse of the new sociology of education. Instead, blame was now allocated variously to teachers, to schools, to unequal power relations attributed to colonisation, or to capitalism in general.

The role of schools in transmitting disciplinary knowledge to the next generation came under this general attack. The attack ignored the fact that it was this knowledge and the advanced literacy that accompanied it that were essential resources in generating the occupational incomes required for professional status in the expanding social and administrative structures of the nation-state. The children of the new professional class already had access to higher-order knowledge at home as a result of parents who were educated in a system that valued knowledge. For their parents the child-centred approach that characterised progressivism then constructivism was seen as providing the "authentic learning" denied by the teacher transmission model they now turned against.

Yet, for working-class children, the access to academic knowledge was available only at school. Roy Nash (2001a, 2001b) drawing on the writing of Basil Bernstein (1971) refers to the types of cognitive socialisation and associated practices of the working-class home as a barrier to acquiring what was available at school. What matters though is that it *was* available at school if not at home. By providing access to the intellectual resource of disciplinary knowledge for increasing numbers of working-class people in the modern period, education was a means for resource re-distribution and social mobility. It was indeed "powerful knowledge" that empowered by giving access to the unknowable and providing the means with which to think the unthinkable (Young, 2008).

Unfortunately the value of disciplinary knowledge for many young people was lessened by a Gradgrind pedagogy that seems to have been commonplace—although the many who remember inspiring teachers suggests that good teaching was also widespread. Unfortunately the bad teaching of the incompetent teacher does tend to be remembered. It has wider implications than just spoiling a child's interest in a subject. Poor teaching can strip science, humanities, and the arts of their creative beauty. It can also undermine confidence in the knowledge itself. It was the "Gradgrind" image that became the caricature of disciplinary-based teaching. It provided fuel for the constructivist argument that students would be motivated to learn not by "irrelevant" ideas but by knowledge constructed from their own experience. Combined with the metacognitive thinker thinking about his or her own thoughts as the new type of critical thinker, this shift to constructivism confirmed the child-centred approach as the orthodoxy. Michael Matthews's (2000) hope, expressed at the end of the 1990s, that social constructivism 'will eventually be seen as a passing fad' (p. 343) was a forlorn wish.

The consolidation of constructivism in education came on the back of another attack on education—its supposed failure to provide social mobility for marginalised groups. Led by intellectuals of the new middle class in the social sciences, education was accused of reproducing capitalism's inequalities; its emancipatory rhetoric merely a contribution to the liberal "myth" of equal opportunity (Shuker, 1987). Yet this was a class that had itself benefitted from the twentieth-century commitment to the rational autonomous individual and to faith in education as the means by which circumstances could be changed. The post-war children of the working class who became, because of their education, the privileged new middle class from the 1960s were doubly blessed. They were well educated in a prosperous age. Although education may not have caused post-war prosperity, it was certainly the means by which a generation raised by parents committed to education's transformative power were able to enjoy that prosperity and enter the globalised professions of the post-1980s decades. It is therefore profoundly ironic that it was the generation whose circumstances were changed because they had access to higher-order disciplinary knowledge who led the move against reason, to postmodernism, and to the commitment to the social construction of knowledge.

Many Left-wing humanists of the new professional class turned in disillusionment from class to identity group politics as the prosperity that had improved the lives of working-class people throughout the developed world came to an abrupt close with the global economic crisis of the 1970s and beyond. The enthusiasm of the post-war generation that had initially thrown its weight behind Left-wing class politics was directed instead to the group identity politics of race, religion, tradition, and the essentialisation of gender and sexuality. For liberal feminists, equal rights for women had been fought for within the framework of universal human rights. With the turn against universalism by radical feminism, gender was essentialised within the politics of identity. Girls were regarded as members of the localised cultural group before they were acknowledged as universal human beings with rights based on that status. This led to the unconscionable position of liberals who had spent their lives committed to human rights and social justice defending appalling acts against women and girls on the basis that they were "cultural". In any other circumstances, these acts would be condemned as torture.

The "cultural turn" of the Left and its reactionary effects have been identified by a number of commentators (Parkin, 1968; Gouldner, 1978; Rata, 1996; Jacoby, 1999). This was a new professional class with universalist ideals but localised economic interests. As those economic interests became more acute, commentators such as Russell Jacoby (1999) could confidently announce the death of a class that had been over a century in the making. In his words: 'We are witnessing not simply the defeat of the Left, but its conversion and perhaps inversion' (p. 11). The intellectual Left's cultural turn in support of localisation has had numerous consequences. In the political domain, it produced the alliance with neoliberalism. Its descent into the confusion of postmodernism and the fence-sitting of cultural relativism has damaged the social sciences, perhaps irrevocably. Adam Kuper (2005) argues that the 'obsolete anthropological notions' and 'romantic and false ethnographic vision' in anthropology that 'justify "indigenous" land claims' 'foster essentialist ideologies of culture and identity' that 'may have dangerous political consequences' (p. 218).

The same is true for education where the relativism of localising ideologies provides support for social constructivism and localised "knowledges", such as Maori knowledge, Bantu knowledge, and Hindutva knowledge (Nanda, 2003). The discipline of history too is affected as accounts of the past are used to justify localised politics. The group's self-image often draws on a heroic mythological past, so one of the tasks of knowledge production is to re-create that past, a task that involves distinguishing the knowledge of the localised group from universal knowledge in revisionist histories. For that reason, localised knowledges, whether based on religious or racial or traditional cosmologies, attack the idea of universalism with vigour, even with fanatical fervour. How this is done and with whose support is the subject of the next chapter.

3 Trust and the National Imaginary

The previous chapter discussed the political and economic forces behind localisation explaining how structural changes to the global economy led to the reconfiguration of class relations and to a shift away from universalism. Those changes to the division of labour are implicated in what knowledge is taught in schools and higher education and to whom. The role of the symbolic "product" of knowledge in class relations of production was of course as much a feature of industrial capitalism as it is of contemporary financial capitalism. This means that understanding education's role in society requires a sociological understanding of economic processes and how those processes are regulated at the national level. This is the reason I focus on explaining those processes in these first few chapters before discussing the nature of the knowledge that should be taught in schools.

The expansion of education to national populations during the late nineteenth and twentieth centuries was within the period of the 'collective class project of the historic modern middle class' (Turner, 2003, p. 58) when the middle class grew exponentially and acquired power from its base in the democratic nation-state. Many in that new middle class had come from the working class, so its politics remained connected to working-class aspirations for social justice. However middle-class progressivism was disrupted by the contraction and de-centralisation of capitalism in the late twentieth century. Since that time, the squeeze on those who made it into the middle class during prosperous times has intensified. Not only is there little social mobility, but those in the new middle class are vulnerable to downward social mobility—a disturbing contrast to the upward mobility that had characterised the period of industrial capitalism, particularly the prosperous post-war decades.

In addition, that class has lost its power base as the old Labour parties replace social democratic policies with a soft neoliberalism. Here liberalism's equality of opportunity ideal is distorted as governments abandon *governing* society for *managing* it on behalf of an amoral and rapacious market led by unaccountable elites. Nowhere is this distortion more pernicious than in education, where disciplinary knowledge is increasingly available only to a section of the middle class. These are the upper-level professionals and managers who can afford years of advanced schooling at the top end of the education market for their children. It is a task that often requires being financially responsible for adult children who may not become earners themselves until they are into their mid- or even late twenties.

The widespread acceptance of the globalised market as the framework for, and controller of, political society has led to a greater acceptance of instrumental knowledge—to the "knowledge business". This is at the expense of the moral and aesthetic dimensions of knowledge that are located mainly in the arts and humanities, but that also inform how the physical sciences are applied to the natural and social worlds. These dimensions are required for the social polity, for how a population that does not have a shared history comes together and understands itself as a modern democratic nation. Social cohesion is not to be found in the past—it requires a vision of a shared collective. That is the imaginary of the modern democratic nation. It is created in the building of a shared culture, one that does not have organic origins in centuries, even millennia, of an imagined race, or in the naturalised conformity of a religio-cultural group.

The disciplines of the arts, music, literature, language, architecture, philosophy, and the social sciences contribute to the imaginary of the modern society because creating and distributing knowledge is a profoundly social act. Modern societies are held together by trust, a trust found not only in Voltaire's (1637/1994) recognition that capitalism requires that people of differing backgrounds 'transact together' (p. 30), but also in the trust generated by the social production of objective academic knowledge. Steven Shapin (1994) identifies this contradictory feature of knowledge in his comment that 'the very power of science to hold knowledge as collective property and to focus doubt on bits of currently accepted knowledge is founded upon a degree and a quality of trust which are arguably unparalleled elsewhere in our culture' (p. 417).

In agreeing with Shapin about the remarkable power of knowledge to balance the opposing forces, whereby the knowledge that is created by people located within society must at the same time be independent of that society, that is, be objectified, I would add that Voltaire was also correct in identifying trust as the balancing principle between contradictory forces in capitalism. Those doing business must trust at the same time as they compete. Those creating knowledge must trust the procedures that criticise the knowledge. The function of trust in maintaining these contradictory elements in a delicate balancing act is due to the mechanism of "partial loyalty". (This is such an important concept that I devote most of chapter 6 to its analysis.)

The future-oriented nature of scientific knowledge and the contribution of its critical faculty to democratic politics through the increasing availability of scientific knowledge to the wider population played a central role in creating the trust required for democratic nations to maintain social cohesion. It is likely that the decline of that availability will lead to a related decline in the trust required for the national imaginary as people withdraw to the localised understandings of social knowledge. This chapter is about how that withdrawal occurs.

Strategies of localisation draw on all the identity spaces of modernity conceptualised by Jonathan Friedman (1994) to shift peoples' identification from the progressive liberal democratic nation to pre-modern status societies. According to Friedman's (1994) theory, the four identity spaces of modernity—primitivism, postmodernism, traditionalism, and modernism—combine in different ways and strengths within global hegemonic cycles. The current breakdown of Western hegemony has produced localised identities where ideologies of primitivism and traditionalism are strengthened. These are supported by the relativism of postmodernism. Friedman describes how the economic decline in ancient Greece, initially an expansionist and hence modernist period, produced a similar response to that occurring in the current period of economic contraction. He observes that 'protests against an emergent modernity come from all sectors of society, but they can only have their day when real development is jeopardized by systemic crises'. These protests 'dwell on the negative aspects of the modern, the alienated individual devoid of a larger cosmological identity, the lack of fixed roots, the destruction of the social fabric and the disaster of poverty' (Friedman, 1994, p. 26). An outcome of this pre-occupation with the negative aspects of modernity is localisation, caused by people identifying with pre-modern forms of social organisation as they turn to primitivist and traditionalist ideologies. It is a re-racialisation of society, a process that moves against the de-racialising tendency of modernity and its reliance of trust as the bond to unite diverse peoples.

Localism has received its most enthusiastic response from the relativism promoted by postmodernists. This has its ancient Greece comparison. There too, as modernism lost its hegemonic power, the Greek Sophists, precursors of today's postmodernists according to Friedman (1994), promoted the relativism of many diverse viewpoints.

> A taste for subtle and arbitrary distinctions and the multiplication of differences and points of view is not a purely contemporary phenomenon. Plato had already criticised the sophists of his time of the same failing when he said that "the attempt to separate all existences from one another is a barbarism, and utterly unworthy of an educated and philosophical mind". (Culliver, 1983, p. viii)

Relativism is a fundamentally anti-intellectual approach to knowledge because it rejects the demarcation between objective scientific knowledge and subjective social knowledge. In the latter the authority of the knower replaces the procedures of reason, including scrutiny and critique, procedures which are the source of the authority of disciplinary knowledge. The authority for social knowledge can be quite arbitrary. It may be the cleric, the tribal chief, the priest, or any manner of person who claims the "cultural" authority to know. At its extreme it is the cult leader of the fascist collective. This approach to knowledge is, as Moore and Muller (2010) recognise, a 'pre-modern strategy' that attempts 'to reinstate "who knows" as the authority for "what is known"' (p. 66). The damage is not confined to education. In New Zealand "cultural authority" is now recognised in the legal system. A recent court case ended with a Maori spiritual leader escaping a fraud conviction on the grounds that his actions were culturally defensible. The judge accepted the spiritual leader's self-declared status as 'an upoko—a spiritual and cultural repository of knowledge handpicked from birth'. The defendant's lawyer referred to 'the special nature of Maori culture and Maoridom in particular' that 'is recognised by legislation' (Booker, 2011, p. A7). His convicted non-Maori co-defendant was less fortunate.

The turn against their own source of reasoning by intellectuals in times of economic contraction is not new. Describing Cynic ethics as reducible to primitivism, Lovejoy and Boas (1935, p. 118) regard 'Cynicism [as] the first and most vigorous philosophic revolt of the civilized against civilization in nearly all its essentials—except "philosophy" itself'. It is a tendency that has reached full fruition in today's postmodernism, as Friedman (1994) notes. The irrationality of postmodernism's seductive appeal can be seen in the enormous, and still ongoing, influence of Lyotard's 1984 seminal essay, 'The Condition of Postmodernity'. Lyotard provided intellectual support for the retreat from universalism in his assertion that 'postmodernism rejects the idea of objective truth in favour of local versions, the metanarrative in favour of local version' (1984, p. xxiv).

It was a position reinforced by Foucault's (2001) concept of 'genealogy'. Here was the clear statement of the intellectual turn to the 'local' as the source of knowledge and to the idea that localised knowledge was constructed to serve the interests of the knower. In other words, it is 'knowledge-power'. Accordingly, genealogy is 'the union of erudite knowledge and local memories which allow us to establish a historical knowledge of struggles and to make use of this knowledge tactically today' (p. 71). To pursue that struggle, according to Foucault, 'genealogy must wage its struggle' against the Enlightenment 'metanarratives' (p. 71). This was the call to arms that galvanised the social sciences. It attacked the Enlightenment commitment to reason and to the individual that characterise modernity's ideals and underpin its liberal democratic politics.

Foucault's advocacy for 'the amazing efficacy of discontinuous, particular and local criticism' (2001, p. 69), for 'subjugated knowledges' and 'for 'local and specific knowledge' (p. 71), not only reduced knowledge to political manoeuvring, or 'knowledge-power', but contributed to the romanticisation of the local. This point was not lost on historian Peter Munz. For Munz (1992, 1999), Foucault's genealogy ignored the function of local knowledge as social cement for a closed society. I would add that it denied the vested interests of local power elites and the dark side of localised uncritiqued knowledge in providing what Hobsbawm calls the 'raw material of nationalist and ethnic ideologies' (cited in Turton, 1997, p. 37). By supporting localism, postmodernism played into the hands of global neoconservative forces. It provided the intellectual justification for the ideologies of culturalism and constructivism that weakened the trust of the modern national imaginary.

The belief that "culture" is primary and determining can lead to increased racial identity, higher racial and religious boundaries between groups, and to the entrenchment of the elites who claim the authority to decide who belongs and who doesn't. Meera Nanda (2003) provides a sobering account of the 'culturalist turn' by both the Right and the Left in India, which she argues 'has bred a reactionary variety of modernity' (p. 6). Like Friedman's identity spaces of postmodernism, primitivism, traditionalism, and modernism, Nanda shows how in India, a 'complicated politics of resentment and cultural redefinition has come to be adopted by all three intellectual-political currents i.e. postmodernist, postcolonial, and Hindutva'. She contrasts these with the progressive forces found in the 'core values of democratic individualism and skeptical Enlightenment' (2003, p. 6). Her book *Prophets Facing Backwards* (2003) is an account of the 'betrayal of the clerks'. These are the 'men and women of secular learning', now 'postmodern intellectuals and activists' (p. 1) who have turned against scientific reason, modernity, and the Enlightenment. They are the liberal-Left described by Jacoby (1999) and referred to in the previous chapter, those that have turned against the source of their own success.

Postmodernism, primitivism, and culturalism are all ideologies complicit in the transformation of the political imaginary and the trust that holds together that imaginary. The creation of the modern liberal-democratic nation brought formerly separate populations into that new socio-political entity—the universal *demos*. Friedman (2006) locates the developmental cosmology of modernity in that integration. It is based on an orientation to the future that is an integral feature of scientific knowledge. A modern cosmology is, by its very nature, an objectified cosmology. It is the imaginary of a new and progressive future captured in an idealised model of the social polity. Friedman describes it as a cosmology in which action is channelled to a 'politics of transformation' (2006, p. xvi). It is the opposite of the tendency towards fragmentation into imaginaries of revived premodern socio-political units. By abandoning class analysis for culturalism, the liberal-Left joined reactionary forces in clearing the way for 'new forms of integration between the individual and the smaller entity' (p. xvi). The associated weakening of class politics strengthened the nation-state as the regulatory tool for global neoconservatism but weakened its role as the site for the playing out of the contradiction between the classed worker and the liberal citizen—the dynamic of democratic politics.

While the main reason for the liberal-Left's implosion lies in the new middle class' material insecurity, the seductive appeal of postmodernism provided its justification. The writings have a mystical quality—absolute, authoritative, and ultimately incomprehensible. Indeed, the very incomprehensible nature of the ideas combined with the religious certainty were part of postmodernism's seduction of a recently secularised class. Just as the exoticism of cultural difference generated a quasi-religious response from the new middle class (an evangelicalism noted by Roger Openshaw [2009a] in his description of the support by white professionals in New Zealand for Maori culture at the height of biculturalism in the 1980s), so too did postmodernism's relativism. Its support for "anything goes as long as it's exotically different", proved compellingly liberating. All that was required was the passion of faith to justify the commitment. Without the standards and justifying procedures required by the "old" disciplines, the social sciences could produce any amount of "mumbo jumbo", as Francis Wheen noted (2004). Postmodernism had plenty of that. Indeed, the philosopher, Mario Bunge (2001) analysed the nature of that "mumbo jumbo". He described postmodernism as the 'counter-revolution in philosophy of recent decades', consisting 'of irrationalism, wild speculation, apriorism, subjectivism, conventionalism, relativism, and pragmatism, combined with intellectual laziness and an obsession with words and metaphors, symbols and myths' (p. 454).

The cultural essentialism and ethnic primordialism that now permeates the social sciences, especially educational studies, employs 'what Seyla Benhabib has called a "poor man's sociology"—a misconceived, because far too holistic, notion of culture' (Lukes, 2003, p. 34). It ignores the fact that

> cultures are always open systems, sites of contestation and heterogeneity, of hybridisation and cross-fertilization, whose boundaries are inevitably indeterminate. The important thing to see is that cultures are never coherent, never closed to the outside, never merely local, and never uncontested from within and without. (p. 34)

Yet the descent into irrationalism posed by intellectual relativism (Friedman, 1994; Lukes, 2003) appears not to have unduly disturbed its proponents despite the numerous lessons from history about its dangers. Meera Nanda (2003) following Jeffry Herf's study of 'reactionary modernism' in Nazi Germany, shows how 'the embrace of modern technology by those who reject Enlightenment reason' (Herf, 1984, p. 1) has led to an Indian version of Goebbels 'steel-like romanticism' (Nanda, 2003, p. 7). Like contemporary Hindutva clerics, German intellectuals promoted 'immediacy, experience, the self, soul, feeling, blood, permanence, will, instinct and finally the race, rather than what they viewed as lifeless abstractions of intellect, analysis, mind, concepts, money and Jews' (Herf, 1984, p. 224).

Although postmodernism inserted relativism into the social sciences as respectable scholarship (despite some opposition), the support for localisation from the progressive Left cemented it in. In its shift from a Marxist commitment to class analysis and the socialist solution the social Left became the cultural Left. It was a radical shift, jettisoning the Enlightenment commitment to universalism and individualism. There was now no universal standard—a position that has ultimately compromised the standard of human rights. Modern scientific reasoning was seen to be a cultural process, not the reasoning capacity of all people, and for some it was a Western colonising one. In this romantic view of tradition, turning to the past was seen in progressive terms as providing freedom for cultural groups to decide their destiny, not as a return to the oppressive hierarchies of tradition.

At its most extreme, "culture" was a romantic Arcadia. Like the turn against reason and the relativism of the postmodernists, such

> primitivism is one of the most commonest forms assumed by the polemic of a number of different types of would-be reformers of society. Egalitarians, communists, philosophical anarchists, pacifists, insurgents against existing moral codes, including those of sexual relations, vegetarians, to whom may be added deists, those propagandists of 'natural religion', who also had their ancient counterparts, all these have sought and, as they believed, found a sanction for their preachments and their programs in the supposed example of primeval men or of living savages. Most primitivism, especially in poetry, has, no doubt, been rather the expression—often the pessimistic expression—of an emotional nostalgia or an idyllic day-dream. But when it has been concerted into a practical program it has necessarily been a program of reform wholly through elimination and reversion. (Lovejoy and Boas, 1935, p. 16–17)

The cultural turn by the more extreme elements of the Left in liberal democratic nations is in this long line of 'hankering for an Arcadia' (Sayer, 1991, p. 13), a hankering that includes the early nineteenth-century romantics (Sandall, 1999). Derek Sayer, in his immensely readable sociology of modernity, notes Marx's recognition of such romanticism as part of the 'susceptibility of society to its [i.e., modernity's] ideological substitutes' (1991, p. 12). The Arcadian longing that characterises the Left's cultural turn is one such substitute. Class politics was replaced by the group identity politics of radical feminism (although not liberal and socialist varieties of feminism which retained a universalist ethos) and ethnicised cultural rights. Victimhood was understood as oppression by colonisation, the patriarchy, and Western culture generally—an oppression experienced by ethnic groups, indigenous peoples, women, gays, and religious minorities—rather than the capitalist exploitation of working-class people. New Zealand historian Kerry Howe recalls how

> We were involved in a post-imperial/ post-colonial sentiment that started sweeping through western universities from the late 1960s. The

> focus shifted from the colonisers to the colonised (as it did from the powerful to the poor, from white to black, from male to female). Generally we were all caught up in an intoxicating dose of decolonisation. (2009, pp. 18–19)

The intellectual Left's support was crucial to the politics of localisation. Here was a class that was well-educated and committed to social justice and the redistribution of wealth now pledging support for "culture" as the political framework. Not only was the support total, but so too was the Left's active participation. These were the social scientists of the era. They deconstructed the "texts" (now no longer separable from the "context"), produced the localised "knowledges", and vilified the Enlightenment. In an awful irony, it was a support that has ultimately contributed to the redistribution of wealth into greater inequalities.

Modernity and the Enlightenment as modernity's intellectual source were demonised as the destroyers of a more humane, more spiritual, way of living. This view appealed not only to re-racialising groups, particularly those emphasising place as with indigenous groups, but to those in the new middle class whose economic security was threatened by global financial capitalism. Those who were thoroughly modernised and could not claim either an ethnic or a religious identity found a spiritual harmony between humans and nature in various forms of eco-fundamentalism in the tradition of early nineteenth-century romanticism. A fascinating example of a contemporary non-ethnic middle class finding refuge in becoming "ethnic" is from New Zealand. There some members of the new middle class did try to construct themselves as an ethnic category in relation to Maori by identifying as pakeha (British settler-descendants) rather than choosing a national identification as New Zealanders. In a move that shows the underlying contradictions affecting this group, at the same time its members were re-racialising, they were actively involved in the major protests that occurred in New Zealand against racial separation in apartheid South Africa.

The tendency to find meaning in the exotic has a long history. Lovejoy and Boas (1935) refer to 'the primitivistic form of exoticism', a process they trace to the 'author of the *Iliad* or with the state of mind that he reflects' (p. 288). In the case of those New Zealanders identifying as pakeha ethnics, the attraction of the exotic has proved a dual-edged sword. In the wave of enthusiasm in the 1980s and 1990s for the more dramatic forms of Maori culture, a number of Maori rituals were appropriated to demonstrate the country's commitment to biculturalism. A decade later however, where welcome ceremonies in government institutions require women to sit behind men and where God is invoked in prayer in secular courthouses, it seems less of a good idea.

The comparison with New Zealand's progressive history is stark. This was the first country in the world to legislate for the female franchise (in 1893). Secularism has been an essential part of the public sphere since the late nineteenth century (for example, the 1877 Education Act secularised the country's education system). The secular public space had been useful in enabling groups with a history of conflict to establish peaceful cohabitation. This was as true for groups within the settler population as it was for the Maori population. For example, Irish Catholics and Protestant English as well as Maori of the various northland tribes and those of the east coast of the North Island (groups renown for killing one other during the early nineteenth century) now met in a public sphere that was secular in terms of cultural affiliation as well as of religion.

The tolerance for practices that are unacceptable or even illegal in the public sphere, such practices as discriminatory gender roles for women, could still occur within churches or on the Maori marae (meeting place) but that remained a matter for those of the group to decide in these "private" spaces. Similarly a degree of tolerance has been retained for religio-cultural practices that have lost their traditional religious meaning but retained an historical ritualised significance. These include a prayer at the opening of Parliament and the reference to a deity in the country's national anthem. Such pragmatism in these grey areas of public life is a characteristic of New Zealand. As long as the practice does not push the social contract too far, New Zealanders tend to "let it go".

However bringing religio-cultural rituals into New Zealand's secular sphere during the height of Maori revivalism in the 1980s as an attempt to add Maori rituals to those established during the colonial period did test those limits. The practice has proved a double-edged sword. On the one hand, it enabled Maori cultural practices to become known by other New Zealanders, surely an integrating factor. On the other hand, these rituals become less exotic as they become more familiar, especially as they were not mere rituals emptied out of their original meaning but practices that retained meanings for their adherents.

The inclusion of gender-differentiated practices in the public sphere led to considerable disquiet. This was particularly the case with Maori welcome ceremonies that were increasingly taking place in government circles. Here, women are required to sit behind men, and males have the speaking roles. The impossibility of reconciling the legal requirement for gender equality, especially as the practice occurs for women in government employment, with a practice that is discriminatory means that these experiences test the limits of tolerance.

In addition, with familiarity comes scrutiny, but because cultural knowledge does not have procedures of critique, criticism is perceived to be criticism of the people who hold the beliefs, not of the objectified ritual itself. This lack of objectification has ensured that the cultural debates in New Zealand remain personalised. In an unfortunate twist of logic, those who object to the sexism in Maori ceremonies are accused of racism, that is, of being anti-Maori, rather than commended for their anti-sexism. In this way, the discussion is distorted and polarised before it can begin. The "grey area" has become black and white, pushing New Zealand pragmatism to its limit. The likelihood of a discussion occurring is compromised by the weakening of the very social contract that allowed a degree of compromise in the first place. The standardising framework of the national imaginary, operates in the secular public sphere on the basis of trust. When people are separated into ethnic categories, there is not only a weakening of trust between the re-racialised groups but there are no longer ways to communicate across the divide given that the social contract which enabled the integration with all its helpful "grey areas", is also weakened.

The shift to localised "knowledges" where one can only critique the culture from the inside, as an insider, contributes significantly to changing the imaginary of the people from *demos* to *ethnos*. The authority over knowledge is in the hands of those who know rather than in the procedures that authorise and regulate knowledge. The building of the ethnicised local group as the imaginary of the people requires criteria to include those in the group and criteria to identify the excluded. Any threat of criticism from within the cultural boundaries can then be deflected by setting up the straw man of the racialised "other" as the enemy. Framed as the "other", the strategy draws attention away from the privileged position of a group's elites, who remain in their self-representation as the leaders of "their people" (Rata, 2011b). It is only when knowledge is separated from the knower and made an object that it can be subjected to the procedures of reason rather than to the authority of tradition. When knowledge is tied to the knower, as in the case of social knowledge constructed from experience, the authority behind the knowledge is the "knower"—not the scrutinised logic of the ideas. This subverts 'the very power of science' to hold knowledge as collective property that Shapin (1994) identifies and the trust that these collective bonds engender in the national imaginary. The source of authority over knowledge, either the authority of the knower or the authority that comes from procedures of reason is the subject of the next chapter.

4 Knowledge and Authority

In the preceding chapters I have argued that changes to the type of knowledge valued in the education systems of modern democratic nations are the result of major structural changes to the division of labour in global capitalism. The shift in education from a focus on the transmission of disciplinary knowledge to one that emphasises the everyday social knowledge found in students' experiences is justified in ideologies that promote localised identities. Jonathan Friedman's (1994) identity poles of modernity provide a useful model with which to theorise the possibilities available for these particularised forms of identification. In that model the poles are conceptualised as primitivism, postmodernism, traditionalism, and modernism, with each pole or space assuming greater or less significance according to the degree of political and economic pressures on peoples' lives.

Those in retreat from modernity's technological excesses may turn to a primitivism which promises spiritual harmony between humans and nature. Those in retreat from the constant uncertainty and change that characterises modernity may adopt traditionalist identities in the belief that there is a more enduring security in an authoritative culture that prescribes what is to be known and believed. Religions that offer unchanging stability in a world of unceasing and often threatening change are attractive for this reason. Intellectuals, enticed by the romantic ideal of the local, yet resisting both race and religion as potential identities, find the mysticism they desire in a cynical detachment from the material world. The rise of postmodernism from the 1980s was within this tendency. These poles of identity are not new. Prior to the current increase in localisation tendencies, Karl Popper (1972) recognised its precedent in Hegelianism idealism, what he disparagingly referred to as 'Hegel's "mystifying cant"' (p. 31), and in the associated localism. For Popper, that localism was the extreme monoculturalism of the Nazi regime—a blood and soil ideology supported by the romantic idealism of the nineteenth century. He described 'Hegelianism [as] the renaissance of tribalism' (p. 34).

Within each identity pole there exists a relationship between the type of knowledge valued and the type of authority for that knowledge. This chapter traces the nature of that relationship to argue that in periods when the modernity pole is strongest, one sees the strengthening of the authority of knowledge based on its own procedures, methods, codes, and principles. In contrast, when postmodernism, primitivism, and traditionalism are resurgent as in the last four decades, the source of the authority for knowledge shifts to "who knows" rather than to an authority located in the procedures of knowledge itself. The authority for knowledge may be that of localised elites, one justified in ideologies of tradition. For primitivists, it may be one found in various forms of mysticism, from new age cults to revived pagan rites. The cynicism of the postmodernists leads to an imploding relativism where no one "knowledge" has value greater than any other. Ultimately, in this view, no knowledge can be trusted. This means, of course, that those who hold the knowledge cannot be trusted either. It is a position that subverts the very trust required for the unity of modern contractual societies.

Jonathan Friedman (1994) argues that periods such as the fourth century BC in Greece and the period from the seventeenth century are characterised by a strong modernity identity pole underpinned by expanding economies and increased individualisation. These modernist periods are also characterised by a shift in the authority for knowledge from external agents to the internalised procedures of knowledge production. This has huge implications for authority more widely. It is a profoundly democratising process because anyone, regardless of age, gender, race, or birth-ascribed status can follow the procedures by which knowledge is created and justified.

In addition the ability to reason enables people to objectify experience. By conceptualising the unknown, we are driven to change the way we look at the known. In other words we turn to our own experience and see it with new eyes. This is a radical capability in that the individual can step outside his or her social world and by objectifying it, criticise it. Not only is the object criticised using concepts and methods from the disciplines, but those methods of criticism are also open to criticism. This two-tiered criticism makes the authority of disciplinary knowledge subversive of the external authority claimed for social knowledge, that located in the "knower". There authority is justified by the status of the knower not by anything intrinsic to the systems that test the knowledge. How can we know if the knowledge is right or wrong? We can trust the authority of course, but given the vast inequalities that exist between elites and subjects in status-based societies, this would be a misguided trust.

There is sound historical evidence to be wary of knowledge that has nothing more than the authority of those with a self-interest in its preservation to recommend it. The authority may be that of religion, where supernatural forces are believed to authorise the clerical power on earth. Or it may be the authority of "culture" or experience; that which claims "I know because I belong" or "I know because I was there". Equally insistent on claiming authority over knowledge are political elites whose position and wealth depends on controlling the type of knowledge that can be produced and disseminated. Or it may be the authority of science itself that has lost its capacity for self-critique. In that case the 'public arenas of collective judgement' where the 'objectivity of knowledge' is guaranteed by 'the specific practices of the disciplinary field—procedures, codes, systems' (Moore, 2010, p. 30)—are replaced by a closed system of moribund science.

In contrast to the authority behind ideological knowledge, the authority that justifies disciplinary knowledge may not be found in the practices and beliefs of a social group. Knowing about one's experience is, of course, a form of knowing. The knowledge about one's life is true for that person, but academic knowledge about society is fundamentally different from social knowledge about society. While disciplinary knowledge objectifies society, social knowledge maintains a subjective tie between the knower and the object so that the process of objectification does not occur. The next chapter is about the difference between disciplinary and social knowledge, particularly the vexed questions: If disciplinary knowledge is not social knowledge, then how does one explain its production by people located in their social world? What is the point of demarcation between the two forms? The focus in this chapter, however, is on the authority of knowledge and how that authority plays a vital role in setting the conditions for the demarcation.

Social knowledge is important knowledge in that it provides the commonsense understanding of the world that make everyday life possible. It also provides the foundational beliefs and values that contribute to a group's unity—it is a group's "culture". This in itself is a process common to all societies. It becomes a problem when the knowledge is used as a political strategy to create divisions in multi-ethnic populations. In such cases social knowledge is used to activate ethnicity and religio-culture as strategies of localisation and boundary making. That activation was widespread and intensive during the 1990s when ethnic boundary making reached its apotheosis in the genocides of Rwanda and Yugoslavia. The building of boundaries that became rigid divisions went through several stages, all of which involve using social knowledge to justify the politics and create the new imaginary.

In the first stage of ethnic boundary making, multi-ethnic populations are classified into primordial groups that are placed into the nation's institutions as distinct categories for policy-making purposes. This involves creating social knowledge about membership criteria. Who is an "authentic" member of the group? Who is an outsider—the "Other"? These are questions that contain the implicit threat—"what race are you?" Whether that threat is activated depends upon the type of politics; a politics that recognises ethnic categories or a politics based on the category of citizen. In the latter, individuals may identify with a religious or ethnic group, but their political and legal status is not the basis of that identity.

The political recognition of distinct groups based on ethnic or religio-cultural criteria is what distinguishes multi-cultural democracies from the secularised liberal democracies of the pre-1970s' period. It remains a highly contested issue in those societies today as debates rage about the nature of the secular public sphere as a site for social integration. Multiculturalists who support the political recognition of ethnicity and culture in the public sphere do so within the logic of progressive politics. The recognition is seen as a means to target groups to ensure the group is included within the redistributive and participatory politics of the nation. However this understanding is opposed by others who also work from a progressive logic. They argue that participation is better achieved through the liberal approach of limiting religion and culture to the private sphere so that the secular public sphere is the site of integration. According to this argument it is through integration that social justice will be achieved.

Although liberal-democratic societies debate how progressive politics are best played out in countries with increasingly multi-ethnic populations, there is no doubt that the recognition of ethnicity as a public category for targeted policies carries with it the potential for deep and permanent division. In such cases tradition is used to justify the criteria for belonging to the "insider" group or being excluded and marginalised. The authority for interpreting tradition may be claimed by or on behalf of the elder, the priest, the cultural authority, or those with the "loudest voices" and can be reinforced by threats or even real acts of intimidation and violence.

There are a number of possible scenarios that develop from the use of tradition as a political resource. Indeed for historically oppressed groups, tradition may be a legitimate resource in overcoming injustice. Ivor Schroder (2003) describes tradition used for political purposes as 'a resource in locality production', an 'important strategy in the tribal struggle for the reproduction of locality through representation. What is represented, both to the local society itself and to the outside world, is a claim to history that is different from national history and serves as the basis for further claims in the fields of economy and politics' (2003, p.451). In this way the use of tradition and the setting up of insider-outsider criteria for belonging are strategies that may be used in the service of progressive or reactionary politics. The problem is that because the knowledge used to produce and justify the traditions and criteria is social knowledge it is not subject to the scrutiny and criticism that is required for scientific knowledge. Even if the initial intention of the group using tradition for political means was progressive, once unquestioned and unquestionable beliefs become the only authoritative knowledge, the potential for the distortion of the knowledge and the distortion of the politics that the knowledge serves is always present.

It is not only traditional beliefs within social knowledge that contain the potential for ideological misuse. An uncritiqued history may be employed in a revised version to validate the "evidence" of tradition. What Lakatos (1980/1995) refers to as 'degenerative science', the science that no longer subjects itself to disinterested criticism within disciplinary procedures, may be used for ideologies of social division. The absence of a demarcation between social knowledge and disciplinary knowledge provides the conditions for knowledge to become ideology. Without the demarcation, beliefs that claim the status of knowledge with the power to back the claim can be considered "science" with the authority that the term implies. In this way, social knowledge claiming to be scientific knowledge is eligible for a place in the university—the home of science.

This has occurred with the inclusion of various forms of "indigenous knowledges" in the university. These include Sandy Grande's 'red pedagogy' (2004, 2009), the 'indigenous episteme' of the 'logic of the gift' theorised by Kauna Kuokkanen (2007, p. 2), and the indigenous methodologies proposed by Linda Smith (1999), Marie Battiste (2000), and Margaret Kovack (2009) which I discuss in greater detail in chapter 9. Indigenist theorists, like others in the relativist tradition, claim that all knowledge about society is socially constructed and therefore remains tied to the knower. The problem with indigenous knowledge is not the knowledge itself. The beliefs of indigenous groups are as valid and important as are the beliefs of any social group. The problem is that, like all forms of social knowledge and like degenerative science, the knowledge can be used as a political instrument either for or against the people. It is in the permanent link between knower and known, one claimed by indigenist theorists as its strength, that indigenous knowledge fails its claim to be science. This is so because without the independence of the "text" from the "context", there is no system for scrutinising and criticising the knowledge itself.

While the approach that what people say about themselves is the same as what is really the case (Babdazan, 2000) contributes to a group's cohesion, it is as a mechanism for ethnic and religious boundary making that it deserves critique. The use of social knowledge in this way is a valid subject for anthropological research. This focus contributes to that discipline's renewed relevance as an important social science following its near implosion on the petard of postmodern relativism in the 1980s. There is a growing body of literature about the politics of culture, including cultural closure, inventions of tradition, reconstruction of the cultural past, and the strategies of cultural elites (for example, Hobsbawm and Ranger, 1983; Kuper, 2001; Rata, 2003a, 2003b; Larson and Zalanga, 2003). It is a literature to which this book and my previous research belongs.

Unfortunately in contrast to the strengthening of objective critical research in anthropology, there is also the literature being developed by social scientists that rather than use social knowledge or "culture" as the object *of* research, instead use it as the means *for* research. This includes the interpretativist methodologies used by qualitative researchers in educational studies as well as the relativist approaches found in types of sociology where the researcher accepts uncritically the social knowledge of a particular group. Examples of this type of inquiry are Africana sociology, red sociology, Pacific knowledge, and radical feminist scholarship. What each has in common is the belief that research is and should be subjective; that the researcher is tied to the knowledge, and that the knowledge should be in the interests of the researched.

This voice discourse approach (Moore and Muller, 1999) restricts who can undertake the research to those either from the group or authorised by the group. For example, Maori researchers in New Zealand who follow the "kaupapa Maori" or cultural approach to research 'are differentiated according to kinship links to the research' with 'age and gender (possible) factors in the research process' (Jahnke and Taiapa, 1999, p. 48). In contrast the scientific approach to research recognises the researcher as someone with the conceptual tools to investigate the objectified social or natural phenomenon; an investigation with methods and findings that will be subjected to the procedures of criticism universally accepted within the discipline. The ethnicity, gender, and status of the writer is not implicated in the knowledge that is produced (though it may be a factor in motivating the researcher to investigate that particular topic—but that is not part of the knowledge "product" created by the researcher).

The existence of these two opposing views about what knowledge is and who may produce it is illustrated by another New Zealand example. That country has gone through the stage of classifying the "insider" and the "outsider" in terms of who is considered Maori and who is not, a process that has a number of implications for knowledge production. In the wider New Zealand society the first round of classification occurred during the height of the bicultural period in the 1980s and 1990s, where many government officials, professionals, and academics particularly in the social services, teaching, the media, and the church, either self-identified or were identified as "Maori" or "pakeha" (British settler-descendant). This was not a clear-cut process by any means, given the complex reality of ethnic fluidity in the country with 'all Maori hav(ing) some degree of non-Maori ancestry' (Butterworth and Mako 1989, p. 1).

To further complicate matters Maori descent does not necessarily equate with Maori cultural identification. 'Of the 604,113 persons who reported being of Maori descent in 2001, about one in five did not identify as Maori' (Kukutai, 2004, p. 93). Simon Chapple (2000, p. 104) found a range of identifications noting that 'some people of Maori descent have a strong ethnic Maori identity; others have little or none. For some, their Maori identity is central to their lives; for others, different aspects of their social and personal identities seem to take precedence'. The prioritisation principle, which until 2006, meant that individuals with Maori as one of their ethnicities were recorded as Maori only (Callister, 2007) has further complicated the matter with the subtleties of identification being lost in the process of categorisation.

In additional to the Maori-pakeha classification that has occurred in government policy since the 1980s, a further ethnic classification is becoming increasingly noticeable. This is the division into tribal Maori and non-tribal Maori. From the late 1980s, considerable financial and resource settlements have been allocated to tribes and not to pan-Maori. The outcome is an increase in the numbers of Maori who claim tribal affiliation and a change to who these people are. The 2001 census shows the proportion of Maori descendants who do not have tribal affiliation at 25 percent to 30 percent (Statistics New Zealand, 2011). By the 2006 census, however, that percentage had decreased, 'with 17% reporting no tribal affiliation', a group that includes 'some of those most disadvantaged in society' (Gill, Pride, Gilbert, and Norman, 2010, p. 19). Those more likely to put their names on the new tribal registers are the educated middle class, not the impoverished Maori in whose name the politics of wealth redistribution to Maori was initially justified.

The strengthening of tribal affiliation as the criteria for "being Maori" occurs in three main ways: Firstly, through the influence of tribal leaders who speak with both the authority of tradition and the authority of their positions in contemporary tribal development. Secondly, in the requirement that individuals who wish to be eligible for tribal resources must register with their tribes(s); and thirdly, in the increasingly reference to tribal affiliation in institutions such as education. Influential tribal leaders emphasise genetic descent and tribal affiliation as essential criteria for a person's social identity as Maori and for the individual's entitlement to tribal assets. According to Maori political leader and academic, Professor Whatarangi Winiata, '"A person who is 1/1024 requires only nine or ten generations ancestry to be identified with a full Maori. By contrast, a person who does not have one dot of Maori ancestry is unable to do this"' (Winiata, cited in Tremewan, 2006, p. 110). And from Professor Sir Hugh Kawharu, '"membership in the group comes through whakapapa (i.e., genealogy). Living in it—even marrying into it—will not qualify one for the birthright. Property and authority within the group follow the kin principle"' (Kawharu, cited in Sharp, 2002, p. 21).

Given that the non-Maori parents of Maori children have no Maori ancestors but all their descendants are classified as Maori according to the one-drop principle behind tribal affiliation (see Winiata's previously mentioned statement regarding blood classification), then the division between who can identify as tribal Maori and who is excluded occurs *within* families as well as across the wider population. This affects a large number of families because 'the majority of Maori ethnic children growing up today hav(ing) a non-Maori parent' (Chapple, 2000, p. 105) with 'half of Maori living as part of a couple have non-Maori partners' (Callister, 2003, p. 3). Increasingly the emphasis on tribal identity rather than the more general "Maori" identity can be seen in Maori education policy documents, contributing significantly, not only to institutionalising a Maori/non-Maori binary, but to the acceptance of the view that an "authentic" Maori is someone with kinship ties to a tribe.

Re-racialisation in New Zealand is so far free from violence despite the explosive words of Maori leader, Professor Whatarangi Winiata.

> Failure by our nation to take steps in this direction [towards tribal sovereignty] so as to change the management of our affairs and ways

> of governing ourselves, will create the circumstances where the fury of *tino rangatiratanga* [tribal sovereignty] will produce the true believers, namely, those who will die for the cause. (1998, p. 1)

However the experience of Rwanda is one of a number of terrifying examples of the extreme outcome of ethnic classification that may or may not have been intended in the original ethnic classification process. Classification systems become the political reality with real victims proving the truth of constructs. According to Eltringham (2004), the "Hamiti Hypothesis", a ideology that emphasised racial distinction, became institutionalised in Rwanda with the use of identity cards in the 1930s. These cards noted the ethnic heritage that individuals (often with several heritages) chose. Three generations later, the identity cards were used to "prove" the distorted social distinctions of "pure" ethnic identity. The way in which categories are created by including racial and religious classification in institutions is not confined to the extreme cases of Rwanda, Nazi Germany, Bosnia, and in the Hindutva classification in India today. Lorraine Culley and Jack Demaine's (2006) example of the categorisation process in the United Kingdom reminds us that the process is part of multiculturalism in liberal democracies.

> The Department for Education and Skills Race Equality Scheme uses a plethora of classification terms. Within the space of a few pages the reader can find: ethnic groups; Asian backgrounds; Chinese and Indian (in the U.K.); White British; ethnic minority groups; Black Caribbean pupils; Black and Asian students; Black British; Asian British (all on the same page); minority ethnic groups; pupils from Pakistani and Bangladeshi backgrounds; BME which is explained in a Glossary at the end of the document as meaning Black and Minority Ethnic; BEMG which is said to refer to Black Ethnic Minority Group; Traveller; Irish heritage; Gypsy/Roma; individual minority ethnic groups; Black young people; White British young people; Black young males; and Ethnic Minority and ethnic diversity; Black, Asian and people of mixed ethnic origin. (Department for Education and Skills, 2005, cited in Culley and Demaine, 2006, p. 130)

While the intention of the policy is to identify groups that are underachieving in education in order to provide targeted assistance, such official ethnic categorisation contains within it the potential for boundary making and for the political distortion of the differences that are emphasised in order to shore up the boundaries. The approach belies the complex social reality of societies with multi-ethnic populations. This includes the presence of families within those categories who are as different from one another as they are from families in other ethnic groups. It also includes the degree of social integration that occurs as minority indigenous and migrant groups engage with the wider population. Unfortunately, once the distinction is given its own official reality, it becomes difficult for the actual social reality to be acknowledged. Social life is just too messy to capture in official figures.

The potential contained within the official ethnic classification policies and practices is a real dilemma for those who support multiculturalism for progressive reasons. For these people, recognising difference is seen as a means to identify and assist disadvantaged groups within either the liberal ideals of the integrative social contract or within the socialist ideals of re-distributory social justice. The motivation may be a combination of these two progressive ideals. But there is a reactionary form of multiculturalism referred to in chapter 1 that justifies the official recognition of ethnic or religio-cultural difference for quite different reasons. In this case, the difference to be recognised is a primordial racial one. Social division is to be encouraged according to this approach in order to protect a difference valued for its own sake.

The multicultural dilemma is that recognising ethnicity for the "right" purposes has the potential to lead in the same direction as recognising ethnicity for the "wrong" reasons. Adam Kuper (2001) points out that 'those anthropologists who repudiate the popular ideas that differences are natural, and that cultural identity must be grounded in a primordial, biological identity, but a rhetoric that places great emphasis on difference and identity is not best placed to counter these views. On the contrary, the insistence that racial differences can be observed between peoples serves to sustain them' (p. 239). Who is to say that the names on (or indeed off) the tribal registers in New Zealand will not be used in ways for which they are not intended in the future? In real life where populations are mixed and physical appearance and daily lifestyles may not always provide clues as to a person's heritage, the official recording of "race" is a potentially dangerous instrument. This is the case because the recognition of ethnicity by the "other" or the assertion of ethnicity by "insiders" is always about who controls the understanding of social difference. Ethnic recognition is a political act with the potential for consequences that may not be intended.

The activisation of culture may be the result of official policy, or come from "outsiders" who either support (e.g., progressive multiculturalists) or oppose another group's ethnic difference (e.g., neo-fascist organisations), or be the 'deliberate mobilisation of culture' (Kolig, 2006, p. 37) by those on the inside. Erich Kolig's (2006) study of Muslim students in Vienna provides an example of the latter. Contributing to the students' choice of identity as Muslim was a tendency to iconise those cultural feature, such as clothing and food that set up barriers between them and other students. This practice helped to delineate 'religio-cultural identity that cannot easily merge with the Other'. Kolig describes it as the

> valorisation of cultural features to act as boundary devices (that) deliberately and emphatically mark cultural identity and its distinctiveness against others'. Significantly 'the reason may be not only for

> the sake of preserving the integrity of culture and self but also for oppositional motives, and as expressions of rejection and even provocation. (2006, p. 37)

A fourth group that has contributed to activating culture as a political strategy is made up of social scientists who promote relativism. The 'search of the cultural Other' (Abaza and Stauth, 1990, p. 213) requires affirming the group's cultural distinctiveness by emphasising what the group is not, its "otherness". David Cannadine refers to the attraction for academics of the 'beguiling binary' 'built around the notions of collective categories eternally in conflict' (Cannadine, 2008, p. 34). It is an attraction demonstrated by educational sociologist Alison Jones's plea for researchers to 'work the colonizer-indigene hyphen' (Jones and Jenkins, 2008, p. 473). According to Jones, 'in indigene-colonizer research and teaching work, the hyphen is to be protected and asserted and is a positive site of productive methodological work' (Jones and Jenkins, 2008, p. 475). This is an argument for the maintenance of a permanent tension in an ahistorical present between two groups regarded as separate on the basis of different ethnic heritages. It is one attractive to 'Western-educated third world scholars who today, after years of engagement in modernity, argue for a re-establishment of other forms of knowledge production and rules of discourse' (Friedman, 1994, p. 122). According to Turton (1997) indigenous academics may create, through self-consciously traditional discourses permanent ethnic divisions. Such divisions are then used to justify the conflation of social knowledge with scientific knowledge.

The use of ideas by academics to support ethnic politics is illustrated by the way in which New Zealand ethnic politics is represented to the outside world. The idea of a Maori revolutionary struggle against structural oppression established during the colonial era is taken for granted in the international literature (for example, see Kincheloe, 2008; and Kovack, 2009). Yet, as early as 1989, McCulloch argued that there was actually 'little evidence of this resistance and struggle' (p. 50) in New Zealand education. Elsewhere (Rata, 2010b) I have analysed the 1987 to 1989 campaign to secure legislation for the kaupapa Maori schools as one conducted by a small, highly effective lobby group led by university-educated professionals, including a disproportionate number of academics. It was their networks of influence *within* the state, amongst politicians and government officials, that was the decisive factor in the campaign's success.

The leading role played by New Zealand in developing an indigenous sociology of education is noted in the international literature which tends to accept without criticism the culturalist orthodoxy presented by New Zealand writers. Weis, Fine, and Dimitriadis's (2009, p. 438) reference to the 'intellectual and political ascendancy gained by critical Indigenous scholarship which privileges local knowledge and cross-site Indigenous knowledges' mentions kaupapa Maori theorists, G. H. Smith (2000) and L. T. Smith (1999, 2005). Because there is no attempt to problematise that ascendancy, the reference is an implicit recognition of indigenous scholarship as an authoritative discourse. Similarly Nicholas Burbules (2000) accepts Alison Jones's description of her research as showing Maori students resisting pakeha students' 'cannibal desire to know the other'. She describes this 'desire' as 'a further sort of exploitation' (p. 268).

That powerful, even defiant, 'cannibalism' image, reflects a narrative style that is common to revisionist writing in New Zealand. Much of this writing is contained in the Waitangi Tribunal reports. These have played a major role in creating the revised history that then influences historical understanding more widely. The historian, W. B. Oliver (2001) describes how E. T. Durie, chair of the Tribunal from 1981 to 2000 'made clear his belief that the Tribunal should help to rewrite New Zealand history "from a Maori point of view"' (p. 10). One short section of the Taranaki Report (Wai, 143, 1996: 12.2) shows how the narrative style of the tribunal reports identified by Oliver (2001) evokes the good versus evil struggle found in all mythological epics. The use and number of words and phrases describing the government create a vivid caricature of evil: 'macabre', 'fraud', 'corruption', 'cruel', 'machinations', 'violations', 'war of aggression'. The good versus evil struggle is played out in heightened poetic imagery: 'emblazons in vivid relief', 'protests of desperation', 'to destroy, by stealth and by arms'. The dramatic effect produced by this writing is not just in the word meaning. The rhythmic phrasing and periodic sentences of the syntax contributes to the binary opposition between oppressor and victim with active and passive voices supporting the ascribed roles of each protagonist.

This use of syntactical phrasing to add to the dramatic quality of the writing and to build tension is clearly demonstrated in the following quotation (taken from the same short section of the Taranaki Report, the italics are mine) '. . . . Maori custom, law and institutions were judged by those who did not know them, *and the judgments were wrong*. The right of Maori to make their own decisions about who controlled the dispossession of land and the nature of the interests held was negated, *and the immediate result was war*. The long-term consequence was that the Government enforced a plan to alter Maori land tenure and *to destroy, by stealth and by arms*, the capacity of Maori to manage their own properties and *to determine rights with them*. The relationship the Government imposed was that *of dominance and sub-servience*.'

A final example, also from section 12.2 of the Taranaki Report (Wai 143, 1996), captures vividly the range of language techniques used in the reports (despite being only a sentence fragment). 'the invasion and sacking of Parihaka must rank with the most heinous action of any government, in any country, in the last century.' The build-up of qualifiers 'must', 'most', 'any' 'any' in such a short space empowers the sentence with authority. 'Invasion', 'sacking', 'heinous' evoke poetic epics of battles between the forces of good and evil. Finally, the periodic triple construction of the final phrases 'of any government, in any country, in the last century' is one of the most effective and evocative oratorical devices used in persuasive language.

Such historical and sociological writing contributes to the climate within international educational scholarship that authorises anti-Westernism as 'a new type of "Orientalism in reverse"' (Al-Azm, 1981, cited in Abaza and Stauth, 1990, p. 210). This occurs within the broader context of Occidentalism described by Buruma and Margalit (2004) as 'a dehumanizing picture of the West'. While those writers refer to contemporary Islam, pre-war Japan, Nazi Germany, and Mao's China, amongst others, the analysis is extended by Jonathan Friedman (2009) to include the anti-Westernism of postcolonial critiques, including indigenous scholarship.

Yet Occidentalism is an 'inverted representation of the West [which] is part of the logic of its identity formation'. Just as 'the other within and the external other are constituted simultaneously in the same process of Western expansion' so too is the 'external other' implicated in the decline of Western hegemony (Friedman, 2009, pp. 93–94). Occidentalism is the anti-Western logic of modernity in which 'the Other resurgent and its various expressions are particular versions of the general assault on the Western nation-state' (p. 99). But rather than an opposition to modernity, capitalism, and the West, Occidentalism is within the logic of the modern capitalist world. It allows emergent elites that use ideologies based on ethnicity, religion, and indigeneity to justify traditionalist modes of social regulation. These strategies secure the accumulation of capital for elites rather than for wider distribution in a period of the West's declining hegemony (Friedman, 2009).

In the ideologies that have in some cases (for example, New Zealand and Canada) become included in the university as disciplinary scientific knowledge, the 'mind of the West' unlike the East is presented as 'soulless', capable of 'developing and promoting advanced technology' but lacking in the 'spirituality and understanding of human suffering' (Buruma and Margalit, 2004, pp. 75–76), Like other forms of Occidentalism which reject the West for an idealised view of the East as a symbol of the unity of mind and soul, Maori re-tribalists promote their traditional beliefs as more spiritual and less corrupted by what was seen as the decaying materialism of the West. For example, the 1988 Waitangi Tribunal report on the Maori language referred to the East-West dichotomy in this way: 'The language is the embodiment of the particular spiritual and mental concepts of the Maori, more closely related to oriental tradition than to our western ways' (Wai 11, 1988).

A master's thesis, also from the New Zealand example, portrays a vivid account of what Steven Lukes calls the 'denigration of systematic thought' that exemplifies an extreme Occidentalism. Citing Berlin, Lukes identifies 'the "inarticulate, the mystical, the demonic, the dark reaches and mysterious depths"', the 'view of the world as 'an unordered succession of episodes, each carrying its value in itself, intelligible only by direct experience' as relativism's collapse into irrationalism (Lukes, 2003, p. 89). In the thesis, the writer (Walker, 1996) refers to the way her 'gut instincts scream out!' as she encounters the requirements of a thesis.

> Why this entrenchment in the notion of thesis as argument, as assertion, as proposition to be maintained? This Western Euro-centric notion of a thesis postulates knowledge as brute argument, dictates thought processes as oppositional elements in some theoretical battle' (p. 4).

The authority to set the criteria for who belongs and who is an outsider is one of the first stages in establishing authority over social knowledge. Producing its content and having that content accepted as disciplinary knowledge within the international disciplinary community is the next stage. Despite being unavailable for scrutiny by "outsiders", localised sociologies and histories are produced in the social sciences as a result of the "social construction of knowledge" approach. It is an approach that justifies not only the content itself, but the methodologies and procedures involved in producing the knowledge. More widely, the social construction of knowledge justifies the politics of ethnic boundary making and cultural closure. The next chapter is about the difference between disciplinary and social knowledge to show how the argument for conflating these two different types of knowledge discounts their very real and important difference.

5 Social Relations of Symbolic Production

The relationship between disciplinary knowledge and social knowledge is the central issue for the two opposed factions of social realism and social constructivism in the sociology of knowledge. The opposition rests on this question; how does knowledge that is produced in a social context become independent of its creators? For the constructivists in the sociology of knowledge, it doesn't—the knower remains tied to the knowledge which is understood to be always subjective and context dependent. In contrast social realists argue, as do realist epistemologists, that knowledge can be independent of its producers and therefore objective. (However, the agreement between the social realists and realist epistemologists does not extend to an agreement about the source of reasoning, a point I discuss later in the chapter).

It is the task of understanding the *sociality* of knowledge that divided the sociology of knowledge. On the one side, the various types of standpoint or constructivist theories claim that the knowledge produced by a social group is always tied to that group. This means that there can be no universal standard because all "knowledges" are context bound and therefore commensurate (Moore and Muller, 1999). Such relativism is rejected by social realists within the sociology of knowledge. Theorists such as Rob Moore, Johan Muller, and Michael Young argue that although knowledge is produced in social and historical circumstances, it is a product with its own materiality, and can therefore be separated from its producer. In other words, knowledge can be objective and universal.

How this separation occurs within the social relations of symbolic production is the subject of this chapter. Drawing on the social realist literature (for example, Muller, 2000, Moore and Young 2001; Moore, 2000, 2007a, 2007b; Moore and Maton, 2001; Young, 1998, 2008; Maton and Moore, 2010), I identify two interdependent features of symbolic production. The first is the production of structures, codes, and methods intrinsic to disciplinary knowledge. The second is the disciplinary institutions, systems, and procedures that authorise the generating epistemic concepts, principles, and content that constitute those structures, codes, and methods. These features develop within the specific material context identified in chapter 3—societies characterised by an expansionist economy, an individualised identity, and a universalist cosmology where trust rather than status is the societal bond.

Social realism draws on the school of critical realism in the philosophy of science associated with Roy Bhaskar (1975), Andrew Collier (1994), and Jose Lopez and Garry Potter (2001). Moore (2007a) provides an account of the usefulness of critical realism for education, saying that although 'it has yet to make a major impact in education studies', he sees critical realism as important given what he describes as 'the centrality of its implications for major concerns there' (p. 29). These are the concerns that I discuss in this book—the effects of localising knowledge in limiting opportunities for many young people, especially those in the working class and other localised groups, to use disciplinary knowledge as the means to empower their lives. The social realist approach enables these concerns to be recognised by asking that knowledge be returned to its rightful position as the focus of educational studies.

Social realists' commitment to developing a theory of knowledge is to explain why knowledge is distributed unequally in education and how schools can bring knowledge back in (Young, 2008). Central to the task is the recognition that although knowledge is socially produced and historically located, this does not compromise 'the possibility of rational objectivity in knowledge' (Moore, 2007a, p. 30) and hence its universal availability to all. This position underpins the social realist argument for the importance of disciplinary knowledge in the curriculum. Because that type of knowledge is objective, it has the power to take young people beyond the confines of their own experience. Michael Young (2008) uses the term 'powerful knowledge' to capture this sense of the self-actualising and political potential of objective knowledge.

Those two key ideas in social realism—that knowledge is socially produced but at the same time capable of becoming independent of that social context (i.e., objective) builds on Durkheim's commitment to the sociality as well as the materiality of knowledge:

> Everything in man has been made by mankind in the course of time. Consequently, if truth is human, it too is a human product. Sociology applies the same conception to reason. All that constitutes reason, its principles and categories, has been made in the course of history. That is why I can accept neither the statement of the idealists, that *in the beginning there is thought*, nor that of the pragmatists, that *in the beginning there is action.* (Durkheim, 1983, p. 67)

Constructivists on the other hand, dismiss the possibility of rational objectivity in knowledge precisely because it is produced by humans in social contexts and therefore subject to the culture and interests of its producers. 'Constructivist approaches locate knowledge within the consciousness and subjectivity of knowing subjects sharing an intersubjective social world' (Moore, 2007a, p. 31). Popper (1945/2003) referred to the 'astounding failure of sociologists of knowledge' (the precursors of social contructivists)

> to understand precisely its main subject, the *social aspects of knowledge*, or rather of the scientific method. It looks upon science of knowledge as a process in the mind or consciousness of the individual scientist, or perhaps as a product of such a process. If considered this way, what we call scientific objectivity must indeed become completely ununderstandable, or even impossible. If scientific objectivity were founded . . . upon the individual scientist's impartiality or objectivity, then we should say goodbye to it (p. 240).

It is in the recognition of the sociality of knowledge as 'the public arenas of collective judgement' where the 'objectivity of knowledge' is guaranteed by the 'specific practices of the disciplinary field—procedures, codes, system' (Moore and Young, 2010, p. 30) that Popper and the social realists in the sociology of knowledge are united against the Hegelian (now Foucauldian) constructivists. In his description of how scientific objectivity arises, Popper, like Moore and Young, refers to the 'public character of scientific method' with its 'free criticism' (1945/2003, p. 241) and the 'various social institutions which have been designed to further scientific objectivity and criticism; for instance the laboratories, the scientific periodicals, the congresses' (p. 242).

However, social realists part company with Popper and other rationalists in the explanation for the source of objective knowledge. For social realists, objective knowledge is a material 'product' developed in the 'distinctive modes of production' described by Moore (2007a, p. 30). This is 'an "emergent materialist" approach to the production of knowledge that sees symbolic production as organized through distinctive modes of production parallel to those of material production in the economic sphere' (p. 30). Just as there are social relations of production in that sphere so too are relations of production to be found in the sphere of symbolic or knowledge production. According to Moore,

> all forms of production entail a process of transformation requiring (a) a raw material (whether physical or symbolic); (b) a mechanism of transformation (a technology or theoretical apparatus); and (c) the combination of those things as an enduring systematic process within an organization of the social relations of production (as in a physical plant or an intellectual or aesthetic field) (2007a, p. 30).

It is this materiality of production that enables the symbolic product to be objectified and universalised.

Social constructivists reject that objectivity and view all knowledge as the outcome of the social context in which it is produced. In that line of argument, the disciplines of the arts, humanities, and sciences that have developed since the Enlightenment according to scientific principles and methodologies are simply the 'Western canon and an oppressive colonising one at that'. Indeed, Linda Smith, an influential promoter of "indigenous methodologies", refers to 'objectification [as] a process of dehumanisation' (1999, p. 39). Yet for Moore and other social realists that constructivist approach is 'flawed' (2007a, p. 38) because it confuses the conditions within which knowledge is produced with the knowledge product.

There is no doubt that knowledge is produced by people who have their own interests, concerns, and beliefs but whether those interests and beliefs become included in the knowledge product depends on what happens to the product. Does the knowledge remain tied to the interests of its producers or does it become separated from its originating context? For social realists, the objectivity of the truth claims in any given discipline depends upon the procedures within the disciplinary institutions themselves—those of scrutiny and critique that have been established over time within universities and other types of scientific centres to test the discipline's generative principles, conceptual framework, content, and methods. Scrutiny and criticism ensures that what we claim as knowledge is constantly justified; constantly required "to put itself on trial" in Habermas's metaphor. In addition, those truth claims are always provisional.

It is those procedures of justification that turn belief into knowledge (i.e., justified truth claims) and knowledge into a product that has a materiality separate from its creator—a materiality consisting of the codes and structures intrinsic to any given discipline. Without such procedures, as is the case with beliefs justified by experience alone, by an "I know because it is what we do" approach, knowledge remains as the unexamined beliefs and the tacit knowledge tied to everyday experience—important for its own reasons but different from the knowledge of the disciplines. However for those who take the relativist position, including social constructivists and the local knowledges movement, the 'ultimate source of justification [is] to be found in the prevailing social relations, cultural metaphors, and metaphysics claimed by writers in the various cultural studies and feminist offshoots, combined with postcolonial theory and post-development critiques' (Nanda, 2003, p. xiii).

For this group, even the procedures that justify science, 'the content and cognitive values used for assessing and evaluating the evidence of experiments' (Nanda, 2003, p. xiii) are considered to be non-universal. This creates an impasse between the two positions in the sociology of knowledge. It is an impasse in which the social constructivist argument fails. There are two reasons for the failure. One is the problem inherent to relativism—the claim that there is no universal standard is itself a universal statement. The social constructivist argument also fails because it does not recognise that the material codes and structures that constitute a discipline are neither context dependent nor *content* dependent. The generative principles and concepts that provide a discipline's theoretical tools remain the discipline's intrinsic structure even if the actual content changes, as indeed it must in an ever-changing world.

This is particularly important for the arts, humanities, and social sciences. Can these disciplines, which by their very nature have content that is socially located, be separated from experience and studied objectively in the same way as the physical sciences? It is true that the content of these disciplines and the content of everyday social knowledge may be the same or very similar. However, the codes and structures of the discipline contain concepts and theories which can lead to generalisation so that the content is illustrative of the truth of the concept. As Johan Muller points out, 'theory legitimately drives to generalisation' (2009, p. 506). Take the example of sociology; its disciplinary principles and theories enable the sociologist to understand the idea of social division according to the concepts of social categories such as "class", "caste", and "kinship".

Generalised statements about social division can then be applied to a number of situations, both historically and in the present using those concepts, although the content, the actual empirical facts, will change depending upon the society under examination. Content is of course essential for any discipline. The concepts need to be about something—but their closeness to the social context doesn't mean that the concepts and the theoretical explanation using those concepts are similarly tied. This relationship between conceptual knowledge and knowledge derived or constructed 'in some manner from experience' (Nola, 2001, p. 428)—what Robert Nola refers to as the 'old approach of the Aristotelians' (p. 428) and Kant the 'dogmatical solution' (1781/1993, p. 352)—is a key issue for social realists in explaining how disciplinary knowledge is separated from the original context within which it is produced. It is also an issue in explaining why that separation is important.

Theoretical understanding using a discipline's conceptual tools does what an empirical evidence-based approach cannot do. It captures the social meaning of events and explores causes and processes that are hidden in the phenomenon itself—'inquiring into the basis of the knowledge upon which the question rests' (Kant, 1781/1993, p. 352). For the social sciences, the messy reality of social life cannot be captured at one static moment and remain true for the next moment, yet empirically driven research makes claims based on that static moment. It was for this reason that empiricism was rejected by the rationalist philosophical tradition 'running from Montesquieu through the philosophors of the Enlightenment—Turgot, Condorcet, St Simon—to Comte and then Durkheim, a tradition in which conclusions were reached by analysis of concepts rather than of facts, the facts being used as illustrations of formulations reached by other than inductive means' (Evans-Pritchard, 1954), p. vii).

The impossibility of matching evidence to theorised explanation in any fixed and permanent way does not make social research pointless. If it helps to 'illuminate a range of historical and contemporary data' (Bhaskar, 1989, p. 5) by throwing light on the way various processes come together as social movements embedded in deep globalising transformation, then it serves a useful explanatory purpose. Critical realist philosopher, Roy Bhaskar, refers to the way theory can also play a 'prognostic role in the social domain' by 'situating possibilities long before they are manifested' (1989, p. 5). What examples taken from empirical evidence can do is show the usefulness of the theory to help us understand society, but with the proviso that the meaning of that evidence is analysed critically in accordance with the theoretical concepts of a discipline.

Using idealised models applied in ideal, non-actual or non-real situations, but which, as Nola (2001) points out, also 'take a '"rationalist" stance' in that they 'remain open to comparison with experience' (p. 430) can provide ways into theorising the patterns and processes of causation. Although 'no ideally constructed model will fit reality exactly, there will be better and better degrees of fit' (p. 429). Similarly, Durkheim (1983) had also noted that 'an idea is true, not because it conforms to reality, but by virtue of its creative power' (p. 84). The role of the 'creative power' in producing ideas is one of the features of scientific programmes that Lakatos (1978) identified in his reference to 'novel facts, facts which have been either undreamed of, or have indeed been contradicted by previous or rival programmes' (p. 5). This creative power is the imaginative component of science that Kant (1781/1993) referred to as the 'third faculty' (p. 135). It distinguishes conceptual thinking used to create religious beliefs and political ideologies which enable people to explain their society from the conceptual reasoning required for explaining what is unknown but what humans attempt to explain without recourse to the supernatural or to experience.

Theorised or idealised explanations of what may not be experienced are not only the content of a discipline's intrinsic structures; they are the source of innovation in the disciplines. Galileo's use of geometry and mathematics is referred to by Michael Matthews (2000) to illustrate the significance of idealised models using a discipline's theoretical tools as the means by which new knowledge is created. Another common illustration of rationalist knowledge is Einstein's theory that the 'only true constant, the speed of light meant that time can run faster or slower depending on how high you are, and how fast you are travelling' (Connor, 2010, p. B14). Although this was an idealised model, the exact precision of atomic clocks have recently revealed that the effects of gravitational pull shows how close the model is to reality (Connor, 2010). Aristotle's conceptualisation of the metaphor provided one of the most important concepts in language and literature studies. Similarly, Linnaeus gave botany its classification taxonomy, and Marx contributed the idea of exploitative classed relations of production in the capitalist economic system to political philosophy.

The endurance of concepts is about more than whether or not they fit the real world. Concepts enable us to understand the world and to think about what we don't yet know. They may turn out to fit the real world, as with Einstein's model previously referred to, or they may not, or we may never know. But the applicability of an idea is only one part of its usefulness. Ideas are not isolated. As parts of larger disciplines, they feed into the imagination that gives disciplines vitality. An idea that turns out in the end to be wrong is still important because it is an idea that uses the symbolic code of the discipline. In doing this, it has value. The rejected idea serves its purpose by being tested, its rejection proving the rigour of the procedures of critique and revealing a research programme that is no longer worth pursuing. In addition the act of reasoning using the concepts, principles, and theories of a discipline contributes to building the discipline's symbolic code and its integrating structure.

Although abstract scientific models may be 'empirically adequate' (Nola, 2001, p. 430), both Nola (2001), and Matthews (2000) emphasis that the central feature of science is its ability to 'revise and improve, or reject the models that have been proposed' in accordance with the 'cycle of "conjecture and refutation" that occurs time and time again in the history of science' (Nola, 2001, p. 430), subjective experience is rejected as the starting point for understanding the world because, as Descartes (1637/1956) recognised a century before Kant, 'our senses sometimes deceive us'. His starting point was to 'suppose that nothing is such as they (i.e., our senses) make us imagine it'. Accordingly:

> I resolved to feign that everything which has ever entered into my mind was no more than the illusions of my dreams. But immediately afterwards I observed that while I desired everything to be false, I, who thought, must of necessity be something; and remarking that this truth, I think therefore I am, was so firm and so assured, I judged that I could unhesitatingly accept it as the first principle of the philosophy I was seeking. (p. 53)

The mistrust in our senses as the source of knowledge has a long heritage. David Lindberg (1992) points out that 'Parmenides and Zeno knew perfectly well what experience taught, but the question was whether experience could be trusted' (p. 33). 'Parmenides distinguished between "the way of seeing" associated with observation, and "the way of truth" trod by reason'. In his discussion of the Ancient Greeks' engagement with the philosophy of science, Lindberg passes on the advice that Parmenides gave in his poem where he

> warned against letting 'custom, born of much experience, force thee to wander along this road thy aimless eye, thy echoing ear or thy tongue; but do not thou judge by reason the strife-encompassed proof that I have spoken'. (p. 33)

Like Descartes and Parmenides, Kant (1781/1993) separated sense and experiences from concepts and thinking but went further to link them in a contingent way, that is, in the *a priori* condition. According to Politis (1993), Kant suggested that 'a concept can apply to what we experience even if it cannot be defined in terms of what we experience; it may do so by being a necessary condition for the possibility of experiencing things and of using concepts to describe what we experience. Kant calls this way of establishing objective validity of concepts "the *a priori* or transcendental way". "Transcendental" means "concerning the necessary conditions for the possibility of experiencing things and of describing what we experience"' (p. xli).

Politis (1993) considers that Kant was right in arguing that

> a concept that is a necessary condition for experiencing things that could not be defined by appeal to what we experience. What we experience could always have been different from what we experience it to be; it is contingent rather than necessary states of affairs that we experience. The method is *a priori* or independent of experience in the sense that it does not defend the empirical validity of concepts by defining them in terms of what we experience. (p. xlii)

This is Kant's justification for the *a priori* concept. He argued 'that in order to avoid the separation of appearance and reality, we need to conceive of space and time as essentially tied to our capacity to experience things' (Politis, 1993, p. xlv). The Kantian idea that mental activity is the source of reason is the point of disagreement between realists in epistemology on the one hand and social realists in the sociology of knowledge on the other. For Durkheim (1983), a major influence on social realist ideas, it is the very sociality of knowledge with

> all that constitutes reason, its principles and categories, has been made in the course of history that is the reason he could not accept neither the statement of the idealists, that *in the beginning there is thought*, nor that of the pragmatists, that *in the beginning there is action*. (p. 67)

Similarly Moore (2007a) distinguishes between the 'differing logics of inquiry between the two disciplines' (p. 27), that of the sociology of knowledge (to which the social realists belong) and realist epistemology.

Randall Collins's (2000) position that 'if ideas are determined by social interaction, then they cannot be determined by truth' (p. 7) sums up the difference between the epistemological realists and the social realists in sociology of knowledge. Collins's social realist explanation of the materiality of knowledge production in the various social institutions of academic disciplines is quite different from Kant's categorical apparatus whereby the 'framework of our intellectual outfit, i.e. human reason' (Popper, 1945/2003, p. 237) is the source of objective knowledge. For Kant, knowledge is

> largely the result of our own mental activity, an 'activist' theory of knowledge that requires us to actively engage ourselves in searching, comparing, unifying, generalizing is we wish to attain knowledge . . . He [Kant] made it quite clear that we cannot start from nothing, and that we have to approach our task equipped with a system of presuppositions which we hold without having tested them by the empirical methods of science. (p. 237)

The idea that knowledge originates in the mind of the scientist is captured in Kant's well-known statement from the *Critique of Pure Reason* (1781/1993), where he states that 'all rational knowledge is based either on concepts, or on the construction of concepts' (p. 535). Kant called this faculty *cognito ex principiis* (p. 354)—the intellectual resource of conceptual thinking that enables individuals to 'exercis(e) our powers of reasoning in accordance with general principles, retaining at the same time, the right of investigating the sources of these principles, of testing, and even of rejecting them' (p. 535).

Social realists reject the *a priori* concept of reasoning based in the mental apparatus for the idea that knowledge is created in the sociality of the relations of symbolic production. Moore (2007a, 2007b) explains how the sociology of knowledge, in attempting to 'recover the relationship between knowledge and the social and historical conditions under which it is produced' was unable to accept the claim made by epistemology that 'it is possible to distinguish between those beliefs that can be justified as true and those others that cannot' (2007a, p. 27). However, this disagreement between realist epistemologists and social realists over the source of objective knowledge and the role of the individual should not overshadow the importance of their shared agreement that knowledge can be objective and universal and their opposition to constructivism and relativism. What is important is that both social realists and realist epistemologists support the idea that knowledge can be objective while constructivists reject objective knowledge.

The postmodernist, social constructivist strand of the sociology of knowledge shows a real hostility to the idea of objectification itself—what is often referred to as the "Cartesian binary". This is the separation of the objective from the subjective, of the conceptual from everyday experience, of mind and body that is the crucial idea in social realism and epistemological realism. Popkewitz (2001, p. 327), for example, proposes a 'radical constructivism' to overcome 'the Cartesian binary' that, in 'twentieth-century European social theory' 'separate mind from body and individuality from social relations and history'. These 'binaries', he claims:

> are not just theoretical: they also entail practices. This is evident in school pedagogies. Scientific theories of instruction, for example, have been built on binaries: concepts are separated from methods, and the

> cognitive is separated from the affective. Teacher education courses that separate knowledge about "school and society" from knowledge about learning stand as testimony to the binaries in which the social/personal and mind/body splits are naturalised in teaching. (p. 327)

Indigenous writers tend to locate all "Western" science in the Cartesian binary. Roberts and Wills (1998) for example, set the binary up as the 'other' to 'Maori metaphysics', where 'this Cartesian dichotomy between an observing, thinking self and the outside world cannot and does not exist. . . any understanding of the Maori worldview must come from a subjective approach'. Citing an influential Maori religious leader, Roberts and Wills shut the door on science by saying that 'the route . . . through abstract interpretation is a deadend' (p. 50). This is a powerful statement about the closing down of knowledge. It contains the echo of the clerics throughout the ages who have attacked science and progress (Freeman, 2003). Without abstract interpretation of the natural and social worlds, we are left confined to the world of immediate experience and subject to the interpretations of those claiming a source of knowledge in the supernatural. It is the vision of a dark age.

The rejection of abstract interpretation is not confined to those whose faith lies with the supernatural. It is a rejection that permeates the social sciences, especially educational studies. Critical pedagogy writers Semali and Kincheloe (1999) claim that 'an awareness of the ways epistemological "truth production" operates in the lived world may shake the western scientific faith in Cartesian-Newtonian epistemological foundationalism'. The awareness that knowledge is 'more a socio-political process than an exercise of a universal form of disinterested abstract reason' may help the Western analyst to 'reassess the criteria for judging knowledge claims in light of the problems inherent in calling upon a transcultural, universal faculty of reason' (p. 17). Lest this suggests relativism, the reader is assured that 'in these anti-foundational (a rejection of a transcultural referent for truth such as the Western scientific method) dynamics the hell of relativism is avoided by an understanding of culturally-specific discursive practices' (p. 17). It is not clear in their explanation, however, exactly how this 'hell of relativism' is avoided. The approach is, in fact, relativist despite the disclaimer.

The promotion of localised cosmologies, where knowledge of the world is tied to the experience of that world (with various types of supernatural or mystical justification called upon in some instances), is the defining feature of the constructivist approach. Although the social constructivism that surged in popularity in the social sciences during the 1990s took into mainstream education the 'idea that all beliefs, but particularly scientific beliefs, are constructions out of sensory experience' (Nola, 2001, p. 429), the extreme form of 'radical constructivism' (Popkewitz, 2001) went further. The 'undoing of the Cartesian opposition of mind and body and the distinctions between ideas and material existence' (p. 327) could be achieved in schools by not only using 'learners sense-making processes' but by discarding the notion that teachers have knowledge that might benefit the learner. Accordingly, 'teachers must interact with students in such a way that knowledge is co-created' (Bishop and Glynn, 1999, p. 165). The implications of this are serious. As Nola (1997) points out: 'Constructivists have a distorted conception of knowledge which infects their view of learning', one leading to the state of affairs where 'the role of reason in knowledge and our sciences is quite enfeebled' (p. 81).

In education the 'widespread acceptance of alternatives to objectivism, one of which is constructivism' (Tobin, 1993, p. ix) has reduced the 'universal reason of humanity' (Kant, 1781/1993, p. 491) to experiences to be known. This 'unsatisfactory account of knowledge' (Nola, 1997, p. 55)—is the "I know because I was there", "I know because I feel", "I know because I believe", and "I know because I am" kind (Rata, 2011c). It replaces the systematic critical inquiry fuelled by continual doubt—the science of the Enlightenment heritage. By locating knowledge in the experiences of the "knower", constructivism emphasises the emotional dimension of human existence, regarding that dimension as a part of thinking. Kathryn Ecclestone (2010) draws our attention to the dangers of 'the rapid incursion of an emotional epistemology into formal education' saying how such an epistemology is a 'logical outcome of an education system no longer committed to an externally-seeking human subject and forms of knowledge to foster it'. Her comment that 'it is hard to overstate the extent to which the idea of a universal, externally-seeking human subject is held in contempt' (p. 3) is not hard to accept if one has spent time immersed in the rapidly growing literature of localised epistemologies.

These include for example, "feminist epistemology" (Harding, 1998), "red pedagogy" (Grande, 2009), "southern theory" (Connell, 2009), and "indigenous methodology" (Smith, 1999), among others. The production of an "indigenous episteme" with its basis in Occidentalism is one of the constructivist discourses that have become accepted in academia. One example of many that show its taken-for-granted place in New Zealand is a study of 'the Maori concept of Hauora' (balanced development). This refers to the 'physical, spiritual, pedagogical, and socio-economic dimensions' in a teacher education programme. Despite the legal secular status of the country's education system, the researcher approvingly found that this 'culturally relevant model using Maori epistemological constructions of the world', has a 'strong influence on beginning teacher programmes' (Main, 2009, p. 101).

In social constructivist literature, the Enlightenment universal human subject is replaced by the person "created" in the Lacanian intersubjectivity of social relations (Lacan, 1977). The former is seen as the false consciousness of a socially constructed identity; false because the identity that we recognise in ourselves is merely a mirror image, built within the interactions and language of the social group. Only within that social construction of the recognised image of who we are meant to be can the human exist fully as a social being according to this approach. For relativists 'the "free" and "autonomous" individual is a necessary fiction for enabling modern cultures to function' (Irwin, 2008, p.73). The knowledge produced in each society can therefore be nothing more than the construction of the knower—the product of social groups and their interests—that is, ideological knowledge serving the powerful. Rational human thought developed within the material relations of symbolic production (for social realists) or in the minds of reasoning individuals (for realist epistemologists) is understood in this way by social constructivists. It is mere ideology internalised as false consciousness by less powerful groups and complicit in their subjugation.

A telling indictment of the pervasiveness of the constructivist view that "knowledge is ideology" and the reasoning person an Enlightenment "fiction" is Ecclestone's (2010) account of a collegial exchange. She was asked to explain her attachment to 'the discredited and outdated myth of the universal, externally-facing human subject, and the "failed project" of an education system based on this subject' (p. 14), an incident which indicates the extent to which science is on the defence as it is forced to defend itself against charges of ideology. For sociologists of education like myself, who have taught few post-graduate students not raised on postmodernism, social constructivism, culturalism, and the "truth" of local "knowledges", the Enlightenment human subject is similarly almost incomprehensible to some of my students. Their efforts to find the agent for the discipline's politicised goal of social transformation must, of necessity, fail. Without the human subject who 'releases himself' from 'his self-incurred tutelage' through the 'courage of his own reasoning' (Kant, 1784/1990, p. 1), where is the source of human agency? The rational humanist subject of the Enlightenment is needed both for reasoning and for the democratic politics that promote and safeguard a science that must constantly justify its knowledge against peer critique. That science is based upon the Enlightenment commitment to the superiority of 'a mode of arriving at a settled decision' that is based upon a 'critical investigation of reason itself' (Kant, 1781/1993, p. 490) and not upon the 'injustice and violence that Hobbes maintains is our natural state' (Habermas, 2001, p. 30).

Despite the loud assertion by social constructivists that the autonomous individual is a 'fiction' (Irwin, 2008, p.73), it is that socially located individual who thinks. I have referred in chapter 3 to the political economic context within which individualisation becomes a strong identity pole. Included in the strengthening of individualism in periods of economic expansion is an intellectual individualism. Durkheim recognised this connection between the loosening of social bonds based in religious conformity and the rise of the reasoning individual engaged in symbolic production. 'As long as mythological truth holds sway, conformity is the rule. Once scientific thought becomes paramount, however, intellectual individualism appears' (Durkheim, 1983, p. 91). According to Cullivier in his preface to *Pragmatism and Sociology* (1983) 'Durkheim shows how "intellectual individualism" develops with the arrival of rational and scientific thought, which itself is a correlative of the increasing complexity of societies. He is to conclude that "truth is only ever achieved by individuals"' (p. xx).

The relationship between society and the individual is a major issue for social realists. Given the social realist claim that knowledge is produced within the social relations of symbolic production, what is the role of the individual? Is the intellectual agent the reasoning thinker proposed by Kant and the realist epistemologists? Or do symbolic relations of production determine a "knowing individual" in the same way as the social relations of economic production determine the classed individual in Marxist theory? If so, then the difference between social realism and constructivism collapses within a shared deterministic theory—regardless of whether it is class relations, symbolic relations, or the cultural relations of the constructivists that are determining.

It was a question addressed by Durkheim (1983), who argued that although truth is social, 'even the collective element in it exists only through the consciousness of individuals, and truth is only ever achieved by individuals' (p. 98). That thinking individual who comes from yet criticises his or her society from within uses methods of objectification and ideas developed within the 'coalitions of mind' (Collins, 2000, p. 7) of disciplinary canons. This is the modern individual who exists in a state of partial loyalty to the society, as the next chapter explains. It is here in the concept of partial loyalty that I argue for a non-deterministic understanding of the reasoning individual who engages in the sociality of knowledge production.

6 Social Relations of Trust

The objective knowledge developed in the arts, humanities, social sciences, and sciences is important to liberal democracies for political as well as for educational reasons. This chapter is about the link between the objectivity of epistemic knowledge and the rational thinking required for democracy. It draws on Alan Macfarlane's (2002) ideas about 'partial loyalty' (p. 271), a concept developed in the literature about the role of contractual associations in making the modern world (the title of Macfarlane's book). According to this approach, the partial loyalty of social relations of trust enables the simultaneous attachment and separation towards knowledge that is required for objectivity and criticism. Macfarlane (2002) refers to the development of a world of trust and openness as 'the basis not only for capitalism but also for modern science' (p. 106), a view of science's role in modern society shared by Sharplin and discussed in chapter 3. Along with their importance in establishing and maintaining relations of trust between people in societies based on contract not status, objectivity, criticism, and judgement are also features of democratic citizenship.

The student who 'knows only what has been told him, (whose) judgements are only those which he has received from his teachers (and) has formed his mind on another's. His knowledge has not been drawn from reason. He is merely the plaster-cast of a man' (Kant, 1781/1993, p. 535). Such imbibed understanding is the doxic or embodied knowledge of subjective experience, where 'we accept many things without knowing them' (Bourdieu and Eagleton, 1992, p. 113). It is the commonsense reality of experience that is the source of ideology and the reason for ideology's power. But it is a reality in which our "senses may fail us". Only the provisional truth claims of objective knowledge can reveal the ideological or cultural nature of experience.

This means that the reasoning required for disciplinary knowledge is that which is critical both of itself and of the society which that knowledge serves. It employs the sociological imagination which makes the familiar unfamiliar and enables us to conceptualise that which is unknown to us. Forms of social organisation that have been developed in the academic disciplines over time, forms that arise from the 'cognitive interests' (Young,

2008, p. 31) of intellectualised individuals and that are produced in disciplinary institutions, are intimately connected to the partial loyalty of contractual social organisation. That partial loyalty enables agency—whether the agency of the intellectual individual in knowledge creation or the rational citizen in democratic politics.

Social knowledge and academic knowledge have much in common. Both types of knowledge are produced by people within a social context and in the service of the society. Both have their origin in the sacred of the traditional world where 'in general no distinction is drawn between the natural, the supernatural, and the human; the gods do not transcend the universe but are rooted in it and subject to its principles' (Lindberg, 1992, p. 8). But as David Lindberg (1992) observes, the early 'conceptions of space and time are not (like those of modern physics) abstract and mathematical, but are invested with meaning and value drawn from the experience of the community' (p. 8). With reference to the origin myths of several early societies, Lindberg points to the 'strong tendency in oral traditions to identify causes with beginnings, so that to explain something is to identify its historical origins' (p. 8).

This is a significant observation and helps with the task of delineating one of the major differences between social realism and social constructivism—that of abstract conceptual knowledge. Whereas scientific knowledge is characterised by advanced theoretical and conceptual understanding, social knowledge too conceptualises the world in the beliefs found in religious and cultural explanations for the unknown. However with social knowledge, the meaning and value of knowledge remain tied to the experience of the social group. The beliefs do not become abstract concepts capable of being applied to other times and other situations. They remain experience-based beliefs even if the experience referred to occurred in mythological times. In this way, commonsense knowledge, although located in the reality of experience, is ideological. It is not a "false consciousness", because it is deeply embedded in the reality of everyday life and is a "way of knowing" that arises from that experience. For this reason the cultural beliefs that make up ideology are extremely difficult to change (Shalem and Bensusan, 1999). But although such social knowledge is the "truth" of our lives it is one limited in what and how it can explain the world given that it is always tied to the the world of the "knower".

Like Durkheim, Lindberg (1992) traces the emergence of science from the early understandings of the sacred, describing how the contemplation of natural phenomena led to new sets of questions and new sets of answers with 'personification of nature gradually becoming a less-prominent feature of their (the early philosophers) discourse, and the gods disappearing from their explanations of natural phenomena' (p. 26) as a 'distinction between the natural and the supernatural was emerging' (p. 27). The distinction between the natural and the supernatural, which has enabled the growth of science as objective knowledge, was developed within the canons of the various disciplines. These were communities of scholars across time and space that produced the 'coalitions of minds' described by Collins (2000, p. 7)—a claim accepted by social realists to support the argument that knowledge is produced within social and historical circumstances but not limited to those circumstances. It is in the sociality of the canon that the collective representations of the discipline are generated. According to Durkheim (1995):

> Collective representations are the product of immense cooperation that extends not only in space but also through time; to make them, a multitude of different minds have associated, intermixed, and combined their ideas and feelings; long generations have accumulated their experience and knowledge. A very special intellectuality that is infinitely richer and more complex than that of the individual is distilled in them. (p. 15)

Despite the sociality of the production of knowledge, the "product" is able to be separated from those conditions of production—for reasons that I described in the previous chapter. That is one of the crucial differences between social realist and constructivist arguments. Another distinction concerns the role of the individual in generating knowledge and contributing to the disciplinary canon. Not only must the knowledge be separated from the knower, but that "knower" must have a degree of agency within the social relations of symbolic production. In order to be a critic within disciplinary systems and procedures researchers must be capable of objectifying their own conditions of existence, including the symbolic relations of production within which they are located. In doing so researchers are intellectual agents contributing to producing the collective canon, not to merely reproducing it.

Social knowledge is characterised by its role as the means to reproduce a socio-cultural group. It preserves the "culture" in order to maintain continuity and cohesion. In contrast, modern societies are characterised by internal mechanisms of change, what Alan Macfarlane (2002) describes as 'the unusual properties of the new kind of grouping' to emerge in societies based on contract not status (p. 259). This is the partial loyalty made possible by the fact that individuals can enter and leave social groups according to the person's volition—something not possible with groups organised according to kin and ethnicity. The idea of partial loyalty can also be usefully applied to academic communities. They, like members of socio-political organisations, have an "entry and escape clause". Neither the researchers nor their ideas are required to be totally loyal to the wider group, as is the case with religio-cultural groups. The latter require such total loyalty to maintain social and political cohesion. But it is a condition of the academic system that its members are not "loyal", that they remain critical and judgmental.

For this reason, although ideas are created within the social relations of symbolic production of any particular discipline, those relations are not necessarily determining of the intellectual thinker who produced them. They do determine the systems, methods, and codes that are used, that is true, but the scientist is not restricted to reproducing the theories and concepts of the discipline. He or she is able to change them. While the disciplinary systems and procedures allow for the development of innovative theories, it is the individual scientist either alone or with colleagues whose creativity is "distilled" in the complex intellectuality of the canon.

Michael Young (2008) refers to one of the two goals he identifies for social realism as 'to explore how the forms of social organization that arise from "cognitive" interests may themselves shape the organization of society itself' (p. 31). That exploration is my purpose here to link the type of institutions made possible in contractual societies to those institutions and procedures of science. The link is to be found in the partial loyalty that characterise the social relations of trust required for criticism and judgement. The rise of objective knowledge that contains criticism as a key part of its logic is intimately associated with the shift from status-based to contractual societies and the resulting individualisation of personal identity that followed from the breakdown of the kinship structuring principle. Trust emerged as the unifying device for this new social order.

My interest in this chapter is in examining the relationship between contractual society and objective knowledge to explore the nature of the link. I find it in a politics of knowledge that contains two features; one is the processes of objectivity, criticism, and judgement that allows for the partial loyalty of attachment and distance exercised in the disciplinary canons and in democratic politics. The second feature is the social relations of trust that provide the context for that partial loyalty to operate. The organising principle of liberal democratic societies in the modern world is that of contract, and it is in the making of the contractual relationships and the public sphere as the site for those relationships that objective knowledge plays a major role. It is for this reason that I devote the first section of the chapter to explaining the shift from status to contract—what Henry Maine describe as the 'the greatest of all changes' (Maine, cited in Macfarlane, 2002, p. 16)—before turning to examining how objectivity creates the partial loyalty that is a necessary condition for the exercise of critical reasoning in contractual societies.

How do societies with populations that do not share a common past cohere and hold themselves together? The status to contract issue is an old question for modernity—one asked by thinkers from Montesquieu, Adam Smith, and Tocqueville to Marx, J. S. Mill, and Durkheim. According to Alan Macfarlane a question at the heart of sociology is: What is the 'way in which the individual is embedded in wider groupings'? (p. 5). In *The Making of the Modern World* (2002), Macfarlane traces what it was about the change in the individual-group relationship that enabled the shift to modern liberal democratic societies. Convinced by the nineteenth-century historian, F. W. Maitland's argument that the answer is found in the non-kinship corporations and trusts that characterise English common law and equity from the Anglo-Saxon period, Macfarlane asks the rhetorical question: 'How could civilisations avoid the Scylla of status and also the Charybdis of contract?' His answer is that 'the way lay through some combination of the best of both; the affective, emotional ties of status, the flexibility and efficiency of contract' (p. 259).

In tracing the development of contractual associations as 'a new kind of grouping', Macfarlane brings back into the literature Maitland's ideas about how a new form of cooperation emerging from the early English 'proto-trusts' 'could balance the allegiances of group and individual' and replace societies based on status bonds' (p. 259). According to Macfarlane (2002), Maitland 'finally solved the problem of combining individualism and associations in a new way' (p. 3) in explaining the 'origins and nature of the modern world' (p. 4). This is indeed a powerful statement. If it is the case, then Maitland's insights will also assist those like myself who wrestle with how to explain the relationship between a determinism in the relations of symbolic production and the agency of individuals in creating Durkheim's 'collective representations' (1995, p. 15).

While the canon '*enables* a particular type of activity and its principles are *generative*' given that it is the 'knowledge not the knower that counts' (Moore, 2007b, p. 68), the individual *is* consciously involved in the creation of knowledge. In this way, I would argue, the knower *does* count (although not tied forever to the knowledge as the constructivists would argue). Along with creating ideas that become distilled in the canon's complex intellectuality, the scientist is simultaneously a member of the disciplinary community and its critic. It is this "knower" who enacts the systems and procedures of objectification and criticism authorised by the discipline as well as doing the actual thinking. As Durkheim (cited in Culliver, 1983) maintained, 'truth is only ever achieved by individuals' (p. xx). However, Durkheim traced the condition for individualism in the social division of labour.

My argument that the form individuality takes with its "partial loyalty" under certain political conditions—conditions enabled by the objectivity of knowledge—does not deny the location of individualism in economic relations. However I do argue that the contractual nature of liberal democratic political relations acts as a counterbalance to the determinism of capitalist relations of production. This is the case because the partial loyalty of contractual social relations encourages objectification, and with it, criticism and judgement. It is for this reason that the uneasy but workable settlement between liberalism and capitalism of the expansive industrial period was the condition for the extension of epistemic knowledge to the wider population. The stronger the forces of liberal democracy, the greater the spread of epistemic knowledge with its objectivity and criticism.

However, since the 1970s, the democracy-capitalism settlement of the industrial era has weakened. Reactionary and conservative political forces with their accompanying strategies of localisation have found that accumulation in the era of financial capitalism appears to operate effectively alongside non-democratic polities. The success of capitalist accumulation in countries governed by oligarchies and autocracies as well as the emergence of localised forms of capitalism, such as neotribal capitalism in New Zealand (Rata, 2000; 2011b) would support this view. It would appear that democracy is no longer the price that capitalist elites need to pay by placating the working class in return for expanding profits. This realisation that democracy may not be the only polity suited to capitalist accumulation supports the rise of conservative elites, increasing inequalities, and liberal-democratic nations that govern increasingly on behalf of global capitalism rather than on behalf of the people.

It is a pyrrhic victory for capitalism however. As democracy declines, so too does epistemic knowledge, given one is a condition for the other. Capitalism, by weakening the conditions for objective knowledge through various localisation strategies, weakens its own foundations. The source of creativity required for capitalist expansion is located in epistemic knowledge. The "long twentieth century" settlement between capitalism and democracy was not only a settlement with the working class, it was a settlement with science. While financial capitalism may believe it can dismiss the claims of working people for greater equality, it cannot do without objective knowledge. However, such knowledge also serves democratic aspirations. This means that contemporary capitalism is mistaken to think that its rejection of the settlement with democracy is in its best interests. Creative capitalism still needs the "turbulent individual" who can think objectively. Democracy is the price to be paid for science.

But before continuing with the idea that the objectivity and critical reasoning developed in the disciplines is made possible by the social relations of trust in liberal democracies—I indulge in an intriguing tangent—one that also fascinated Macfarlane. Given the importance of Maitland's contribution to explaining the modern world, what accounts for the amnesia surrounding his work? Macfarlane attributes that amnesia to 'the way in which earlier knowledge of a high quality is quietly forgotten' (p. 7). I include these comments here as a further reason for the importance of the structuration of disciplinary knowledge with its procedures of building on the work of earlier thinkers through processes of scrutiny and criticism. The collective representations developed over time that become the disciplinary canon are undermined by the constructivist conflation of knowledge and the knower. It means if one does not approve of the politics of the philosopher or the politics of the age in which the philosopher worked, then one also rejects his or her ideas. This has enabled the dismissal of earlier thinkers as "dead, white men" and of their ideas as well. It means the generation of students raised within postmodernism miss out on the philosophical heritage that underpins today's social sciences.

I recall one of my postgraduate students justifying her refusal to read anything from the "dead white male camp" by saying that not only did those writers contribute to Western patriarchy but so did their writings. For her, the knower and the knowledge were inseparable. Because she refused to read the work of Enlightenment thinkers, she missed out not only on understanding the historical context of today's sociological theories but also on those works with which she would have a degree of sympathy. These would, I have no doubt, include Kant's essay *On Enlightenment* (1784/1990) and Mills's *The Subjugation of Women* (1869/1999). She also missed out on acquiring the historical way of thinking required for the sociological imagination. Most unfortunate of all is that she will never know what she has missed. Although that student was at the extreme end of the postmodern generation of graduates, her dismissal of the knowledge of the last three hundred years on the grounds of the sex of its producers captures the intransigence and irrationality of the postmodern fundamentalist that I referred to in chapter 4. It is also a real problem for emerging researchers in indigenous studies, where a hostility to "Western" ideas can mean that the young researcher is confined to an ahistorical intellectual context.

To return to the amnesia surrounding Maitland—a silence that cannot be blamed on postmodernism since Macfarlane identified it in the 1960s. The silence suggests a larger problem; how to maintain disciplinary knowledge down through the generations without important ideas becoming lost, or alternately, other ideas taking over as an authoritative "creed" in the manner of moribund degenerative science. When the latter happens, disciplinary knowledge is reduced to stultified and stultifying "truths". Indeed that is a charge levelled at the traditional school curriculum by social constructivists—one not without some foundation—although the answer lies in re-vitalising the knowledge that is taught and in teaching it well, not in rejecting it. In the case of the former, when ideas are simply lost, as exemplified by the amnesia concerning F. W. Maitland, it was not that Maitland's ideas were abandoned because they had been tried and found wanting. That would suggest a vibrant discipline doing what it should do—testing and discarding as warranted. In this case it appears that the ideas had simply been overlooked and then forgotten. Yet, like Macfarlane, I also consider Maitland's ideas insightful, finding in his explanation of a new form of social organisation based on trust and its institutional expression in legal trusts a powerful explanation for the emergence and resilience of contractual societies. This includes the "contractual" society of the scientific community. Their "discovery" by Macfarlane and my own use of the ideas may well exemplify the cooperation over time that may be seen not only as a continual process, but as one that has its stops, starts, and disjunctures.

Maitland drew on earlier ideas about the role of trusts in the modern world and contributed to taking the ideas further. Voltaire (1647/1994) had, as early in the modern period as the seventeenth century, identified the emerging new forms of association based on trust (in his case a trust engendered by common business interests) that overrode race and religion. Accordingly, 'the Jew, the Mahometan, and the Christian transact together, as though they all profess the same religion and give the name of infidel to none but bankrupts' (p. 30). Over three centuries later the two great unanswered questions that Macfarlane returned to remain central to sociological inquiry.

The first concerns the exceptional case of modernity, where civilisation favours the individual rather than the group as the political subject. The second is 'what could possibly hold such a system together? If kinship is restrained, God was kept out of the market, the state inhibited, how and why should people work effectively together?' (2002, p. 257). Given social realism's preoccupation with the sociality of knowledge, these are questions as relevant for that discipline as for political science. For society generally, the institutions of the political sphere—the state—and the institutions of the broader public sphere—civil society—provide the sites and systems for the individual to exercise partial loyalty to the group and, in doing so, enable individualisation and, at the same time, group commitment. For academia more specifically, the institutions of each discipline offer the site and systems for that partially loyal engagement.

The intellectual conversations across time by those in the same or interrelated disciplines are part of the procedures of academic knowledge that guarantee its truthfulness. It is a point made by the social realists in their use of Collins's metaphor "coalitions of the mind" as the sub-title in the edited volume by Karl Maton and Rob Moore (2010) that brings together some of the major articles in the emerging social realist canon. The idea emphasises the importance of scholarship that builds disciplinary knowledge over the centuries. As a relative newcomer to this coalition, my interest in applying the ideas of Maitland and Macfarlane to social realism is because both writers provide insights into the socialising character of contractual associations and it is the very *sociality* of knowledge that is the central issue for social realists. Such associations, which include academic communities, must remain connected to their social contexts if they are to survive, and yet they must also be able to exercise critical judgement within that very context; a criticism that has the potential to destabilise the discipline's existence. What accounts for the stability of that vulnerable state? It is a contradiction that exists in contractual societies as in disciplinary institutions. According to Maitland and Macfarlane, it is the social relations of trust that stabilise the society while at the same time allowing the contradiction to serve as the vehicle for innovation and change. Contractual forms of social cohesion have something very human at the core—trust—a trust that becomes institutionalised as legal trusts, associations, incorporations, institutions, and in the case of knowledge, in disciplinary institutions, systems, and procedures.

Disciplinary knowledge remains connected to its social context yet able to transcend that context in a number of ways: by the sociality of the academic community—that is its "coalition of minds" I previously referred to, and by the partial loyalty of those working in that coalition. The third way in which knowledge both maintains and transcends its social character is in the materiality of the knowledge "product". Moore (2007a, p. 38) draws a distinction between 'constructivism' and 'emergence' to explain the materiality of scientific knowledge. He describes constructivism as reductionist in that 'knowledge relations are reduced to power relations between social groups and their specific standpoints and interests and any autonomy of knowledge is denied'. In contrast, the disciplines are 'concerned with the emergent properties of knowledge producing practices and their capacities to transcend their immediate contexts of production (allowing for autonomy)'. Accordingly, 'whereas one is concerned with the social *construction* of knowledge (and is a form of idealism) the other is concerned with the social *production* of knowledge (and is a form of materialism)' (p. 38). I understand that 'autonomy' to be the partial loyalty of social relations of trust found in institutions that have mechanisms enabling change (in contrast to the stasis that characterises the institutions of traditional societies). In the knowledge disciplines, the mechanisms of change are the thinker's objective reasoning and critical judgement. These are faculties enabled, rather than determined, by the procedures of the disciplines.

It is the structuring relations of trust that enable the otherwise de-stabilising forces of change to operate in disciplinary institutions and in the wider contractual society itself without destroying institutions from within. Scientific knowledge serves that society through processes of objectification that enable change to occur within institutions that guarantee continuity. Social knowledge also serves society. It is important primarily for its role in providing the cement that holds the society together and maintaining stability and continuity. This role of disciplinary knowledge, on the other hand, is as the agent of change. But to understand the changes made possible by science in Heideggerian terms as 'a machine-like "total mobilization" of technological enframing' (Irwin, 2008, p. 73) is to confuse knowledge with how it is used. That application is to be found in the motives and interests of real people.

Knowledge is, as Moore (2007a) suggests, a symbolic production that is 'organized through distinctive modes of production parallel to those of material production in the economic sphere' (p. 30). If its use is corrupted, then it is to those who control knowledge to whom we look, not to the knowledge itself. In chapter 10, I take up Moore's identification of the issue for the sociology of education—'to investigate the historical and sociological conditions under which the possibilities (of modes of symbolic production) are realised and distributed' in an account of the production of indigenous knowledge. It is in the specificity of those conditions that one finds the ideological strategies of knowledge production and application.

Where the science "product" is controlled by a political group acting in its own interests, knowledge production and reproduction, like any economic resource, serves that elite. In such cases, erudite knowledge loses its partial loyalty character and becomes social knowledge—a total loyalty.

This is the case because the authority over the knowledge has passed from the disinterested systems and procedures of the discipline reliant on trust to maintain their stability to the interested strategies of an economic elite or an ideological driven group. We see this with religious and cultural "knowledges", where the criteria for who can produce the knowledge is based on the knower's status as a group member rather than developed through procedures integral to the discipline. These are the procedures that scrutinise and test the knowledge.

Objective knowledge contains moral and aesthetic as well as economic dimensions. The arts and humanities are as important in their potential application to society as are the sciences from which technologies are developed. Objective knowledge with its inherent reasoning and critical features has the potential to ensure that science is directed towards sustaining the natural world and improving the lives of human beings. This is in marked contrast to societies that value knowledge for its economic worth only. With only an instrumental rationality as the guiding principle for existence, a society becomes lost in the reactionary modernism that Jeffrey Herf (1984) identified as Germany's fate in the 1930s. It is the other side of modernity; soulless, sterile, and ultimately self-destructing. It is the price to be paid for rejecting the Enlightenment ideal of knowledge as capable of containing the moral and aesthetic means by which we become fully human, means that are intrinsic to the judgement function of criticism.

Contract societies need all three dimensions of knowledge to provide the material for "trust" that integrates individuals into the social contract. The individual is the social and political subject of the modern world, and it is for the individual that the concept of human rights was developed. It is the individual who holds those rights in liberal democratic nations. This fact makes nonsense of the belief that the modern individual is 'a fiction' (Irwin, 2008, p. 73). The social contract between individuals that arises from the individual's political subjectivity is the condition for social and political agency. Whether the explanation for individualisation is a Marxist or liberal one, the process of becoming individualised means separating from the status-based social group in order to re-connect through contract (the liberal explanation) or class social relations (the Marxist understanding). Ulrich Beck (1994, p. 13) uses the terms 'disembedding and re-embedding' to describe that process of individualisation. It contains the same idea of attaching, separating, and re-attaching—the process by which partial loyalty is created.

The struggle to be free from cultural tyranny, to cast off the prescriptive template laid out for people in status-based societies is not only about what is to be rejected. It also involves ways of re-connecting. For Marxists the individual is re-connected through capitalist social relations of production that are considered to be alienating in their exploitative character. For liberals, the re-connection is the partial loyalty enabled by the contractual social relations of trust. It is when the re-connections fail and the individual is left isolated and atomised that we see the rise of traditionalist ideologies, of re-racialisation movements, and of romantic dreams of Arcadia. Although these are all part of modernity—in the logic of its negation—they are understood as a return to the more humanised world of an idealised tradition. Yet it is a world that lacks the means of progressive change. That is found in the partial loyalty of individuals within institutions, including disciplinary institutions, and operating according to social relations of trust.

Individualisation enables people who are not from the same racial and religio-cultural heritage to unite within the modern imaginary of the liberal democratic nation. How this happens is, as Macfarlane (2002) points out, the task of sociology—to understand 'what it is that unites people in the modern, industrial, world' (p. 109). While Marx argued that the new form of social relations are to be found in the exploitative relations of production, Macfarlane, drawing on Maitland's insights, looks to trust-based forms of association for the explanation of reconnection. The key feature of the associations that sustain individualisation while simultaneously relating the individual to others within a social entity is the partial loyalty of the individual. That person, while belonging to the group through relations based upon trust—a relationship institutionalised in various ways and all with their codes, systems, and practices as with the institutions of academic practice—is also free to join and leave.

The processes involved in developing objective knowledge provide the mechanisms that connect people into the non-status associations of the disciplines in the arts, humanities, and social and natural sciences. The same procedures also provide the wider society with the mechanism for the unifying trust that enables the simultaneous stabilising continuity and the destabilising but transformative change of contractual social organisations. That mechanism is objective critical reasoning. It is a process developed within the scientific disciplines but of huge importance to modern societies based on the delicately balanced social contract. The trust between individuals that creates the society, a trust institutionalised within the systems, procedures, and practices of social organisations, ensures the existence of the society as well as the existence of the individual. It is a trust that is only as sound as the institutions that provide its structures and systems. The processes of objectification, scrutiny, and criticism, processes developed as mechanisms in disciplinary knowledge production, are as important for all forms of contractual social organisations as they are for the disciplinary communities. They play a crucial part in maintaining trust because they are procedures that enable the connection to—yet, at the same time, the separation from—the social context.

It is in these ways that scientific knowledge contributes to uniting people so that non kin-based associations are possible. Epistemic knowledge, while located in the social context, is directed to its criticism and transformation. The type of knowledge that can unite the non-kin, non-ethnic associations of the modern world must be knowledge that enables 'communities not based on blood and place, but communities of sentiment as well as purely instrumental and practical goals' (Macfarlane, 2002, p. 269) to cohere. Any society with groups placed on the margins and not fully integrated into the national imaginary struggles with that unity. And yet what is the 'trick' of unity? Macfarlane speaks of the concept of 'trusts' as 'islands of fellowship in a sea of atomistic, contractual, market society' providing the possibility and the resolution of the logical contradiction of self-love and social'—a 'trick' he calls the 'mysterious essence of modernity' (p. 272). These 'new flexible institutions', whose 'prototype is the trust', enable a 'civilisation to emerge which "has separated off different parts of life"—power, economics, religion, and kinship' (p. 272). I would add that the 'trick' he identifies is one made up of objectification, doubt, and criticism—strategies first developed within and protected by the institutions of science.

The new ways of uniting people that don't come from one's status in the kin group, in the religious order, or in other traditional hierarchies of power and wealth brings people together in the sports clubs, the music and arts fraternities, the political groups, the endless number and type of community organisations based on anything from gardening to sexuality to child care, and central to all—the school. The public school in the national education system—one with a common curriculum that teaches academic knowledge—is at the heart of the "trick" of unity. Public schools have the potential to create the social links that are vital to unifying each new generation in the act (and art) of association—one that ultimately depends on trust. Trust only develops where there are shared values, behaviours, and aspirations, but it is a sharing that is not mandated by kinship and the need for total loyalty to ensure the group's survival.

To have a "heart", these associations must have internal links but be able to link to the wider contractual society in ways that command both loyalty and criticism—in other words "partial loyalty". Public schooling and public universities are not only institutions where the contract is developed and strengthened, their importance lies in their role as contractual institutions based on the "raw material" of association—the methods of producing and reproducing abstract objective knowledge. That knowledge is, or should be, produced and reproduced in public education, thereby providing the instrumental means for social coherence but also providing the affective and moral ties that make the civilisation worth having. In a world where people without a shared heritage form new bonds, those bonds must have ongoing value from a source other than tradition. It is not enough that epistemic knowledge be instrumental. It must also provide the raw material for social integration, but for an integration that is constantly fluid as new individuals and groups join the society. To do this, knowledge must draw on disciplines from the three dimensions of human life—the instrumental or economic, the moral or spiritual, and the aesthetic. These are found in the symbolic codes of the arts, humanities, and sciences. They form the basis of education in modern democratic nations—all directed towards the universal humanity captured in Kant's (1781/1993) dictum referred to in chapter 1 of this volume.

> What can I know?
> What ought I to do?
> What may I hope? (p. 518)

'What can I know' is the promise offered by objective knowledge. It frees us from the way of thinking that is tied to experience; to a world where "I know because I was there", "I know because I feel", "I know because I am a member of a gender, a race, a religion", a membership that provides certain experiences to be understood only by those in the group. 'What can I know' is the implicit acknowledgement of the key idea of the Enlightenment, the idea of the universal human being who is the author of his or her own destiny, whose self-authority comes from the ability to reason and to criticise—but who exercises the authority within the collective representations of "coalitions of minds". 'What can I know' also evokes an instrumental use of knowledge. It suggests what can I know for what purpose. It is the utility of knowledge; the way knowledge can make our lives better. We don't need to live the brutish and short lives lived by all our ancestors. The science that brings economic benefits is to be welcomed. As David Landes (1998) points out in describing the great technical advances of the nineteenth century, the bringing together of 'instruction in abstract and theoretical matters' with technical application 'opened the way to new branches of knowledge of great economic potential' (p. 283).

But that instrumental use of knowledge is only one dimension. It needs the humanising control of the moral and aesthetic dimensions if we are to be more than alienated, mindless machines. It is these dimensions that are expressed in the everyday lives of people as they associate with those to whom they are not bound by ties other than their universal humanity. The contractual society cannot do away with the human need for emotional warmth and for a life with meaning and value. Indeed it needs these values more than status-based societies do because they cannot be assumed but must be constantly created.

'What ought I to do' is the promise of that meaningful future. Disciplinary knowledge is by its nature future oriented. It is about what is not yet known. The very idea of a future is the source of hope. We can think about what is to be valued and why and what we should do to maintain that value and carry it forward into the future. It is for this reason that a national curriculum should be the 'knowledge that each country agrees is important for all students to have access to' (Young, 2011). The universality and future orientation of epistemic knowledge means that all individuals are seen as contributors to this future. It has a moral message: That we have an obligation to contribute to making a better world, and that what we do, however small, does matter. Indeed, it is the idea behind the growing contemporary commitment to a sustainable world, a commitment to redress the excesses of industrial capitalism and the narcissistic greed of financial capitalism. The final line of Kant's dictum, coming after the first two suggesting that knowledge is behind action, is a political message. Hope implies a purpose; hope for a better society. Politics is about making that society. In this way, Kant's dictum links knowledge and politics.

The mechanisms for the link between knowledge and politics are the partial loyalty based on trust and produced by objectivity and critical reasoning. The objectivity and critical reasoning needed for scientific inquiry is also needed for democracy. Young people are prepared for citizenship, not merely by learning about being a citizen and what democracy is, but by being trained in the practices of objectivity and critical reasoning. Their understanding of the world cannot be tested against experience because "experience fails us". It requires "testing" using the abstract concepts of political and civic engagement. In this way, the objectification required for scientific knowledge is a source for the institutions and systems of political citizenship. It is also a source for the systems and institutions of social citizenship. It provides the material for the partial loyalty that links people across the enormous range of interests and activities in modern societies.

Although loyalty to the contractual group is only partial, this does not mean that societies are simply collections of individuals. The structures of the institutions and systems of association exist independent of the individuals who belong to them. Liberal societies are constituted by social relations of trust. This is not an idealised mechanism but has its own materiality in those social relations of trust. Like knowledge, "trust" is a "product". There is a difference, though, in terms of the type of "product". Unlike academic knowledge, which has a specific product in terms of ideas, the component of the trust product is affective and social—it is the emotional ties and the belief in the efficacy of those ties. It is also the practices of social interaction that occur in contractual organisations. Where abstract knowledge and trust have a similar materiality is that both are produced in systems that operate according to the mechanisms of objectification, doubt, and criticism.

By producing the intellectual means for the individual to be at once separated from yet partially loyal to the group, disciplinary knowledge is intimately tied to democratic politics. This means that the attack on objective knowledge by relativists and constructivists has implications for society far wider than the "dumbing down" of the curriculum. The dominance of constructivism in educational circles contributes to what Durkheim described as 'one of the great obstacles which constrict the development of sociology' (1983, p. 91). Durkheim's insight that 'for a long time to come, there will be two tendencies in any society: a tendency towards objective scientific truth and a tendency towards subjectively perceived truth, towards mythological truth', captures the impasse that the sociology of education found itself in at the end of the century. By denying the objectivity of knowledge, the discipline lost its own object of study. How this was resolved by social realists in the discipline is the subject of chapter 7.

7 Social Realism and the Sociology of Education

The social realist "coalition of the minds" in the sociology of education places knowledge as an object at the centre of the discipline's inquiry. In a little over a decade, books and articles by Michael Young, Rob Moore, Johan Muller, John Beck, Leesa Wheelahan, and Karl Maton among others have addressed the topic of knowledge in education to ask about knowledge production and reproduction. Their question is the one with which I began this book—what should be taught in schools? The inquiry ranges across a number of themes. They include theorising the sociality of knowledge, identifying and explaining the influence of social constructivism, identity, 'voice' or 'standpoint' approaches and their role in the influence of relativism in education, along with trying to understand why educational studies has not developed a theory of knowledge despite the centrality of knowledge in education.

Following Emile Durkheim and Basil Bernstein, social realists argue that the public arenas of collective judgement about truth claims cannot be reduced to the cultures of social groups. They are, instead, the specific practices of a disciplinary field—procedures, codes, systems by which knowledge is objectified. As Moore and Young (2010) point out, it is the 'specialist forms of social organisation that remain the major social bases for guaranteeing the objectivity of knowledge' (p. 30). What happens when those disciplines do not reach students in schools? They do not, to use Bernstein's words, become "recontextualised" as school subjects. The example of the New Zealand national curriculum which has adopted the constructivist approach to knowledge is a cautionary tale about what happens to the curriculum when it is mistaken for pedagogy. In that country the emphasis tends to be on student competency with knowledge rather than the content knowledge itself.

Learning theories and pedagogical practices that enable students to be skilful and competent with knowledge are important of course, but the actual content knowledge with which a student "thinks", "understands", "examines", "explores", and all the other verbs that denote doing something with knowledge is equally important. *What* knowledge should be taught matters as much as *how* it is acquired and *how* it is taught. For example, the competency for level six social sciences in history requires students 'to understand how people's perspectives on past events that are of significance to New Zealand differ' (Ministry of Education, 2009, p. 37).

This approach is focused on student learning not the actual knowledge itself. What is the historical material about 'past events'? Who decides what is taught? Is the selection of past events left to the schools, to a teacher's arbitrary knowledge, or as happens increasingly, to the national assessment system? In the case of the latter, because the national assessment system does refer to actual content it may serve as the *de facto* curriculum. (McPhail, 2011). The dilution of specific content knowledge particularly in subjects from the arts, humanities and social sciences is the result of the shift from the "what"—what knowledge should be known, to a focus on "how" the knowledge is to be known. It is a shift that can be traced to the increasing influence of social constructivism with the emphasis on the pedagogical relationship between teacher and student as well as to the turn against universal knowledge.

What has led to the current position whereby *how* students learn has become the focus of the curriculum replacing the focus on *what* they learn? This chapter traces the role played by the sociology of education in contributing to that state of affairs. In the absence of a theory of knowledge that could have provided the argument for the centrality of concepts and content in the curriculum, the various approaches that have come to characterise the sociology of education have reduced knowledge to political standpoints (Moore and Muller, 1999) or to a narrow technical-instrumentalism (Moore and Young, 2010). That absence has combined with the focus on politicised goals to contribute to the discipline's implosion, to cynicism amongst its practitioners, and to the creation of a vacuum ready to be filled by less progressive forces.

Since the 1970s, what was called the Marxist 'New Sociology of Education' theorised education in Althusserian terms as an ideological state apparatus, an institution reproducing the power relations and ideology of the dominant class (Althusser and Balibar, 1970). Ideologies of class, and from the 1980s, the power relations of cultural and gendered identities, became the discipline's focus. As 'knowledge relations came to be written as power relations between groups' the 'possibility of knowledge that is rationally objective in a culture-transcending manner' (Moore, 2007a, pp. 32–33) was rejected by many social scientists working in education. What happened in schools was seen as the expression of these wider unequal power relations. In this reductionist approach, knowledge was conflated with politics (Foucault's knowledge/power).

The task of the sociology of education was to reveal these sources of educational inequalities in order to transform them. As a consequence the discipline was shaped around the political goal of social transformation rather than the academic goal of investigating and explaining the relationship between society and education, and theorising the production and reproduction of knowledge in education (Rata, 2010b). The result was the over-politicisation of the discipline. Indeed no discipline has been more exposed to self-politicisation than the sociology of education with the result that the discipline, along with 'cultural studies among other social sciences have torn themselves to pieces' (Maton and Moore, 2010, p. 10). The broader outcome has been, as Derek Sayer (1991) notes, a loss of confidence in the social sciences as a consequence of its relativism which has put 'the status of social science seriously in doubt' (p. 1).

The politicisation of educational studies continues today in 'the empty rhetoric of much of what passes for critical pedagogy' (Young, 2010a, p. 21) and in the post-Marxist relativist identity approaches of feminist, cultural, indigenous, and queer theories. For education more generally it has meant that the sociology of education can offer little except the pessimistic view that education reproduces society's inequalities. The idea that knowledge itself may provide a way to address those inequalities is dismissed by politicised sociologists of education as liberal ideology, one based on the Enlightenment's "fictional" subject. Accordingly, the only solution for critical pedagogy writers is the overthrow of Western capitalism itself (McLaren and Jaramillo, 2007).

Along with critical pedagogy, the various identity "voice" or "standpoint" approaches also offer "solutions" to the putative failure of liberal education. The production and reproduction of various ethnic "knowledges" are within this trend. In New Zealand for example, Maori academics are developing the disciplinary infrastructure for "indigenous knowledge"—a topic that I turn to in greater depth in the next three chapters. In the schooling sector, a whole new "kaupapa Maori" (Maori culture) system from early childhood to tertiary education has been developed. It includes not only a curriculum with "Maori science" and "Maori mathematics", but a Maori pedagogy based on the belief that Maori children learn best in kinship-styled groups. Social realists fully acknowledge the inequalities in society and the crucial role of education in addressing these inequalities. There is no less a commitment to the ideals of freedom, equality, and justice than that promulgated by critical pedagogues and relativist theorists—a commitment used as rationale for the politicised approach. However, unlike critical pedagogy and identity forms of the discipline, social realism is interested in *how* education can contribute to a better world rather than in ways to transform the world.

There is no disputing the overwhelming evidence that socio-economic class affects educational achievement, as those with more resources do better in education than those with less (e.g., Davis, 1995; Snook and O'Neill, 2010; Nash, 2003). Roy Nash's (2001a) comment that 'the reason for the sociology of education was the real existence of socially differentiated access to education' (p. 55) is one with which many in the discipline would concur. However there are two conflicting ways in which the issue is currently theorised. The first is the politicised and relativist approaches of critical pedagogy and identity theories found in the writings of Peter McLaren, Joe Kincheloe, Michael Apple, Henri Giroux, Linda Smith, Sandy Grande, Sandra Harding, and Raewyn Connell, amongst others. The second is also concerned with politics but as an object for investigation rather than the means with which to theorise education. Two areas of study have emerged within this second approach; one focuses on policy, and the second, the social realist "school", focuses on knowledge. Both are informed by a critical approach which aims to understand the deeper forces behind the social phenomena that shapes education. It is this critical approach combined with a focus on policy and knowledge which contain the promise for the discipline's re-vitalisation.

For those studying the effects of policy on education, the questions asked by Snook and O'Neill (2010) map out the field. 'To what extent can achievement be improved by changes to educational policy? Can educational policy alone close the achievement gaps or must the solution be found in wider social and economic policies?' (p. 4). This renewed 'critical dialogue with government policy, especially that concerned with marketisation' was identified by Young (1998, p. 174) as a strength of the discipline. It is found in the writings of Geoff Whitty, Roger Dale, Susan Robertson, Mark Olssen, John Codd, Hugh Lauder, Gerald Grace, and Stephen Ball, amongst others.

The policy approach retains its critical interest in politics but as an object of analysis rather than as the solution. According to Young (1998), it addressed the weakness of Marxist sociology of education by reversing the concentration of theory that led 'Marxists to neglect how capitalism was changing and how these changes were transforming the terms of policy debates and struggles' (p. 175). It is worth noting that critical policy analysis is not the same as the type of educational studies of 'those with a more pragmatic involvement in various kinds of policy analysis and evaluation' (p. 169). The latter takes a technical approach to policy. Ministry policies are taken as "given". What is investigated is their implementation and success, rather than a critical approach that investigates the reasons and effects of the policy in terms of wider political movements.

The increasing shift to critical policy analysis occurred within the context of changes to the politics of global capitalism, particularly after 1989. Apart from those in critical pedagogy, Marxist analysis in the sociology of education shifted from a rejection of capitalism to the transformative possibilities within capitalism. The approach by Fischer and colleagues (1996) that inequalities are caused not only by the exploitative capitalist economic system but also by 'purposeful, and alterable, policy' (p. 10) captures the increased interest in education policy. Because education's role is in 'constructing the right sort of egalitarian social relationships so that people have equal standing in public life' (Kymlicka, 2002, p. 196), policy is conceptualised as the means for transformation. This is a more sober and restrained notion of "transformation" than the overthrow of capitalism promoted by the critical pedagogues with their 'commitment to socialism' (McLaren and Jaramillo, 2007, p. 197). The former "transformation" approach accepts that 'sufficient social equality is possible by accepting the market-based inequalities in the economy and looking to other spheres for social justice—for example, education and public recognition' (Kymlicka, 2002, p. 198).

Social realism with its focus on theorising knowledge in education is the second strand in twenty-first-century critical sociology of education. Like the strand that focuses on educational policy, social realism also addresses the fundamental question in the sociology of education—what are the causes of differential achievement in education?—but does so by focusing on knowledge production and reproduction. It is in these two analytical strands—policy and knowledge—that the critical character of the sociology of education is retained.

The "original" Marxist New Sociology of Education (NSOE) with its "critical" claim, as opposed to mainstream sociology of education (Davies, 1995), emerged in the 1970s within the same context that produced the new professional class of well-educated idealists that I discussed in chapter 2. It is within the context of this class's emergence that one finds the source of the discipline's tendency for politicisation. Like other social sciences that developed in the same period, the sociologists of education were, in many cases, from amongst the ranks of the working class. Their upward mobility into the new professional class was a result of their education and the expansion of middle-class employment in the prosperous 1950s and 1960s. Indeed the discipline was so resolutely political because the new sociologists of education were, as with other social scientists, members of this class, a self-conscious membership prior to the "cultural turn".

The new Marxist sociology of education was about the transformation of society. It was also the result of society's transformation. The discipline's radicalisation resulted from its historical location within, and contribution to, the 'unprecedented commitment by successive governments to supporting a national, university-based intellectual class in both the sciences and the humanities—something that had never happened before' (Cannadine, 2008, p. 24). Roger Dale (2001, p. 8) uses the term 'redemptive' to describe the emancipatory political goal of the new sociology of education, a term that captures the moral imperative of the new intellectual class's project in the two post-war decades. Yet it was a compromised moral imperative—caught as this group was in the ambivalence of the 'goodness and power' (Gouldner, 1979, p. 36) paradox of political idealism and economic particularity (Rata, 1996).

There are a number of accounts (Davies, 1995; Young, 1998; Dale, 2001, 2009; Rata, 2010b) of the NSOE in the early days of reproduction and resistance theories where its Marxist agenda was to put 'liberal-pluralist accounts of education clearly on the run' (Aronowitz, 1981). In New Zealand the opposition to a liberal understanding of education as providing opportunities for social mobility was captured in Roy Shuker's influential

1987 book, *The One Best System?: A Revisionist History of State Schooling in New Zealand*. Sociology of education courses had fully incorporated Shuker's message when I began teaching pre-service teachers in the early 1990s. We taught our students that there were two opposing ways to understand education; liberal-progressivism and critical 'radical revisionism' (Coxon, Massey, and Marshall, 1994). The former was 'essentially the liberal ideology that has pervaded our schooling practices in New Zealand with its mythical belief in 'equality of opportunity' (p. 27). This was obviously the wrong approach, we told our students.

Its 'ideology' was uncovered as 'radical revisionists vigorously questioned the traditional view that the school has contributed to the evolution of a more equitable society [arguing] instead that the school was in fact about the reproduction of dominant groups within society' (Simon and Massey, 1994, p. 36). Subordinate groups—'women, working class and minority ethnic groups, including Maori' (p. 36)—on the other hand were marginalised and oppressed. Radical revisionism laid the ground for a relativism that was fully fledged by the end of the decade. It insisted that 'History is seen, not as an objective recording of (alleged) facts but rather, as the shaping of "facts" and their presentation in a narrative, through the theoretical perspectives of the writer' (p. 37). Such intellectual relativism reaches its nemesis in the New Zealand history curriculum; where 'students will gain knowledge, skills and experience to: Understand how peoples' perspectives on past events that are of significance to New Zealanders differ' (Ministry of Education, 2009, p. 37).

A generation of student teachers in New Zealand as elsewhere were taught the "truth" of radical revisionism. I was reminded of the intense fervour of the times when selecting the previous quotations about the dangers of "liberal-pluralism" from Coxon and colleagues (1994). This was the main textbook for students studying for degrees in teacher education in Auckland—there was no alternative view given. A sub-heading in the textbook's introduction 'How Am I Involved in Creating a More Equitable System?' encouraged students to see the interaction of theory and practice as the means by which they can be 'involved in emancipatory change individually as teachers, and collectively as members of staff and wider community groups' (p. 18).

Michael Young (2010b), too, recalls the way in which he, like so many of us at the time, endorsed an uncritical oppositionist politics which he now describes 'as a kind of naïve radicalism' (p. 11). Now a leading social realist, Young (2010b) recalls arguing in his influential 1971 book, *Knowledge and Control*, that the distinction between knowledge and experience was ideological and relied on the power of those defining what counted as knowledge rather than any objective criteria. Linked to a radical educational politics, this emphasis on subjective experience as the source of academic knowledge led many teachers to an uncritical identification with subordinate groups, whether students, the working class, or indigenous or minority groups (Young, 2010b). The belief that educational studies, indeed all the social sciences, should conflate theory and practice in the interests of political change is expressed in Raewyn Connell's (2009) words: 'Social science as a whole is embodied practice (p. 217). This approach makes the objectification of knowledge impossible because knowledge is always tied to experience.

The influence of Marxist critical theory and its descent in post-Marxist relativism contained a pseudo-religious, almost evangelical character. Indeed the politicised social sciences of the times provided a secular religion to a class that was revolutionary in its ideals but conservative in its economic particularity. In "doing good by doing well" (Tom Lehrer's brutally incisive line), the new professional class appeared to have the best of both worlds. Given these pseudo-religious underpinnings, it is not surprising that this class adopted a moral position towards equality and was prepared to use education as the means to engine the "good" society. Gouldner's (1979) reference to the 'goodness and power' character of this class captures the same paradox (p. 36). This was a group with the power to put their ideals into practice and the moral conviction to make it happen. Not only had the shift to equity enabled the new professional class to maintain their socialist ideals from a position of relative wealth, but for a radicalised generation who wanted to socialise the world and overcome the limitations of liberalism that had outlived its day in their service, "equity" was more satisfying than "equality of opportunity". The political and intellectual elite of the new generation, these 'legitimate defenders of the common good' (Kellner and Berger, 1992, p. 11) were to do well by doing good.

However, the fundamental changes to the class's prosperity during the 1980s dampened the intensity of the desire for transformation. Rather than a universal class movement, the new professional class's politics and its understanding of those politics in the social science disciplines became localised and fragmented in the various voice perspectives of identity politics. The paradox of "doing well by doing good" was resolved for many in the victory of the class's economic interests over its idealism. This was the profound shift to left-wing politics that enabled various social democratic parties like the New Zealand Labour Party to embrace a neoliberal understanding of globalisation. Here the universalism designed to unite workers for a better world is replaced by a globalisation that unites consumers in the market of unsatiated desire. The large numbers of left-wing academics in the social sciences meant that class analysis was best avoided; least the analysis explained their own abandonment of this basic premise of Left-wing politics. The gap was filled by the "loud voices" from constructivists exclaiming that identity and cultural politics were the way to the new equality.

By the 1990s the extent to which the new sociology of education had incorporated those wider changes could be seen in the way 'justice was imagined' (Nancy Fraser, cited in Apple, 2003). Post-Marxists, such as Michael Apple, Henry Giroux, Peter McLaren, and Joe Kincheloe, championed the shift from class to cultural politics in the discipline under the rubric "critical pedagogy" (Giroux and McLaren, 1989; Apple, 2003; Kincheloe, 2008). In emptying out critical theory of the very idea that made it progressive—the concept of class inequality for cultural determinism, critical pedagogues abandoned progressivism while keeping its emancipatory rhetoric. The resulting shrillness of a message without substance can be found in McLaren's most recent book (2007, written with Nathalia Jaramillo). The writers call for a 'new critical humanist pedagogy' that is

> an approach to reading the word and the world that puts that struggle against capitalism (and the imperialism inherent in it) at the center of the pedagogical project, a project that is powered by the oxygen of socialism's universal quest for human freedom and social justice. When the Bean Chaointe (keening woman) announces the death of humanity, it will not be a eerie wail from the flapping criss-crossed jowls of Barbara Bush, but the slow rasp of an emphysemic, dying planet, a planet failed by the human consciousness to which it gave birth. (p. 20)

The earlier alliance between critical pedagogy and identity theories, one built on a shared claim to the emancipatory project, weakened in the face of eclectic and contradictory theories and politics as critical pedagogy struggles to return to class politics while retaining its commitment to cultural determinism (Rata, 2011e). This can be seen in the rejection of Western critical sociology by Native American Red sociologist, Sandy Grande (2004, 2009). Grande (2009) acknowledges that 'Indigenous and critical scholars do share a common ground' (p. 199). However she draws a distinction between critical scholars' 'vision in Western conceptions of democracy and justice that present a "liberated" self' and 'indigenous scholars (who) ground their vision in conceptions of sovereignty that presume a profound connection to place and land' (p. 200). Yet critical pedagogy and indigenous theorists still have much in common, including a politicised rhetoric. The former sees indigenous education as sharing its political agenda for rights-based social justice, a peoples' revolution, liberation from oppressive colonial power relations, ideologies, and structures, and the rejection of Western capitalist hegemony.

Such a vision is echoed in Grande's (2009) statement that Red 'pedagogy (is) inherently political, cultural, spiritual and intellectual, an education for decolonization (through a) praxis of collective agency (based upon) indigenous knowledge' (p. 210). Identity theories are based on an immanentism that assigns a progressive force to indigenous movements, yet ignores the potential for all political forces, even those that begin in peoples' revolutions, to become reactionary and oppressive. However this 'practice of asserting a necessary movement of history that confers subordinate groups with objective interests in radical change' (Davies, 1995, p. 1448) ensures that indigeneity is interpreted as always and necessarily a progressive force. Yet the use of indigeneity as a means to categorise social groups in respect to place and time may be used as a political instrument of possession or dispossession (Li, 2010) according to specific historical circumstances. Indeed legal and administrative processes in the neoliberal era support the type of indigenous politics identified by Luisa Steur as 'indigenism'; that is, 'the cultural identity politics of indigenous people where class is the determining element in identity construction and political alliance building' (2005, p. 175).

In this era of globalisation, the market, rather than the nation-state, provides the neoliberal hegemonic framework for political society. Indigenous politics that originate in peoples' movements for greater access to resources are subsumed into this hegemony. Indigeneity develops a double duality as a consequence of its strategic role in regulating social organisation and resource distribution in the global market. In one duality, indigeneity remains a source of identity and empowerment for indigenous people generally, but it also serves to divide indigenous people from the working class and provide greater power and legitimacy to the emergent indigenist elite as a capitalist class. The second duality occurs within that growing class division and reflects the globalisation-localisation dialectic of global capitalism. In their role as representatives of the indigenous group, the elite share in the mobility of global capitalism as 'a travelling class of tribal representatives as opposed to those who stay at home' (Friedman, 2003, p. 18). Those 'at home' are localised, permanently fixed into an ahistorical present bound to the imaginary of the primordial place.

Davies's (1995) reference to the 'dramatic interpretations over slender evidence' of which 'resistance theorists have been accused (p. 1459) is also the case with indigenous education. This tendency to cherry pick the statistics can provide an incomplete, even distorted, picture as this example from Maori education illustrates (Rata, 2011e). The UNESCO Report, *Education for All* (UNESCO, 2010) notes that the kohanga reo or Maori language early childhood centres began in 1981 and 'thirteen years later there were 800 kohanga reo catering for 14,000 children' (p. 206). But although numbers did grow rapidly following the establishment of the first centre in 1982 to a peak of 767 in 1996, since the mid-1990s, there has been a decline to 464 kohanga in 2009 (Education Counts, 2009a). This is a considerable decline, yet despite the fact that those figures were available to the UNESCO report writers, the decline was not included. The picture to be shown was one of a successful peoples' movement that continues to attract the support of the people.

Another example of 'dramatic interpretations over slender evidence', also from New Zealand, concerns the comparisons made about the achievement of Maori students who undertake the National Certificate of Educational Achievement (NCEA) in year 11. Once again, the 2010 UNESCO report makes dramatic claims. Accordingly, 'Year 11 Maori students in immersion schools have recorded *significantly* better achievement rates than their Maori peers in English-medium schools' (United Nations Educational,

Scientific and Cultural Organization, 2010, p. 26, my italics). This finding appears to be confirmed in a recent report by Takao and colleagues (2010). These researchers claim that 'recent NCEA results *confirm strongly* the academic success of kura graduates (p. 18, my italics, "kura" are Maori-medium schools).

Yet, as Murray (2007) points out, comparisons between Maori students in Maori-medium education with those in English-medium education are 'difficult and sometimes misleading' (p. 3). Given the small numbers of students in Maori medium education it is not yet possible to say that Maori medium education offers greater success to Maori students, if that is indeed the case. The 2007 comparison is between only 509 Year 11 students in Maori-medium and a much larger number (11,079) of Maori at other schools (Education Counts, 2009b, p. 26). Given these figures the most accurate statement that can be made is that *we don't know* whether Maori-medium or English-medium schools are more successful. Terms such as 'significantly better achievement' and 'confirm strongly' are not correct, yet their 'dramatic' flavour means that these are the findings that appear in the media and reports, such as the UNESCO one, to gain widespread currency.

Despite the ongoing politicisation in the sociology of education from the relativist strands, the discipline's current revival with the resurgence of critical policy analysis and the social realist inquiry into knowledge production and reproduction indicates the discipline's re-vitalisation. The remainder of this chapter considers the social realist claim that by bringing back knowledge into the sociology of education (the phrase used as the title of Michael Young's 2008 book to which I have already alluded), social realism positions itself as a real alternative to the politicised and relativist critical sociology of education. By doing so it breaks down the 'impasse that has debilitated sociological thinking about knowledge and education for decades' (Maton and Moore, 2010, p. 10). Social realism offers a way forward for the sociology of education by proposing and developing the framework for a sociology of knowledge for education.

Its object of inquiry is into 'how is knowledge created and developed, modes of the creation, forms knowledge takes and effects for policies and practices' (Maton and Moore, 2010, p. 10). To undertake this inquiry, social realists need to distinguish between social everyday knowledge and disciplinary knowledge and to justify their claim that knowledge is *emergent from but irreducible to* the practices and contexts of its production and recontextualization, teaching and learning' (Maton and Moore, 2010, p. 5). The distinction is crucial to the social realism case given that its main claim is the identification of separate social and epistemic relations in the production of knowledge (Moore and Young, 2010). It order to do so, two questions must be addressed; firstly, in what way is knowledge as an object (its intrinsic or epistemic character) distinguishable from the socio-historical conductions in which its production is located? Following from this question; given that distinction, what is the relationship between the social and epistemic codes in knowledge production?

In the aptly titled article, 'Why Educators Must Differentiate Knowledge from Experience' (2010b), Michael Young provides a succinct account of 'Durkheim's distinction between the practical and the everyday (the profane) from the theoretical/intellectual/conceptual (the sacred) that was originally expressed in religion or theology but historically became secularised to include science and any intellectual activity' (2010b, p. 14). Young describes the resulting 'basic distinction between theory and practice as a feature of all societies for Durkheim' and contrasts it with Marx's view of the theory/practice issue. 'Whereas for Marx philosophers only interpret the world, when the point is to change it, for Durkheim the knowledge (or theory) that we need as a basis for changing the world must be separate from and prior to the practical activities involved in social change' (p. 14). This is quite different from the conflation of theory and practice which led to the over-politicisation of the sociology of education, the approach first advocated by the new sociologists of education in the 1970s and taken up by identity theorists from the 1980s.

In this section, I extend the discussion that began in chapter 5 about how social realists account for the truth claims of esoteric or disciplinary knowledge. According to social realism, disciplinary systems, codes, and procedures, that human 'effort to create a conceptual framework and a vocabulary for investigating the world' (Lindberg, 1992, p. 44) ensure that the content of a particular discipline remains contestable and subject to change. In this way, disciplinary knowledge does not become fixed in immutable ways as *mythos*, that is, in the beliefs and ideologies of particular social groups. But the question about how the cumulative knowledge develops remains a complex problem for theorists. The answer is fairly straightforward for disciplines such as physics, chemistry, and mathematics that are characterised by a weak social relation and a strong epistemic code. But how do disciplines with knowledge structures characterised by a strong social relation (e.g., the arts, humanities, and social sciences) accumulate knowledge structures within the specialised procedures required for the creation of a canon of objective knowledge?

Karl Maton (2010) asks the question succinctly. 'If the arts and humanities are not based on explicit structures of knowledge specialised to clearly defined objects of study, then what are they based on?' (p. 176). This is a question central to the sociology of knowledge. If the arts, humanities, and social sciences are simply the result of a social group's culture or of an individual's personal choice, what is left when that social group disappears or changes, or individuals' tastes move on? How is the epistemic character of knowledge in the humanities, arts, and social sciences maintained given the challenge to epistemic structures from social knowledge?

Recent research by Graham McPhail (2011, in press) addresses this question in the light of changes to the music curriculum with the inclusion of popular music over the past few decades. McPhail (2011) investigated how teachers manage the relationship between classical and popular music in the school curriculum by using Basil Bernstein's (2000) horizontal and vertical differentiation concepts to distinguish between the two types of knowledge. He found that elements of popular music practices (Bernstein's horizontal or social discourse) are adapted for the educational context by being linked to the more vertical or systemised processes of 'academic' learning. He describes how teachers work as recontextualising agents with relative autonomy in creating a curriculum that combines popular music drawn from the students' social experiences with the classical canon. It is in 'linking the contextual (horizontal) knowledge to other knowledge and concepts within the discipline, that students' understanding and application of knowledge can be extended' (p. 3).

McPhail (2011) suggests 'that teachers further manage the relationship between classical and popular music through the weakening of boundaries, but not their dissolution' (p. 3). The importance of this research is the finding that teachers' knowledge is significant to maintaining the epistemic integrity of a discipline that is strongly "horizontal"—that is, susceptible to socio-cultural influences. The central role of teachers' knowledge becomes more critical when the curriculum itself does not specify what knowledge is to be taught. In that case the teachers' knowledge becomes the *de facto* curriculum, often drawing on assessment requirements to ensure which specific content is taught.

The New Zealand Curriculum Guides (Ministry of Education, 2009) provide a clear example of what happens to an educational system when the curriculum document is based more on a theory of learning rather than a theory of knowledge. That curriculum emphasises *how* students learn, not *what* they learn. There is sometimes little detail about the actual content to be learned, instead the curriculum document is written according to what students will "do", "observe", "explore", "understand", "compute", "recognise", "demonstrate", "identify", and other verbs that focus on how the student learns. Some examples of this competency, skills approach to learning are: in level 1 and 2 science, with respect to 'properties and changes to matter, students will observe, describe, and compare physical and chemical properties of common materials and changes that occur when materials are mixed, heated, or cooled'. Under the heading 'Chemistry and society', students will 'find out about the uses of common materials and relate these to their observed properties' (2009, p. 12). In the Personal Health and Development curriculum at level 4 concerned with personal growth and development, students will 'Describe the characteristics of pubertal change and discuss positive adjustment strategies' (p. 22). In level 7 of the English curriculum, regarding speaking, writing, and presenting, students will 'Integrate sources of information, processes, and strategise purposefully, confidently, and precisely to identify, form, and express increasingly sophisticated ideas' (p. 38).

The New Zealand national curriculum (Ministry of Education, 2007, 2009) is an impressive document of sequential learning development. Unfortunately it is not a curriculum document that describes the content knowledge that young New Zealanders will learn. The approach is heavily embedded in the constructivist view that knowledge is drawn from the student's experience and created within the student's activities, including being 'co-created' with the teacher who acts as a facilitator to that learning. This gives a fairly arbitrary character to learning with students often dependent upon having teachers with a comprehensive knowledge of the subject they teach. With disciplines that have a strong social content like history, if the curriculum does not specify what is to be taught and the teacher does not know the generative principles and concepts, then it is likely that students will learn very little from the disciplinary canon itself. The content they acquire is likely to come from their own or the teacher's social knowledge. This will take the form of personal experience, local stories, and opinion.

The case of the history example from the social science curriculum guide, which states that students need to 'understand how people's perspectives on past events that are of significance to New Zealanders differ' (Ministry of Education, 2009, p. 37), simply reinforces the idea that knowledge comes from people's perspectives, including their own. There is a danger that history is what the person telling the narrative says it is. In this extreme form of intellectual relativism, the discipline of history is reduced to who is telling what to whom. It is a view that can be traced to the highpoint of relativism in teacher education programmes in the 1990s to which I referred earlier in the chapter. Over a decade later influential positions in the Ministry of Education and other educational agencies are occupied by those who were students in the teachers colleges at the height of relativism. It is now that we see the ideas of influential officials, ideas acquired as students, becoming placed into the nation's institutions. The relativism and experience-centred beliefs of constructivism may be strongly criticised by social realists in the growing debates within the sociology of education. However these ideas are firmly positioned in the practice of policy making as this generation of government officials embed the relativism they acquired in their student days into education policy.

The history curriculum provides a clear example of the constructivist view that knowledge is reducible to the knower. History that shows how different perspectives of the past differ will no doubt have some entertainment value as storytelling and be engaging pedagogy. After all, young people enjoy narratives with clearly defined villians and heroes. But that relativist approach will not produce students who know the principles, content, and concepts of history in any depth. When the constructivist approach is applied to other subjects, it will not produce students who can, to paraphrase Gramsci (1986, p. 38, cited in Muller, 2000) 'reason, think abstractly and schematically while remaining able to plunge back from abstraction into real and immediate life, see in each fact or datum what is general and what is particular, distinguish the concept from the particular instance' (pp. 7–8).

There are any number of outcomes of a curriculum without content. One is that we are all authorities—this may give people a misguided sense of the power of their own specified content knowledge as well as leading to doubts about the superior explanatory power of disciplinary knowledge. Another outcome is described in John Beck's (2010) analysis of the development of competency training in teacher education. Beck describes how the weakening of the 'sacred' (the intrinsic or esoteric value of knowledge) contributes to the market-oriented instrumentalism in education. Drawing on Bernstein's ideas, Beck explains the consequences for education. Because knowledge production, as something with its own procedures, insulates objective knowledge from the 'profane' sphere of economic production, the breakdown of that insulation between knower and knowledge leads to the empty receptacle of the trainable learner.

In this scenario, there is little to be transmitted to learners, only atomised content and the process of knowing—the "identify", "demonstrate", "describe", "experience", "recognise" approach that characterises the New Zealand national curriculum. Like Beck, Lisa Wheelahan (2010a, 2010b) addresses the consequences of hollowed-out knowledge using Bernstein's (2000) analysis of structures of knowledge and ways in which access to structured knowledge (the content of canons) is differentially distributed. Wheelahan argues that the trainability approach of competency-based training excludes the working class and other disadvantaged social groups from access to powerful knowledge. It is the very hollowness of knowledge, that is knowledge without an intrinsic or epistemic code, that denies students access to structuring principles of disciplinary knowledge and hence to the world of concepts, theoretical explanation, and understanding.

The dissolution of strong boundaries between social knowledge and disciplinary knowledge diminishes the chances of students acquiring those capabilities. If the curriculum is based mainly on social knowledge, students will remain tied to the local world of experience. Here knowledge is meaningful because it is socially contextual. In contrast to knowledge based on experience, disciplinary knowledge or 'collective representations' are the means

> societies use to transcend the limits of individual experience to see beyond appearances to the real nature of relations in the natural and social world. All societies need to connect the material and immaterial, the known and unknown, the thinkable and unthinkable, the here and the not here, the specific and the general, and the past, present and future. (Wheelahan, 2010a, p. 95)

It is epistemic knowledge that has the potential to challenge distributions of power. This is the basis of the social realist claim that the approach is progressive. It is precisely because objective knowledge has the power to "think the unthinkable" by taking people outside the naturalised world of their own experience, that access to it is regulated through the division of labour. Accordingly, marginalised and disadvantaged groups need more of this type of knowledge, not less, if they are to challenge embedded power and improve their own life circumstances. Yet, competency-based training provides only atomised fragments, while standpoint relativism closes off esoteric knowledge by claiming that knowledge is only ever the voice of the dominant group, to be known by those of the group. For social realists, denying students access to the structures of epistemic knowledge relevant in their field and social access to the "unthinkable" reinforces class divisions. As Muller (2000) explains, the epistemic is not just the specific content of a subject. It is the style of thinking *found in the generative principles* that underpin disciplinary knowledge. A curriculum requires all three components: the style of thinking, the generative concepts and principles, and the content knowledge within which those concepts and principles are expressed.

Social realism's focus on knowledge takes up the progressive vision traditionally associated with the sociology of education; namely, a commitment to the ideals of social justice and democratic principles. It does this not by politicising the discipline's goals, as did the new sociology of education, but by providing the conceptual means to extend our understanding of the way access to education is distributed unequally across social groups. As Roy Nash argued, 'there are powerful forms of knowledge' that are not reducible to 'the knowledge of the powerful' (cited in Lauder, 2010, p. 3). However many educational officials and teachers today believe unquestioningly in the constructivist views that knowledge based on experience is the basis of a sound curriculum and that learning which uses students' experience is sound pedagogy. In this way, curriculum (what is taught) and pedagogy (how it is taught) are conflated. The task of social realism is to show how curriculum and pedagogy are to be distinguished and to bring epistemic knowledge back into education, into its rightful place in the curriculum.

8 Knowledge and Culturalism

The inclusion of social knowledge into the school curriculum and the corresponding decline of the importance of disciplinary knowledge is the result of a number of forces—ones traced in the preceding chapters to the decline of universalism within the context of a new form of globalisation. Where people are united across the world is as consumers in the global market. Those workers who produce the consumer goods are confined to the factories of the Third World, while the brands they produce move into that global market. The commitment to universalism that was used by democratic movements in the nineteenth and twentieth centuries to justify human rights for all people has been replaced by a global unity of consumption, to be enjoyed by a few. This process occurs within the larger shift to modernism's negative logic that I discussed in chapter 3; the shift to primitivism, traditionalism, and postmodernism that pull against universalism in favour of a return to pre-modern localism (Friedman, 1994). Contributing to those forces of localisation is the culturalist ideology that promotes a belief in the foundational status of racial/ethnic or religio-cultural groups with their distinctive "knowledges" and ways of being. Of significance is the idea that follows from this belief—that political rights should adhere to foundational groups.

Since the 1970s that belief in the foundational group as opposed to the universality of human beings has informed various forms of cultural politics—from multiculturalism to biculturalism (in New Zealand), to mono-culturalism. It has served to localise people by breaking down the modernist commitment to universalism. The concept of a politicised category of people classified according to their racial ancestry is common to all forms of culturalism and is the defining idea in this ideology. The important differences between the types that I identified in chapter 1 are briefly summarised here.

Mono-culturalism is the recognition of one racial or religio-culture group only as the rightful political and social category. Its politics is used to discriminate against those perceived not to belong to the essentialised racial category—to the *volk*. In this way racial categorisation is used to support racist politics of exclusion and discrimination. Multiculturalism, on the other hand, while also using racial categorisation along with religio-cultural categories, does so by appealing to the Enlightenment ideal of human rights, in this case, rights for social group recognition. Therein lies the fundamental contradiction for bi- and multiculturalism; a social group created in the past and with a membership classified according to the principle of birth-ascribed status claims political recognition according to principles of universal human rights. This chapter traces the effects of this inherently flawed culturalist approach on the politics of knowledge in education. Drawing on the New Zealand example, I illustrate the role that culturalism has played in supporting the dominance of relativism and constructivism in education.

The contradiction between the foundational group and the universal individual has caused unease amongst those liberal progressives for whom bi- and multicultural politics was the solution to the problem of minority group marginalisation. Here was to be a new way to interpret the social contract, one that still recognised "rights" but "group rights" rather than those based on the individual. However, the failure of culturalist politics to achieve its progressive aims and the use of multicultural rights language in support of reactionary beliefs and practices, especially towards women and girls, has undermined its supporters' faith that "culture" is the solution to society's inequalities. That failure of confidence in multiculturalism is symbolised by British Prime Minister David Cameron's (2011) speech given in Munich in February 2011. In calling for 'a much more active, muscular liberalism', Cameron drew attention to the unintended outcomes of state multiculturalism. He spoke of 'segregated communities', the lack of a commitment by some groups to 'equal rights regardless of race, sex or sexuality', and the dangers of 'passive tolerance' in the face of bigotry and racism.

It is likely that the Cameron speech will be seen in hindsight as signalling the beginning of the end of the liberal support for multiculturalism in the Commonwealth Anglophone countries of New Zealand, Australia, Canada, and the United Kingdom. This does not mean the end of support for the progressive principles that first attracted the Left to multiculturalism, but it does suggest that the Left may return to a solution based on class politics. Liberals may re-affirm their commitment to the integrating potential of a social contract that actually works for all groups. Indeed the liberal response to the August 2011 riots in London along with the atrocity in Norway in that year may well be the revival of universalist democratic principles. This is likely to be a twenty-first version of liberal idealism for a post-multicultural era. It may combine the commitment to individual autonomy with the social justice ideals promoted by socialism along with the more recent sustainability approach to global integration.

The disillusionment with culturalism in New Zealand is fairly muted in comparison to the United Kingdom and other European countries. This relative silence is probably the result of the comprehensive inclusion since the late 1980s of principles relating to the 1840 Treaty of Waitangi in government institutions. Yet despite successive governments' insistence that the treaty is the nation's founding document and must be honoured in a bicultural partnership, about half of all New Zealanders remain unconvinced that the treaty is the means for progressive politics despite intensive educational programmes designed to convince people that this is the case. A 1999 survey of attitudes to the treaty and the Waitangi Tribunal found that the treaty 'is a major point of division within the country'. Only 5 percent of those surveyed 'think that the Treaty should be strengthened and given the full force of law'. 'About 34 percent want the Treaty abolished' (Perry and Webster, 1999, p. 74). A decade later, the Human Rights Commission's annual progress report on treaty issues (Human Rights Commission, 2011) found that '60 per cent of people agree that the treaty is New Zealand's founding document. However only 51 per cent of all those polled consider the treaty is for all New Zealanders' (p. 21).

The 1840 Treaty of Waitangi was the instrument of annexation by which the British government established sovereignty over New Zealand. In recent decades it has acquired a new interpretation. It became the symbol of Maori cultural revivalism in the 1970s and the document of inheritance for an emerging Maori re-tribalised elite in the 1980s. The concept of a treaty "partnership" between the revived tribes and the "Crown" was coined as recently as 1987 when the notion of the treaty having 'principles' was developed (Ministry of Maori Development, 2001, p. 78). The concept of partnership gained widespread acceptance despite its illogical premise, something noted by legal scholar, David Round. "If there were to be a partnership of Maori and the Crown, then by definition Maori could not be subjects of the Crown. One cannot be a partner and a subject at the same time. If there were to be a partnership of Maori and the Crown in the government of New Zealand, then it must follow logically that the only people who would be subjects would not be Maori—They would be partners—but rather non-Maori, who would be the subjects of the Crown and also the subjects of the Treaty partner who shares the Crown's authority" (Round, 2011, p. 538).

Despite this inherent problem with a "treaty partnership", the concept was embraced by the liberal-Left who made up the majority of politicians, government officials, academics, media, and social service professionals in the 1980s and 1990s. It was justified in terms of the bicultural ideals of social justice for Maori people. Treaty grievance settlements for historical injustices were intended to redistribute economic and social benefits and the inclusion of the treaty principles into government institutions would give effect to the "partnership" by bringing Maori fully into New Zealand society. However, the decision to award treaty settlements to tribes rather than pan-Maori subverted the redistribution goal and led to the emergence of the corporate 'neotribe' (Rata, 2000, 2003b, 2011b).

This is now the unit of governance for the devolution of public services to Maori and the incorporated body for the ownership and management of privatised resources that were previously in public ownership. The growing interest by the neotribal elite in claiming further public resources such as geothermal power, the foreshore and seabed, and the radio spectrum is justified by the concept of the tribe as the revived socio-political unit of a distinctive indigenous people. This is a new concept of the "people" who comprise the "public", with rights that are seen to derive not only from the Treaty of Waitangi but from that indigenous status. It is a discourse that sidesteps 170 years of New Zealand history, which, from the 1852 Constitution Act, established the concept of a New Zealand public based on universalist principles together with the concept of a public domain managed by the democratically elected government.

Yet the justification for the transfer of public resources to the corporate tribe still draws on the social justice and redistribution ideals of biculturalism, despite the fact that the process has led to growing inequalities amongst Maori. According to Chapple (2000), treaty settlements 'risk being captured by the considerable number of Maori who already have jobs, skills, high incomes and good prospects' (p. 115). For Poata-Smith (1996) the emphasis on culture in the struggle for equality 'resulted in a dramatic expansion of opportunities for middle-class professional Maori in the state apparatus, education system, health and the media', but has been 'an unmitigated disaster for the vast majority of working-class Maori whanau [extended families]' (p. 110). Indeed after four decades of biculturalism, there is increasing disparity within the Maori population. The number of Maori in severe poverty has increased from 7 percent in 2000 to 17 percent in 2004 (Callister, 2007, p. 24). There is an increasing Maori middle class, and a small but powerful Maori elite (Lashley, 2000; Webster, 2002).

Concerns about the extensive economic and political influence of the neotribal elite are no longer confined to critical researchers. In a recent lecture given at the University of Auckland, a Left-wing Maori activist referred to the 'self-anointed Iwi [tribal] Leaders Group' whose commercial deals for acquiring geothermal resources, national parks, private prisons, and mining were 'harnessing Maori to a global capitalism that impoverishes the mass of working class Maori' (Sykes, 2010). Similarly, a Right-wing activist refers to the 'Maori tribal elite' [which] is pursing the country towards a future where corporate iwi [tribes] will control our key institutions and resources' (New Zealand Centre for Political Research, 2011).

Tribal claims for treaty settlement depends upon the acceptance of the communal people discourse used to justify the revived tribes and their leaders as the legitimate inheritors of those settlements. Yet deep class divisions exist amongst the Maori population. It is Maori with no tribal affiliation who are 'some of those most disadvantaged in society' (Gill et al., 2010, p. 19). However as early as 1983, Roy Nash astutely observed the use of cultural theory in the political interests of this elite. Referring to 'what is now very much the party line', Nash (1983) explained 'the silent exclusion of class from the discourse' about Maori education as being in the interests of 'the programme of ethnic compensation on which the entire political strategy is based' (p. 82).

The link between appeals to community, tribe, and custom on the one hand and class politics on the other was also made by Basil Bernstein (2000) in his references to ideologies as ways to 'prevent, limit or otherwise manage dynamics of class formation' (p. 72). Within the classed indigenous group are those on the fringe of the capitalist economy: unemployed, expendable, and fixed in a localised ahistorical present; for whom 'protection and incarceration are two sides of the same coin' (Li, 2010, p. 399). This fate is poignantly described in Peter Sutton's 2009 account of the misery of Australian Aborigines where 'care and compassion' are sidelined by policies 'dominated by cultural relativism' (p. 11).

The belief that Maori are a communal people sharing the experiences of an oppressive colonial history is the dominant discourse in the New Zealand social sciences. The claim is that Maori subordinate status was established by colonisation and is maintained in the social and political relationships between subsequent generations descended from coloniser settlers and the colonised indigenous by being built into New Zealand's social and political structures. Individuals, as a result of their Maori ethnicity, inherit and are locked into the inferior and unequal status of these structures (Bishop and Berryman, 2006). The structural oppression is expressed in a number of ways at both individual and group level, in mental and physical illness, educational underachievement, imprisonment, and welfare dependency. Because colonisation is considered to be the cause of the structural inequality between Maori and non-Maori, the solution is the decolonisation of social and political structures by establishing separate Maori systems, such as Maori mental health programmes (Durie, 1999; 2011), Maori education (Smith, 2003), and Maori research (Cunningham, 2000).

Indeed Linda Smith's influential 1999 book, *Decolonising Methodologies*, one translated into Spanish, Chinese, Arabic, Italian, and Bhasa Indonesian, works from the premise that universal knowledge is another of the West's ideological claims to superiority over non-Western peoples, with that ideology justifying colonisation. Even the disciplines are implicated. In her statement that 'underpinning all of what is taught at universities is the belief in the concept of science as the all-embracing method for an understanding of the world' (p. 65), those who had not read the book would at first assume that Smith concurs with the accepted view of the purpose of the university as the place for the creation of knowledge. (See for example, Grace, 2010). But they would be mistaken. According to Smith, the purpose of the university is to colonise, hence her call for indigenous "knowledges" to act as the instrument of decolonisation. In this view colonisation is always destructive.

The late New Zealand historian, Peter Munz (a student of Karl Popper at the University of Canterbury in Christchurch) would disagree. In explaining why the West become 'Westernised, that is, modernise, Munz

(1991) locates 'a general law which would enable one to deduce from the initial conditions the prognosis that growth had to occur and would have occurred in other places had the initial conditions been similar' (p. 261). Like Smith, Munz recognises the importance of colonisation and decolonisation. Unlike her, however, he regards colonisation as 'beneficial and a precondition for growth, not because of the positive advantages it bestows but because of the corrosive effects it has on traditions' (p. 262). It is colonisation that, by breaking down societies based on status leads to modern societies like New Zealand, where, while 'one cannot "become" a Maori, one can "become" a New Zealander' (Munz, 1994, p. 75).

Despite the growing disillusionment with culturalism amongst its advocates in the liberal-Left, its legacy in education will be less easily dismissed. As I explained in the preceding chapter, relativism, a key premise of culturalism and constructivism, has had a major effect on education systems, including the curriculum, through the influence of the liberal-Left students of the 1960s and 1970s who became key decision-makers in government ministries in later decades. In New Zealand schools social constructivist ideas have hollowed out the curriculum and permeated the pedagogy. When culturalism is combined with social constructivism, the result is to enclose young people in the restricted world of "culture". It is assumed that, because the individual is "constructed" within the social relations, language, and ways of the communal group, that person's education should remain within those boundaries.

To impose the curriculum of others, especially the coloniser, is considered an act of "symbolic violence", one that leads to alienation, low self-esteem, and poor achievement. Given this argument, and despite it leading to the restriction of knowledge to those young people, New Zealand has established a separate Maori education system (kaupapa Maori) from early childhood to tertiary. According to the Ministry of Education these institutions have 'made a major contribution to the education system as a whole by giving learners a new means through which to achieve education success' (Education Information and Analysis Group, 2009, p. 2). In chapter 7 I argued that it is not possible to make this claim because we simply do not know whether Maori students achieve greater success in Maori-medium education or in English-medium education. What is significant here and demonstrated by the ministry's statement, is the uncritical embrace of culturalist ideology by government officials.

The public judgement of knowledge through testing and criticism is at the heart of the process by which disciplines validate their knowledge claims. But when public judgement is withheld in the belief that knowledge is reducible to the cultures of social groups (or to the individual scientist) the integrity of knowledge production is compromised. This is the case with the production of indigenous knowledge today, an issue to which I turn in detail in the next chapter. Here my interest is in how culturalism weakens the commitment to universal knowledge. It does so by rejecting the idea of objectivity and by conflating what is known with who knows it.

Cultural theorists (e.g., Connell, 2009; Smith, 1999), however, argue that this decolonising process is necessary because it exposes the inherent ideology of knowledge. Accordingly, it will lead to the emancipation of minority and indigenous peoples from the imperialism of universal knowledge. Karl Maton (2010) describes how 'such discourses are legitimated on the basis of the inability of existing knowledge to articulate the voice of this previously silenced knower' (p. 53). He points out that in this line of argument, 'the potential categories of new knowers is hypothetically endless' (p. 54). 'With this proliferation of knowers, where each new knowledge is defined according to the criteria of articulating each knower's specialised voice, and truth is defined as whatever may be said by that voice, then it is not *what* has been said that matters, it is *who* has said it' (p. 54).

Objective knowledge, in contrast, is defined by its epistemic character, by the separation of the knowledge from the knower through disciplinary institutions and procedures. This was not always the case, as Daston and Galison (2010) point out in their fascinating account of scientific objectivity discussed with reference to pictures drawn from the long tradition of scientific atlases. Importantly for my purpose here, they point to a key feature of objectivity saying that 'To be objective is to aspire to knowledge that *bears no trace of the knower*—knowledge unmarked by prejudice or skill, fantasy or judgement, wishing or striving' (p. 17, my italics). As I argued in chapter 5, traces of the knower are removed in the social institutions and procedures that guarantee objectivity. In this way, the claim for scientific objectivity is not attributed to the scientists' impartiality.

One of the flaws in the relativist argument is that because the "knower" and "knowledge" are not separated, there is no source for objectivity other than in the scientist him or herself—a source easily rejected. Karl Popper (1945/2003) traced the 'attitude which considers the person of the thinker instead of his thought' to the 'abandonment of the rationalist attitude, of the respect for reason and argument and the other fellow's point of view' to the 'stress upon the "deeper" layers of human nature'. He argued that 'all this must lead to the view that thought is merely a somewhat superficial manifestation of what lies within these irrational depths'. In turn this attitude 'must produce the belief that "we think with our blood", or "with our national heritage", or "with our class"' (p. 260). In cultural theory it is the belief that we "think" with our cultural group.

It is a way of knowing available only to the insider. This determinism may be presented, according to Popper 'in a materialist form', as in the belief that class determines ways of thinking or in a 'highly spiritual fashion'—the idea underpinning the culturalist approach that '"we think with our race"' (p. 260). For fundamentalist Maori, it is the belief that there is a Maori way of knowing according to a Maori worldview (Durie, 2003). Nowhere is this racial belief that knowledge comes from a group's ethnic genetic heritage more clearly expressed than in this statement by Roberts and Wills (1998). The writers say that genealogy

> provides a grand, unifying framework for understanding the origin and appearance of regularity in the entire universe, one that in the process unites the biological with the social and cultural. (p. 61)

Ironically, while culturalism rejects the concept of universalism, it is itself a universalist movement. The call to "culture" in the service of various types of nationalist, ethnic, or religious political movements has a long heritage. Although dominant in certain periods—the late twentieth-century and the nineteenth-century romanticism that opposed the Enlightenment's commitment to reason—cultural ideology draws on the irrationalism that remains a strong undercurrent in modernity. It feeds the identity poles of traditionalism, primitivism, and postmodernism (Friedman, 1994), freeing us from 'the strain of individual responsibility' by, as Popper (1945/2003) recognised, allowing us to indulge our 'nostalgic desire to submit to the passion and prejudice of our tribal instincts' (p. 54). These 'instincts', or more specifically, fears of insecurity that shook the previously unbounded confidence of the new professional class from the late 1970s, fuel the desire for Arcadia.

In contrast to the commitment by liberalism and socialism to the Enlightenment ideals of equality (despite interpreting the idea differently, Kymlicka, 2002), culturalism is in the tradition of the counter-Enlightenment. It looks backwards to traditional pre-democratic forms of political organisation that are believed to provide stability within the continuity of tradition. It is a stability yearned for in periods of crisis, a yearning not new to the late twentieth and twenty-first centuries, as Edmund Burke showed in his call for continuity and tradition following the French Revolution. For Burke (1790), the overthrown of established order was 'unnatural'. It produced 'laws overturned; tribunals subverted; industry without vigour; commerce expiring; the revenue unpaid, yet the people impoverished; a church pillaged, and a state not relieved; civil and military anarchy made the constitution of the kingdom; everything human and divine sacrificed to the idol of public credit, and national bankruptcy the consequence' (paragraphs 50–74).

While Burke argued for continuity, other counter-Enlightenment thinkers sought that continuity in the foundational group as the primary unit of political and social organisation (Herder, cited in Lukes, 2003). This group is involuntary, indissoluble, and irreducible to its individual members (Sharp, 2002). Its ethnic or religious criteria for membership is a birthright and it is from the blood connection that the individual is "constructed" within the social relations and practices of the primordial ethnic groups. Adam Kuper (2001) compares the two traditions of thinking about culture in this way. 'A central theme of the Enlightenment thinkers was human progress, whereas their opponents were interested in the particular destiny of a nation. In the Enlightenment view, civilization was engaged in a great struggle to overcome the resistance of traditional cultures, with their superstitions, irrational prejudices, and fearful loyalties to cynical rulers. For the party of the Counter-Enlightenment, the defining enemy was rational, scientific, universal civilisation; the Enlightenment itself' (p. 7).

The idea that people are constructed within the social relations of their culture owes much to counter-Enlightenment writer, Johann Herder. He believed that 'to belong to a given community, to be connected with its members by indissoluble and impalpable ties of common language, historical memory, habit, tradition and feeling, is a basic human need no less natural than for food and drink or security or procreation' (Herder, cited in Lukes, 2003, p. 87). This approach considers status hierarchies and rule by birth-ascribed elites as the "natural" way to distribute authority. It regards individual citizenship, universalism, and equality as a corruption of the natural order—the inviolate ethnic group (Kuper, 2001). Popper (1945/2003) refers to Kant's recognition of his long-term friend, Herder's 'dangerous irrational romanticism' (p. 57). Herder had, in 1785, a year after the publication of Kant's 'What Is Enlightenment', published his theories of nationalism in *Ideas Towards a Philosophy of the History of Mankind*. He (Herder) referred to the 'most natural state . . . as a state composed of a single people with a single national character . . . a people is a natural growth like a family, only spread more widely. . . . As in all human communities . . . so, in the case of the state, the natural order is the best—that is to say, the order in which everyone fulfils that function for which nature intended him' (cited in Popper, 1945/2003, p. 57).

Kant's response to Herder's desire to fix people in primordial bonds of kinship—whether as the race-based nation, the ethnic group, or the religio-cultural group, is as fitting a response for the varieties of relativism today as it was for Herder's romantic nostalgia. Kant spoke out strongly (and in doing so lost his friend), against this essentialist determinism, saying:

> A Sagacity quick in picking up analogies and an imagination audacious in the use it makes of them are combined with a capability for enlisting emotions and passions in order to obtain interest for its object—an object that is always veiled in mystery. These emotions are easily mistaken for the efforts of powerful thoughts. . . Synonyms are passed off as explanations, and allegories are offered as truths. (cited in Popper, 1945/2003, p. 57)

A contemporary example of such "audacious" explanation is Huia Jahnke and Julia Taiapa's (1999) account of who should do Maori research. It appears in a popular textbook used widely for over a decade now in research methods courses throughout New Zealand. Drawing on a number of authoritative Maori researchers, the writers describe the criteria for undertaking Maori research.

> Maori researchers are differentiated according to iwi [tribe], hapu [subtribe], or whanau [extended family] links. Furthermore, age and gender

> may also be a factor in the research process. In terms of empowerment, it cannot be assumed that it is the researcher who is necessarily doing all the empowering. Within a Maori context, mana or power remains with an individual and is not something that can be given. (p. 48)

In this account, knowledge is based on "blood"; on the birth, age, and sex of the "knower"—all that science and reason rejects. The fundamental criteria for research—objectivity, public accountability, the universal criteria for researchers—are dismissed without explanation. The easy displacement of science by superstition, of the rational by the irrational, shows how the 'rationalization and secularization', which after 1650 'rapidly overthrew theology's age-old hegemony in the world of study, slowly but surely eradicated magic and belief in the supernatural from Europe's intellectual culture (Israel, 2001, p. 4) may be rolled back by the resurgence of the irrational into science.

The amazingly rapid inclusion of Maori knowledge and cultural processes in New Zealand universities and science institutions in just over a decade (Rata, 2010a; Openshaw and Rata, 2007, 2008) owes its success to postmodernism's embrace of Hegelian essentialism. This is a strand that Popper (1945/2003) traces to Hegel's romantic theory of Fate (p. 10). He noted that even Greek philosophy's beginning as a rationalist movement contained 'streaks of mysticism'—'the yearning for the lost unity and shelter of tribalism', that, in the Middle Ages became 'an open conflict between rationalism and irrationalism in the opposition between scholasticism and mysticism' (p. 253).

For philosopher Mario Bunge (2001), irrationalism is 'not just one more philosophical school; it is antiphilosophical, in rejecting clear and cogent discourse, and consequently in being dogmatic. This holds even for the mildest form of irrationalism and the most prevalent one in social studies, namely intuitionism' (p. 452). Bunge blames two major moral culprits for the backwardness of social studies; denying universal knowledge and replacing the authority of scientific procedures with the authority of culture. Culturalism in the social sciences would meet his criteria for the 'frequent violation of the ethos of science'. According to Bunge, this violation occurs 'when the universality of scientific knowledge is denied, dogmatism is substituted for "organized scepticism"—that is rational discussion, in particular criticism—and rigorous testing, or at least testability, is jettisoned' (p. 453).

In New Zealand, Christopher Tremewan (2005a, 2005b) laid the blame for the culturalist 'ideological conformity, [that as] a dead hand has stifled rather than promoted critical debate' at the door of New Zealand's social sciences. He accused this discipline for not only its 'failure to provide an adequate critique of social norms in this country' but for its complicity in a process of racial categorisation that may well have destructive consequences for those it is meant to help and for the whole society' (2005a, p. 2). The source of that conformity in the social sciences can be traced to the shift to postmodernism by influential anthropologists such as Anne Salmond. The meanings-based anthropology that Salmond (1982, 1985, 1991) introduced to New Zealand provided sufficient emotive mystery to seduce a generation of adherents. Roberts and Wills (1998), with reference to Salmond, declared that their aim was

> to present an understanding of Maori epistemology from the perspective of scientists engaged in teaching indigenous worldviews (namely, that of the peoples of the Pacific) alongside that of Western science. (1998, p. 67)

They explained the fundamental difference between Maori knowledge and Western knowledge as a lack of a distinction between subject and object. This is the ultimate abandonment of objectivism that I discussed in chapter 5. There can be no objectivism *when even the object itself is discarded.* Although the passage quoted below is rather long, it is important because many of the ideas promoted by advocates of indigenous knowledge may be traced directly to this and similar ideas. It shows the return of the supernatural to "science" in New Zealand.

> Knowledge is a sacred power that belongs to a group rather than to a particular individual who may hold it for a time, and can only be passed on to chosen members of the group. As a sacred power knowledge can be 'talked into' physical objects as in the blessing of a building or a ceremonial ornament. Likewise, stories are told of how ancestors, in claiming territory, named landmarks, rocks, trees, waterfalls, and so on, and thereby locked together tribal understanding with the entities themselves so that a place and its knowledge could not be separated. In this way, the tribe's heritage and the local environment come to share in a single whakapapa [genealogy], and the world is not separated into a hierarchy of ontological categories corresponding to things of physical, biological and cultural origin. The cosmic generative power, the common dynamic process in which all things unfold (tipu), already contained the form of every possible being. Consequently, all things in the phenomenal world alike unfold their nature (tipu), live (ora), and have form (ahua) and so come to possess a body (Tinana), an immaterial self (wairua), and an abiding place of divine power (mauri), and characteristic vitality (hau). (p. 61)

Nowhere is Bunge's (2001) accusation that the ethos of science is violated by a mysticism with its insistence on emotions and passion rather than reason more clearly demonstrated than in these examples.

> Maori epistemology is based on a view of the world in which the unifying ontological principle is whakapapa (manifesting mauri and wairua)

> rather than matter (driven by mechanism). Manifestations of mauri and wairua arise as a result of influences and 'laws' whose meaning cannot be expressed in terms of pure mechanism or contingency. It is tempting to make a comparison with the Western concept of teleology, but any 'purpose' apparent in the unraveling of Maori whakapapa is driven by knowledge of the past, rather than being directed towards some future goal. For this reason it is sometimes said that Maori are a people who walk backwards into the future, meaning that it is the deeds of the ancestors (real and mythical) that control and guide the present generation and help determine the fate of future generations. (Roberts and Wills, 1998, p. 61)

But the influence of the irrational mysticism that underpins culturalism is not confined to New Zealand is the past four decades. It has a long history. Popper traces the culturalist belief that knowledge is a social product, determined by and determining of people within a particular foundational group to Plato via Hegel. He refers to Hegel and the Hegelians 'who considered knowledge to be a social product and indeed as a kind of department of the soul or the spirit of society (for example, of the nation, or the class) and who emphasise. . . our nearly indebtedness to our social heritage' (1945/2003, p. 250). Writing in 1945, Popper was not to know the 'uninhibited gobbledygook' (Bunge, 2001, p. 453) of late twentieth-century postmodernism, although as a German-Jewish refugee to the University of Canterbury in Christchurch, New Zealand, he had personally experienced the consequences of irrationalism. However, Popper (1945/2003) did identify the precedents of contemporary postmodernism, noting that the 'tide had turned, and "profoundly significant allusions. . . and allegories" (as Kant puts it) have become the fashion of the day' (p. 254). He was spared reading Linda Smith's influential *Decolonizing Methodologies* (1999), although his former student, historian Peter Munz, was particularly critical of the book saying that it:

> is likely to obfuscate politico-social debates in New Zealand because it maintains that acquiring knowledge about indigenous peoples, as distinct from the stories these people themselves are telling, is a way of colonizing them and amounts to imperialism. (1999, p. 4)

Munz (1999) rejected Smith's claim that Maori research is by Maori for Maori, along with the idea that research should be confined 'to the discovery of what people are saying about themselves so that their self-image remains intact and shielded from the corrosive extension of knowledge' (p. 5). According to Munz, 'indigenousness is not a sensible criterion of distinction between research methodologies. Indigenous people can pursue both kinds of research into their own belief system' (p. 5).

The most comprehensive critical analysis of the Maori culturalist research, known as kaupapa Maori, has been undertaken by Dannette Marie and Brian Haig (2006, 2009). They

> contend that a significant feature of the politicisation of science in New Zealand involves the requirement that research scientists uncritically accept the tenets of relativism that the ideology of biculturalism harbours and the Maori renaissance project actively promotes. These tenets of relativism can be observed in the notion that the epistemic worth of 'Maori knowledge' can only be comprehended and evaluated from within the Maori cultural framework (or world-view). (2009, p. 117)

The authors (2009) provide examples of the extent to which the culturalist knowledge approach pervades New Zealand science, saying that:

> areas now regarded as being of specific relevance to Maori are unbounded. Various New Zealand acts of legislation including the *Health Research Council Act 1990*, the *Crown Research Institutes Act 1992*, and the *Foundation for Research, Science and Technology Amendment Act 1993* all express relevant provisions for Maori research' (2009, 120). Of particular interest is their discussion of the Ministry of Research, Science, and Technology' document '*Vision Matauranga: Unlocking the potential of Maori knowledge, resources and people*' (Ministry of Research, Science and Technology, 2006) which refers to 'indigenous innovation and knowledge'. The document states that although indigenous and scientific knowledge should be regarded as distinct knowledge systems or epistemologies, a relation between the two is required in order that issues of mutual interest can be discussed in a culturally appropriate manner. Like the parallel systems of education and health in New Zealand, science must reflect the bicultural orthodoxy. This requires the unconditional acceptance of relativism and allows the science system to be used as an additional platform to further facilitate special Maori identity rights and claims. (pp. 118–119)

They refer also to the significant 'moral pressure, which has led to individuals conforming to doctrines including kaupapa Maori research methodology that fundamentally reject orthodox science' (2009, p. 127). Similarly, Chris Tremewan alludes to the moral pressure that keeps academics silent, and therefore complicit, in the institutionalisation of indigenous ideology into the university. He (2005a) also hints at the fate awaiting those who are critical.

> There is nothing as implacable as academics, NGO activists or government policy analysts policing their colleagues for political conformity under the guise of academic rigour. The New Zealand research

> community, from the biomedical sciences to the social sciences, is almost inured to ideological imperatives in funding applications and conference paper selections. Those critiquing the dominant culturalist paradigm, even obliquely, are likely to miss out on funding or be excluded from presentation roles at multi-sectoral policy conferences. (p. 13)

It is here that culturalism threatens science itself. The integrity of scientific objectivity is only as sound as the integrity of academia's institutions and procedures. Chapter nine is an account of how these institutions and procedures can be compromised from within.

9 Localised Knowledge

The objectivity of epistemic knowledge is developed in the codes and structures of the disciplines of the arts, humanities, and social and natural sciences, and guaranteed by the procedures and systems of the disciplines. It is found neither in the individual scientist nor in the determinism of class, race, sex, and religio-cultures. (The argument for a non-deterministic understanding of the reasoning individual is found in the concept of partial loyalty discussed in chapter 6.) For these reasons, the integrity of those disciplinary institutions and procedures cannot be overstated. These are the procedures within which, as Diderot (1759, 1995) asked; 'All things must be examined, debated, investigated without exception and without regard for anyone's feelings' (p. 18). Yet in the past four decades, those institutional procedures for the production of objective knowledge in the natural and the social sciences, developed in the three centuries since Diderot's call for the processes of objectivity have been weakened. This has occurred with the creation of a knowledge market in the globalised economy as the university becomes a factory in that market and by the conflation of social and scientific knowledge under the pulverising weight of relativism.

Based on his diagnosis of the state of 'social studies', as he calls the various disciplines that make up a unified "social science", Mario Bunge (2001) predicts two possible outcomes from this conflation. The first is the disciplines' decay in 'irrelevant and arbitrary "postmodern" (in particular "constructivist-relativist") speculation, or even degeneration into uninhibited gobbledygook'. The second more optimistic prediction is that 'the study of society will eventually mature into full-fledged science' (p. 453). Of Bunge's five recommendations, one is to *'adopt scientific realism'*. This is also the plea of social realists in the sociology of education who acknowledge that our confidence in the way knowledge is produced depends upon the rigour used to test and criticise knowledge. According to realism 'all knowledge is ultimately provisional and open to revision (and in this respect, it is "critical"), but some ways of producing knowledge are demonstrably more reliable than others' (Moore, 2007a, p. 35). This chapter is about what happens when ways of producing and testing knowledge according to established disciplinary systems break down.

The analysis uses research that I have undertaken over a number of years into the ways in which culturalism has become part of the New Zealand education system (Rata, 2010a, 2011c, 2011d). My most recent interest has concerned the aggressive move to include indigenous knowledge in the New Zealand university. This chapter is about the first stage in that process—the development of an indigenous episteme and the justification for its inclusion, something not confined to New Zealand. Chapter 10 expands on the analysis to show how the inclusion of a localised knowledge is managed so that it is "protected" from the scrutiny to which other disciplinary knowledge must be subjected. These processes of knowledge production, justification, and control show how the main public institution for the production and guarantee of objectivity is undermined by the politics of localisation.

Both stages are about the two interdependent features of symbolic production (see chapter 5). The first feature is the production of structures, codes, and methods intrinsic to the discipline that are neither context nor content dependent. The second feature is the disciplinary institutions, systems, and procedures that authorise the generating concepts, principles, and content that constitute those structures, codes, and methods. Although indigenous knowledge is concerned with producing structures, codes, and methods to make it an "academic discipline" it remains content and context dependent thereby failing the test of what it is to be a discipline. By retaining an authority for the knowledge based in the 'knower's' status as a member of the cultural group, indigenous knowledge is unable to become context and content independent.

I have chosen the university as the object for analysis, although there are a number of institutions, particularly schools, the health system, and the Anglican Church in New Zealand (Tremewan, 2006) that are also thoroughly permeated by culturalist ideas. My choice of the university is because this is the institution that Moore and Young (2010), following Durkheim and Popper, call a public arena of collective judgement. It is where the specific practices of the disciplinary field—procedures, codes, systems by which knowledge is objectified—are themselves constantly available to criticism. As Moore and Young (2010) point out, it is the 'specialist forms of social organisation' (for example, university disciplines) that 'remain the major social bases for guaranteeing the objectivity of knowledge' (p. 30).

Including belief-based practices into those institutions affects the authority over knowledge, a matter I discussed in chapter 4 and return to in chapter 10. Allowing the production of indigenous knowledge, a knowledge that is neither objective nor open to scrutiny, subverts the integrity of the university as an institution guaranteeing objectivity, but it goes further. By creating an "episteme" that is not objective, the new "discipline" of indigenous studies subverts the very principle of objectivity that is necessary for epistemology. In a word—it is illogical. Indigenous knowledge cannot be epistemic knowledge and, at the same time, subjective social knowledge since the intrinsic or epistemic character of knowledge *is* its objectivity.

In the early 1970s, the trend towards an alternative position to Western methodology had not succeeded in producing a distinctive "indigenous alternative" according to Abaza and Stauth (1990, p. 127, with reference to Mursy and colleagues, 1987). By the turn of the century, the story had changed significantly with the establishment of an "indigenous knowledge discipline". This became possible within the politics of localisation given the status of indigeneity as the most local of all localised ideologies. The creation of the "indigenous episteme" has happened remarkably quickly. Not only is there the episteme claim itself—known as the "logic of the gift" (as opposed to the "logic of the commodity"), there is a well-developed knowledge production infrastructure. Frances Widdowson and Albert Howard (2008) describe the 'huge organizational infrastructure supporting traditional knowledge research around the world. . . all engaged in the global enterprise of documenting and "applying" traditional knowledge' (p. 247) developed out of the anti-colonisation resistance and struggle of the 1970s and 1980s. In the past decade, this infrastructure has been used by academics as the infrastructure for the fledging "indigenous episteme" to become a knowledge discipline.

The infrastructure is comprehensive: comprising networks, journals, conferences, publications, and postgraduate qualifications. The discipline is served by journals (for example, *MAI* and *AlterNative* conferences, the Fourth International Indigenous Conference was hosted by the Maori Centre for Excellence at the University of Auckland in June 2010); and a growing number of influential books, including L. T. Smith's *Decolonizing Methodologies Research and Indigenous Peoples* (1999), Marie Battiste's *Reclaiming Indigenous Voice and Vision* (2000); Sandy Grande's *Red Pedagogy* (2004, 2009); Margaret Kovach's *Indigenous Methodologies* (2009); and Rauna Kuokkanen's *Reshaping the University: Responsibility, Indigenous Epistemes, and the Logic of the Gift* (2007).

Formalised links exist between the University of Auckland and the First Nations House of Learning at the University of British Columbia and professorial positions have been established in a number of universities to serve as a centre for the development of indigenous epistemologies. (For example, the University of Auckland appointed a professor of indigenous development in 2010.) Tania Ka'ai, formerly an indigenous professor at the University of Otago and now at Auckland University of Technology makes it clear that the task of indigenous intellectuals is a political one. She proposes that 'indigenising the academy', an 'axion amongst indigenous intellectuals', means 'to make the academy both responsive and responsible to Indigenous people's goals of self-determination and well-being. According to Ka'ai 'this requires a huge effort by Indigenous scholars to be committed to transforming the academy. To engage in this work, requires a redefining of the academy from an agent of colonialism to a platform for decolonisation' (2005, p. 1).

The development of the discipline's raw material began with an emphasis on theorising the difference between indigeneity and the West, that is, defining indigenous knowledge by what it is not. Grande (2009), in her description of American Indian, 'Red sociology', while acknowledging that 'indigenous and critical scholars do share a common ground' (p. 199), drew a distinction between critical scholars' 'vision in Western conceptions of democracy and justice that present a "liberated' self" and indigenous scholars [who] ground their vision in conceptions of sovereignty that presume a profound connection to place and land' (p. 200). The shift to defining indigenous knowledge by what it is, that is, its episteme, the 'logic of the gift', developed from there. Firstly, it essentialises a group of people as fundamentally different from others because their social relations of production are presented as non-capitalist. Apart from being an extreme form of economic determinism, such essentialism ignores the fact that indigeneity itself is a feature of capitalism. It emerged in the modern period as a strategy enabling the legal and administrative management of labour and land within colonisation (Li, 2010).

Tania Li (2010, citing Henry Bernstein, 2005, p. 72) refers to the use of 'collective tenures over customary land, invented by colonial regimes and the associated ideologies of community, tribe and custom to "prevent, limit or otherwise manage dynamics of class formation"'. Secondly, essentialised relations of production are understood to be caused by an indigenous redistributive mode of production. Reciprocity or the "gift" is considered to be the structuring principle of social relations and of the relationship between humans and nature. It is the system identified by Mauss 'in which exchange of goods [is] not a mechanical but a moral transaction, bringing about and maintaining human, personal, relationships between individuals and groups (Evans-Pritchard, 1954, p. ix). This "logic of the gift" is presented as opposed to the exploitative commodity relations of the accumulatory exchange system, that is, to capitalism.

According to indigenous writers, the knowledge produced by a redistributive reciprocal system is fundamentally different from the knowledge produced for a system based on exploitative relations. In both cases, knowledge is understood to be ideology—and as such, serves the power relations of the society. However the ideology of an exploitative system the "logic of the commodity" creates and justifies its exploitative inequalities while the ideology of the reciprocal system "the logic of the gift" creates and justifies equality and balance between human and non-human forces of production. This gives the "indigenous episteme" a considerable moral edge. Not only it is presented as an equalising force between people, it claims to be the original sustainable discourse—a post-capitalist system for re-dressing the relationship between humans and nature, from one of exploitation to one of reciprocity. There is an increasing use of scientific sustainable discourse in indigenous research that supports both the claims to be recognised as a legitimate science and its claims to a completely different and morally superior type of knowledge.

However in both claims lies the justification for political rights to own and manage resources and the justification for those with access to those resources to exercise power. Kauna Kuokkanen's writing shows the link between the moral position claimed for those operating according to the logic of the gift and its political implications in "responsibilities". She (2007) views the 'gift as a manifestation of reciprocity with the natural environment; it reflects the bond of dependence and respect toward the natural world. From this bond, certain responsibilities emerge,' (p. 33). Similarly, Mason Durie's (2009) trust in the 'wise leadership' (p. 2) of the romanticised indigenous world contains the same idea. A moral position captured in the episteme is used to justify political claims by a classed elite, with the sustainability discourse providing the scientific respectability.

Within indigenous theory, the link between the "knower" and the "knowledge" is determined by the thinker's status within the socio-cultural group. Because the knowledge is reduced to the social relations of production, it is knowledge that belongs to that group and to no other. It means that the knowledge cannot be produced by others (for example, Kuokkanen, 2007; Kovack, 2009). This belief applies not only to indigenous groups. The argument advanced by Raewyn Connell in her 2009 book *Southern Theory* is for the recognition of social knowledge as an episteme with knowledge fixed permanently to its creator. It means that knowledge is always subjective. She rejects as "Western" the institutions and procedures for objectifying knowledge so that it is separated from its creator and made available for testing and criticising, regarding these institutions and procedures as compromised by an exploitative ideology. For indigenous knowledge, as with other types of voice or standpoint knowledges based on gender, religion or ethnicity, social knowledge *is* the episteme. Disciplinary knowledge is always subjective and tied to its creator. It is always the knowledge of the social group and available only for criticism based on that group's frame of reference.

The "logic of the gift" concept embeds the dualism of a spiritual people of the land contrasted with a materialist and exploitative "West" (Rata, 2011a). In New Zealand this dualism was developed in the inclusive bicultural period and promoted in the writings of Ranginui Walker (1982) during the 1980s.

> Indigenous people the world over share a common spiritual, philosophical and cultural base in their mythology, tribalism and relationship to the earth-mother. The colonising Pakeha stemmed from a cultural tradition of west-European origin with its tribal roots attenuated or submerged by the new mythology of Christianity and the capitalist economic system, both of which redefined man's relationship with the earth and its resources. Under capitalism the earth is no longer perceived as a mother to be loved and cherished, but as a commodity to be bought and sold in the market-place. (p. 16)

According to Linda Smith (1994) 'what Maori people have, as with other indigenous people, is a distinct knowledge tradition which lies outside western views of knowledge' (p. 10). Similarly, Mason Durie (2003) refers to 'Maori worldviews, [that] like those of many indigenous people, are based on values and experiences that have evolved over centuries. They form the basis for a knowledge system that is distinctly different from other systems such as science and the Judaeo-Christian philosophies' (p. 13).

The "logic of the gift" episteme is not confined to theoretical discussion. It underpins Maori policy and research in New Zealand (Marie and Haig, 2006). There are numerous examples in education (Openshaw, 2009b), whereas in health, Mason Durie's "Te Tapa Wha" Maori Mental Health model was developed to compensate for what was regarded as a lack of a spiritual dimension in the Western-based secular health services (Maori Mental Health Model, 2010). The new "Whanau Ora" (literally, healthy families) social policy is claimed by its advocates to offer a new concept of sustainability and balance based on indigenous values of 'service to others, thinking of others ahead of oneself and guardianship of the environment'. These are 'sacred and powerful concepts' from

> our ancient ideas and cultures that used these structures for living successfully for many thousands of years. In fact far longer than the economic and societal political and legal structures we use today, that are only several hundred years old and are failing. (n.p.)

The writer, Naida Glavish (2010), refers to the restoration of the natural order and hierarchies of whanau (kinship) of the policy as 'one of the most forward thinking initiatives by any New Zealand government for generations' (p. A13).

While the production of the indigenous episteme is becoming increasingly characterised by the concept of the 'logic of the gift' (Kuokkanen, 2007, p. 2), the Western origins of the concept tend to be ignored. Despite its origins in Mauss's anthropology (1954), the "gift" is re-conceptualised to distinguish the indigenous relationship—one characterised 'by reciprocity and by a call for responsibility toward the "other"' (Kuokkanen, 2007, p. 2) from the commodity relationship of the West. The deepening of the indigenous-West difference at the epistemological level in recent indigenous scholarship has two main purposes. It maintains the difference between the idea of an indigenous episteme in contrast to Western knowledge as I previously mention, but it also establishes a way to cross the divide without weakening the division. This brokerage strategy between the often self-appointed representatives of indigenous peoples and the West is an important strategy in preserving the notion of primordially distinctive people—without whom there could be no representatives. It also enables the various ethnic, indigenous, and religio-cultural leaders to cross the divide as the representatives of their "people". In this role as the legitimate voice of a distinctive people, these leaders are transformed within their brokerage role to become part of the globalised elites of contemporary capitalism (Rata, 2003a, 2011c).

The importance of brokerage is recognised by indigenous academics. Rauna Kuokkanen (2007) refers to crossing the divide as 'mainstreaming' (p. 2). In the New Zealand context the term "partnership" is used. The "gift" itself becomes the conceptual mechanism for the new relationship between the people and the "other". This new concept of social relations is the host-guest relationship, based upon reciprocity, although with the host in the primary position. The guest is to acknowledge the 'gift of indigenous epistemes through reciprocation' (2007, p. 3), a reciprocation that Kuokkanen argues is missing from universities that have appeared to accept indigenous knowledge but more as conformity to rights-based politics than a genuine acceptance of the value of that knowledge. It is, according to Kuokkanen, the means to balance and harmonise the relationship between humans and the natural world.

Elites who rely on their role as representatives of a foundational "people", for whom they serve as brokers, require an ideology of an unchanging collective. For Tania Li (2010), 'protection and incarceration are two sides of the same coin' (p. 399). It is an incarceration of permanence powerfully illustrated in Peter Sutton's recent analysis of the consequences of decades of protection for Australian Aborigines (2009). Although indigenous elites, like all elites, occupy a privileged position by harnessing progress to their own interests, indigenous status incarcerates others. The poor, locked out of modernity's progress by an ideology that dismisses progress as "Western", serve their time in the ahistorical timelessness of indigeneity. Whereas indigenous elites operate in the real historical world, those they represent must remain fixed as the people in whose name indigenous politics can operate.

The logic of the gift versus the logic of the commodity draws on the division and building of boundaries that characterise culturalism more generally. It can be seen in a Maori education administrator's invited speech to senior officials of the New Zealand Treasury.

> The Pakeha world is clearly compartmentalized. There is a compartment for the mundane and another for the spirit. This allows good Christians to rob and pillage during the week and to go to church on Sunday all with a clear conscience. For indigenous peoples the compartmentalization of one's life and mind is not customarily part of their makeup; the world of the spirit and the world of the mundane are not clearly separated although today as a result of colonization separation has begun and sometimes with dire consequences. (Hook, 2006)

This example is of interest not only for its presentation of a crude and inaccurate racial stereotyping of pakeha (settler-descendants) but in the lack of any reaction from the audience. No one challenged the speaker to say that such stereotyping was nonsense. Indeed any understanding of the extent of culturalism in New Zealand must include an analysis of the silence in the face of misleading stereotypes, wrong information (see my discussion of revisionist history in chapter 10), and distorted, even mischievous, explanations of a racially divided and antagonistic peoples. For example, teacher education students taking a separate Maori programme describe how their courses enabled them to 'become more conscious of the ways of the oppressor' (Morehu, Lolesio, Piper, and Pomare, 2009, p. 3). This racial positioning of one people against another from university students is not surprising, however it is when lecturers themselves understand research as 'a research and writing relationship based on the tension of difference not its erasure' (Jones and Jenkins, 2008, p. 473).

According to sociologists of education, Alison Jones and Kuni Jenkins (2008), 'the almost universal indigenous and Other responses to attempts to soften, even erase the hyphen in the interests of seeing us in terms of researchers' enthusiastic all-encompassing visions of humanity' (p. 474) must be 'a firm restatement of the gap'. Otherwise, without the separation of indigenous and Western, 'Western researchers ignore the indigenous-colonizer hyphen as they write across it, recolonising as they go' (p. 474). In this interpretation, research by a non-indigenous person about indigenous people is always colonising. Jones and Jenkins are quite definite about this. They emphasise that 'those colonizer researchers who would dissolve/consume/soften/erase the indigene-colonizer hyphen into a sharing collaboration engagement between "us," there is one, harshly pragmatic, response: *It does not work*' (p. 474, italics in the original.)

In this example of the essentialism of a racialised group, Jones and Jenkins (2008) insist that in response to coloniser people who 'assert the us in a shared modern life, indigenous peoples—as a matter of political, practical, and identity survival *as indigenous people*—insist on a profound difference at the Self-Other border. The hyphen is nonnegotiable. Indeed, in indigene-colonizer research and teaching work, the hyphen is to be protected and asserted and is a positive site of productive methodological work' (p. 475). To make it absolutely clear that the researcher's racial identity is intimately part of the research itself, the two academics refer to another researcher in terms of her ethnicity as 'Settler-colonizer researcher Michelle Fine. . .' (p. 475).

It is difficult not to draw comparisons between this version of a fully ethnicised approach to research and I. L. Kandell's (1935/1970) analysis of Nazi educational theory. According to Kandell this theory requires that the 'bases of education must be the group, ancestral tradition, and hereditary form' (p. 43). All trace of Enlightenment universalism must be removed. Yet as John Clark (2006) shows in his account of the deeply flawed relativist argument, the contradiction implicit to relativism refutes the relativist claim. This means that the Jones/Jenkins 'hyphen of division' is true for all groups—that is, it is universal. 'What the relativist argument does is to assert that the truth of a system of thought is relative to the group but is universally true for all groups (p. 171).

The romanticised view of a permanently fixed indigenous people in touch with nature and the spiritual world that informs the logic of the gift approach ignores the vested interests of those promoting the various standpoint knowledges. The default assumption is that cultural politics, including the production of the knowledge that serves that politics is in the interests of the cultural group—understood as a collective with shared interests. It is built into the approach with its Manichean 'them versus us', an essentialised "West" versus an equally essentialised indigene, dead white men versus contemporary oppressed women, and so on in this permanently divisive story of "Us and the Other".

Raewyn Connell's (2009) *Southern Theory* is built on this Occidentalism. Accordingly, 'northern theory' is about 'modern social science (which) embeds the viewpoints, perspectives and problems of metropolitan society, while presenting it as universal knowledge' (p. viii). 'Southern' is her term for 'the relations of authority, exclusion and inclusion, hegemony, partnership, sponsorship, appropriation—between intellectuals and institutions in the metropole and those in the world periphery' (p. ix). In this unequal relationship, 'alternative ways of thinking about the world, while they persist, are readily marginalised' (p. xi) according to Connell. However, Abaza and Stauth (1990) point out that those 'who claim authenticity by "indigenisation" might not yet be aware of the fact that the local knowledge upon which they want to construct an alternative, has long been part of global structures; or of the fact that they play a part in a global cultural game which itself calls for the "essentialisation" of local truth' (p. 211).

Essentialising difference in a group's primordial origins is a strategy of localisation that enables the group to protect itself from external criticism by being 'quarantined off from legitimate assessment and evaluation by others, being subject only to critical comment from those within the group' (Clark, 2006, p. 171). Indeed indigenous knowledge, by being included in the university yet not subject to its critical procedures has the best of both worlds. It claims the status of epistemic knowledge but acts as social knowledge—by being, as John Clark puts it—'quarantined from external criticism'. Yet it is that very 'external criticism' which, by collapsing the "hyphen" dividing groups each with its own circumscribed social knowledge, enables the testing of truth claims. The production of "indigenous knowledge" consolidates the ideology of historical timelessness. Included as a discipline in the university, it is given respectability and the status of an episteme. However, unlike other disciplines, it is not required to earn that status by being available to all and by being subjected to the academy's scrutiny and criticism. Ideas within the university that are shielded from such scrutiny fail the basis test of what is epistemic knowledge. They remain social knowledge serving the interests of a localised socio-cultural group.

10 Controlling Knowledge

This book has explained why epistemic knowledge, the type of knowledge created in universities and taught in schools, is crucial to modern democratic societies. It has explained why that powerful knowledge has been subverted by the forces of localisation. In education these forces take the form of the various relativisms: constructivism, culturalism, and postmodernism. This chapter examines how the knowledge promoted by localisation—social knowledge or "culture"—that is protected from scrutiny and criticism from "outsiders" becomes accepted as epistemic knowledge despite failing to meet the criteria to support such a claim. I use the example of indigenous knowledge as a type of social knowledge that has acquired remarkable saliency in recent decades to the point where it has developed its own episteme, the "logic of the gift", and a disciplinary infrastructure situated within the university.

Culturalism and the various relativist-constructionist approaches justify the indigenous episteme as scientific knowledge rather than as the social knowledge it is. Such justification must necessarily fail because social knowledge retains its character as knowledge in the interests of a social group. It is profoundly different from scientific knowledge. While "indigenous knowledge" provides the most clear example of the extent to which the boundary between epistemic knowledge and social knowledge has collapsed in recent decades, the argument for the demarcation between disciplinary knowledge and social knowledge as types of knowledge with profoundly different purposes and structures applies not only to indigenous knowledge. All other forms of social knowledge, including religio-cultural beliefs from creationism to fundamentalist Islam and Christianity, and political ideologies, from the cult regimes of Turkmenistan to the neotraditionalism of Tonga use the same criteria to protect the beliefs that protect elites from science's subversive potential. That potential is the constant exposure of epistemic knowledge to doubt, scrutiny, and criticism.

Social knowledge can acquire the status and influence of scientific knowledge without earning that status by being available universally and by being available for criticism. This is happening with the inclusion of indigenous knowledge into the university (Rata, 2011c). The analysis of this process is instructive because it exemplifies how the collapse of the demarcation between epistemic and social knowledge occurs. The first strategy in the production of indigenous knowledge creates the episteme itself—a process discussed in the previous chapter. This is the development of the "logic of the gift"—the idea of a social group with such fundamentally different social relations of production that its study requires a new epistemology to match the ontological beliefs. The second strategy concerns how the discipline is to be controlled and managed.

Systems and procedures are created to frame the indigenous knowledge; to state the criteria for who and how the knowledge is created and used; for what can be said, who is authorised to speak, and the purpose for which the knowledge is developed and used. But why is this a problem? Is the process by which indigenous knowledge becomes a discipline any different to that which has occurred in the centuries following the division of philosophy into scientific disciplines? According to Joseph Priestly in his proposal published as the *History and Present State of Electricity* (1769/1995) systematic scientific research would 'give new life to philosophical enquiries. It would suggest an infinity of new experiments, and would undoubtedly greatly accelerate the progress of knowledge; which is at present retarded, as it were, by its own weight, and the mutual entanglement of its several parts' (p. 70). The same innovative character of disciplines, each with its own intrinsic epistemic structure is something claimed by those establishing the indigenous knowledge discipline.

Priestley gave advice on how to establish the procedures for each subbranch of philosophy—or as they became, each scientific discipline. His suggestion for 'periodical accounts [to] be published of the result of [the] trial of experiments' is the forecursor to academic periodicals. (His advice does contain a criterion that disappeared much later in the wake of a salaried academia. This is that each member of the philosophical companies he proposes 'appoint a director of experiments' and 'let each member have a right to appoint a trial of experiments in some proposition to the sum he subscribes, and let a periodical account be published of the result of them all, successful or unsuccessful' p. 70). Those establishing the discipline of indigenous knowledge would claim that they are doing no less in carving out their disciplinary episteme, in establishing journals, publishing books, and holding conferences, than did the early natural scientists in the eighteenth century and the early social scientists over a century later.

That would indeed be so except that in the case of indigenous knowledge, the purpose and procedures that control and manage indigenous knowledge are the same as those used for social knowledge. Its purpose is to serve the social group and the authority for its management and control comes from those of status within the social group and is restricted to the group's members. (Although Priestley's criteria does restrict those who may experiment to scientists who could afford to do so, this criterion is not set in the past and immutable as is the criteria for the indigenous researcher.) In addition, indigenous knowledge contains the second feature that distinguishes social knowledge from disciplinary science. The meaning and value of knowledge remains tied to the experience of the social group. The beliefs do not become abstract concepts capable of being applied to other times and other situations. They remain experience-based beliefs, even if the experience referred to occurred in mythological times. In that case, genealogical ties are used to connect the present to the past—and indeed, genealogy is a noticeable feature of indigenous knowledge with indigenous scholars refering to their tribal affiliations in order to support their truth claims.

The following example of research into the neuroscience of Huntington's disease by a scientist who identifies as Maori illustrates these features. It shows how the connection is made between the beliefs of the group to which the scientist belongs and the methods used to acquire knowledge. This includes not only practising beliefs associated with the group but also ensuring that the authority for the knowledge is justified by the scientist's membership of the group. Additional authority is supplied by senior scientists who are also group members. The scientist identifies herself as affiliated to two Maori tribes: Ngati Rangitihi and Te Arawa.

Under the guidance of several kaupapa Maori academics (whose names are followed by their tribal affiliations), the scientist explains how she practises her science in accord with 'Tikanga Maori' [Maori culture]. Following consultation with her whanau [extended family] and kaumatua [elders] from her iwi [tribe], the scientist describes the way she has developed 'Tikanga Maori methodologies for working with human brain tissue and primary human brain cells'. She prays, by mourning 'the person who's gone and I use some cultural practices from tangi [funeral ceremony] to say goodbye to that person, to farewell them to Hawaiki, the place we go when we die. And then I welcome the cells to their new function, which is not feeling or thinking any more but growing in a dish to help with my research, which I hope will ultimately help other people' (University of Auckland News, 2011, p. 8).

The scientist's desire to be sensitive and respectful to the families of those human brain tissue and cells with which she works is an ethical approach to research. However, what makes this science "social knowledge" is the socio-cultural form that the respect takes. If scientists can only use human body parts from Maori participants in accordance with prescribed socio-cultural practices, what happens to scientists whose own race or beliefs may prevent them from using a culturally prescribed methodology? Research ethics of respect, disclosure, and accountability should operate regardless of a scientist's personal beliefs. Not only is the inclusion or exclusion of religio-cultural beliefs a problem for the secular science community, so too is the criteria applied to those who undertake research using Maori participants. In this example, the scientist identifies her membership of a tribe. She is authorised by senior researchers whose tribal affiliation is also included and the tribe itself provides the final authorisation.

The problem here is that membership of the group is exclusive. Not anyone can join. Tribal affiliation is established by genetic links to the past. While the actual science in this case may well be rigorous and important science, the socio-cultural criteria being used will limit the extent to which it can be scrutinised and criticised.

Just as criteria are established to define who can be one of the "people" of the indigenous group, so is criteria established to determine who can develop the knowledge of that people—who can be a researcher and under what conditions. Maori academics are very clear about who can undertake research and who cannot. According to Jahnke and Taiapa, 'Kaupapa Maori research models have been developed to ensure that Maori research is 'with Maori, by Maori and for Maori' (1999, p. 45). This restriction extends to the conditions under which the research is conducted. If non-Maori are involved in the research, its purpose and methods are controlled by Maori.

> There is a need to abide by a Maori system of ethics and accountability. Research about Maori requires clear goals and objectives, and reliable information based upon actual Maori experiences. This does require that Maori themselves should be involved in the design, delivery, management and monitoring of the research process. (pp. 49–50)

These controls are institutionalised in New Zealand's universities (Rata, 2011c). For example, the School of Education at the University of Waikato has developed 'guidelines for researchers, supervisors and ethics committee members to ensure that research projects conducted. . . adhere to the ethic and protocols of Maori research methods and philosophies' (Powick, 2002, p. 2). The document includes Graham Smith's four models 'by which culturally appropriate research can be undertaken by Pakeha [settler-descendant] researchers' (p. 8).

The University of Auckland's August 2009 human participants' ethics regulations (Applicants Manual, 2009, pp. 20–21; and Application Form, 2009, p. 12) provides a clear example of the exact mechanisms for controlling research. Outcomes will 'directly or indirectly benefit Maori' (Applicants Manual, 2009, p. 20). Research is

> to empower and build capacity [which] may be by means of: Developing a partnership between whanau [extended family], hapu [sub-tribe], or iwi [tribe] and the university researchers and Involving Maori in the organisation, management, and conduct of the project. (p. 20)

The manual gives detailed instruction about the appropriate Maori groups with whom to consult. Names of local *tangata whenua* (indigenous people) are available from the Office of the Pro Vice-Chancellor (Maori) along with advice on how to consult and people who can help in the consultation process. The manual's reference to the impact of research on the

Maori community, with many 'over-burdened' with consultation requests, shows how deeply entrenched the practice is. The researcher must identify the group(s) with whom consultation has taken place, describe the consultation process, and attach evidence of the support of the group(s). This is closely monitored and the applicant needs to:

> Describe any on-going involvement the group(s) consulted has/have in the project. Describe how information will be disseminated to participants and the group consulted at the end of the project (Application Form, 2009, p. 12).

Control over the research prior to its beginning and throughout the process can be seen in the Applicants Manual (2009) encouragement for 'participants' active involvement in the project at every stage' (p. 20). This emphasis on the participants' involvement at every stage of the research means that the researched, rather than the researcher, will determine what are beneficial outcomes and what are not.

The full extent of the control over Maori research is demonstrated by two statements in the Applicants Manual (2009). One concerns the requirement for Ethics committee approval (and the prior agreement from the Maori community) for research that may be considered 'a topic of particular interest to Maori' (p. 10). This would appear to include information such as the writings, statements, and actions of public figures, information that is in the public domain and not traditionally the concern of university ethics committees. The second is the requirement that researchers declare their racial heritage, referred to in the Applicants Manual as 'background' (p. 10). It is a term that can only mean ancestry.

In this way, valid ethical concerns about the treatment of people being researched are confused with the purpose and nature of scholarship. The findings to come out of the research are already determined by the purpose. What if the researcher produces unexpected, controversial, and critical findings? What if the findings do not support the politics of the researched? The very purpose of research is to acquire deeper understanding of physical and social phenomena. That understanding can never be established prior to the research, only hypothesised. The kaupapa Maori approach to research, by requiring that the research serves the interests of the social group compromises its integrity at a very deep level.

This research approach is not limited to New Zealand's universities. Government research funding agencies also recognise and require a Maori knowledge approach. According to the Ministry of Research, Science, and Technology (MoRST), the government agency formerly responsible for major research funding:

> Maori Development relates to research concerning Maori as tangata whenua [indigenous] and considers, particularly, research by Maori,

> for Maori and possibly employing Maori methodologies. (Ministry of Research, Science, and Technology, 2006, p. 2)

Controls on Maori research extend from approving those who undertake the research to validating the outcome. New Zealand uses a Performance-Based Research Fund (PBRF) system (similar to the British Research Assessment Exercise, RAE) to audit research. Indigenous research has its own category. An article written by the PBRF Education Review Panel (Alcorn et al., 2004) draws attention to the 'high quality of Maori research in education' (p. 281).

> Many Maori education academics were among those receiving the highest quality rating (12% of all A and B grades were in Maori Education). In accordance with TEC [Tertiary Education Commission] guidelines, the review panel members considered the impact of Maori research on iwi, hapū and whanau in forming a judgement on the quality of the research. Perhaps the most obvious feature of the success of Maori academics in education lies in developing alternative and critical epistemological models and research methodologies. (p. 281)

According to this approach it is the very political character of the research and the success of the cultural production of an indigenous "episteme" that receives recognition in the discipline.

While indigenous knowledge production occurs in universities in Canada, Australia, and the United States (Widdowson and Howard, 2008), its highly developed nature in New Zealand is a result of the pervasive influence of culturalism in that country's institutions from the 1980s. Although the belief in cultural determinism was mainly focused on the Maori—non-Maori relationship (now increasingly referred to as the indigenous-coloniser relationship in the indigenous literature), it also permeated interactions between other cultural groups. Along with educational historian, Roger Openshaw, I have described a number of these cases (Openshaw and Rata, 2007, 2008). One referred to the experiences of a senior lecturer in History and American Studies at the University of Waikato. A first-year course in U.S. history included a lecture on Mormonism which was highly critical of the religion and its founder. A formal complaint by students alleging harassment included demands for an apology and equal time in which to present the Mormon view. The lecturer was obliged to consent to a public debate with the Mormon Church, which resulted in a lecture theatre confrontation in which he was accused of being both incompetent and unprofessional. Although the lecturer kept his job and the students later withdrew their complaint, one result of the furor was that several of his colleagues told him that they would drop controversial topics from their programmes to avoid harassment charges (Richards, 2002).

However, the majority of cases in New Zealand concern claims for the inclusion of Maori "world views" into the university. The idea that knowledge is created by and belongs to social groups as a result of their heritage informs governance agreements between local tribes and universities that affect every area of academic work, including research and employment conditions. One example is from an agreement between the South Island Ngai Tahu tribe and several tertiary institutions. Referred to as 'the Treaty Partner', the local tribe 'is involved in the process of appointing staff deemed to be significant for Maori' and 'staff who teach Maori (or any other non-Western world views) can demonstrate their understanding of alternative world views where other specialist practitioners can evaluate them' (Tau, Ormsby, Manthei, and Potiki, 2003, p. 66). Other examples Roger Openshaw and I used to illustrate the reach of the social knowledge approach concerned requirements that Maori research methods be used in health research. We discussed the effect of Maori permission for ethics approval on a student undertaking a master's degree to show how this requirement jeopardised the student's research into rural emergency responses in isolated South Island areas (Openshaw and Rata, 2007, 2008).

Although the main focus of my research is into how localisation strategies have led to ethnic categorisation in New Zealand education, it is difficult to overlook the way the health system, including health research, has been similarly affected. A treaty research model in health has been designed by Wyeth and colleagues (2010) to show researchers a practical means to acknowledge the principles of the Treaty of Waitangi. This involves research that responds to treaty legislation and policies by 'developing methodologies and processes specific to Maori as a collective, while also acknowledging Maori diversity' (Wyeth, et al., 2010, p. 308).

Researchers must refer to the Ministry of Health requirement that:

> All investigators are required to demonstrate commitment to the Treaty through the design and conduct of the research. Issues relating to Maori cultural and ethical values should be discussed with Maori, and Maori should be recognized as *tangata whenua* (Maori that have customary rights in a specific area or region) and indigenous people. (National Ethics Advisory Committee, 2006)

Wyeth and colleagues (2010) claim that 'key to the notion of understanding research invested in indigenous well-being is the way we conceptualize "rights"; that is, as either "individual" or "collective" rights' (Wyeth et al. 2010, p. 306). Marie and Haig (2006) have strongly criticised this rights-based approach in New Zealand health research. Their objection is the same as my own. They argue that political and moral issues interfere in epistemic claims about the nature of reliable knowledge, especially when a rights-based discourse challenges evidence-based assertions. This leads to a lack of scientific scrutiny applied to ideologies of indigenous knowledge and worldviews that justify the model-the very feature that prevents indigenous knowledge becoming a scientific discipline.

Although the conflation of social knowledge with scientific knowledge affects the social sciences in the main, the practice does affect the physical sciences as the discussion about health research shows. A New Zealand's Energy Safety Services household safety pamphlet (Deputy Secretary, Energy Safety Service, 2004) which outlines the current electrical code of practice recently issued for household use contains this bizarre mixture of science and mythology.

> From a Maori perspective, the term "earth" or Papatuanuku translates as Earth Mother—the source of all energy. When aligning this concept to the flow of electricity, a useful parallel can be made to the three-pin plug.
>
> Electricity Maori
>
> Active (phase) Spiritual element, active, tapu [sacred]
> Neutral Physical element, neutral, noa [profane]
> Earth Mauri or life force derived from Papatuanuku or Earth Mother

A second example illustrates several of the problems that arise when social knowledge is considered as epistemic knowledge. The post-modern writer, Ruth Irwin (2010), seeks to justify 'other conceptual paradigms' (p. 21) with reference the half-Inuit, half-Danish woman in Peter Hoeg's 1993 novel *Smilla's Sense of Snow*.

According to Irwin, 'Miss Smilla's conceptual apparatus is figured by genealogy, stories and personal experience'. 'The complexity of her experiences both direct and embedded in the cultural narratives of Greenland and Denmark, inform the countless names for snow (p. 21). The example is used by Irwin to show how a conceptual apparatus is "figured", but it also illustrates the problems that arise when subjective knowledge that is not available for criticism is used as epistemic knowledge.

Research from the discipline of linguistic anthropology would show that the Eskimo snow example is a 'folk myth' (Martin, 1986, p. 419) despite it being "true" in 'Miss Smilla's conceptual apparatus'. Over twenty years ago, Laura Martin (1986) traced the 'sorry evolution of the snow example' within anthropology (p. 421) to '1950s' texts and its adoption into a variety of disciplines in the 1970s'. Pointing out that 'there is nothing at all peculiar about the behavior or distribution of "snow words" in Eskimo languages' (p. 419), Martin refers to 'a creeping carelessness about the actual linguistic facts of the example; this carelessness is no less shocking because it has become so commonplace' (p. 419). In her account of how 'this folklore has been promulgated by anthropologists and linguists who should know better and by professors in other fields who first learned it from them' (p. 420), Martin says how 'years of carelessness of taken their toll' with 'frequent casual classroom use' and the 'gradual filtering of the example into the educated lay population' (p. 420). Her call for 'greater alertness to the dangers inherent in careless disregard for the essential requirements of responsible scholarship' (p. 421) can be disregarded in an approach that takes what people say about themselves as the truth.

The importance of scrutiny and criticism in all research cannot be overemphasised. Lakatos' (1980/1995) degenerative research programmes would remain "degenerative" where there is no system of scrutiny and criticism to reveal their flaws as is the case when social knowledge is accepted as having the same authority as scientific knowledge. Lakatos is no doubt correct when he refers to the ways in which loud voices win out and inaccurate, even incorrect, knowledge maintains its strength within a discipline. Revisionist history is an obvious example of this. The tendency of relativist-constructivists to accept what people say about themselves as the truth with respect to New Zealand history has been attacked by a number of historians, yet with little effect.

The two most infamous examples of the distortion of history that occurs when folklore becomes uncriticised scholarship in that country are the Te Papa Moriori example and the Holocaust on the Wanganui River example. My account of the Te Papa Moriori incident is taken from historian, Peter Munz's (2000) analysis in the scholarly journal *History Now*. Munz described how Te Papa, the National Museum of New Zealand mounted an exhibition of the Chatham Islands and their Moriori inhabitants without reference to the most important event in the history of the Moriori—their massacre by the invading Maori tribes in 1835 where the invaders, following their customs, 'killed and ate, or enslaved the local population' (p. 13). Not only was the 'gross historical misrepresentation' (p. 13) a problem for the historians who drew the museum's attention to that omission, but the museum's claim that 'there are two equally valid systems of knowledge that may be applied to telling our stories' (p. 14) revealed the extent of cultural relativism that pervades scholarship in New Zealand.

Support for the "two ways of knowing" idea came from eminent Maori academic, Mason Durie. Munz (2000) detailed Durie's three justifying points: 'First there are many different standards of knowledge and each standard reflects the cultural situation of the historian. There is no real truth. Second, the Museum is justified in suppressing the truth about the massacre because it accepts the inherent value of matauranga Maori [Maori knowledge]. The Museum is committed to the recognition of different knowledge bases. Third, the exhibition is not about the past, but about Moriori aspirations' (p. 14). Munz devotes the remainder of his article explaining why Durie's argument is mistaken.

It is an explanation against the conflation of social and esoteric knowledge. Munz reminds us that Maori matauranga and scholarship serve two entirely different purposes. The former is a 'belief system designed to bond people into a community, and whether or not it gives a true factual account is irrelevant'. 'Scholarship and science. . . are based on the application of unrestricted criticism and scrutiny to all beliefs, especially those alleged to be taboo. Its purpose is simply to obtain the best possible knowledge of the world' (p. 14). In his analysis of the 'advocacy and propaganda displayed by the exhibition', Munz suggests that 'there seems to be a political agenda and a propaganda campaign which, so it is hoped, will be advanced by the distortion of the truth' (p. 15).

The second example of the disregard for historical truth is the Wanganui River holocaust incident. Historian, Graham Butterworth (2006) shows how Maori politician, Tariana Turia's account of a 'holocaust' on the Wanganui River when hundreds of Maori were poisoned by flour treated with arsenic is false. Butterworth provides the following more likely explanation based on written report from the time. 'Richard Taylor, a nineteenth century missionary, records in his journal a raid on Wanganui where a merchant had to abandon some bags of flour and in anger poisoned them with arsenic. Taylor read the merchant a lesson on the wickedness of his action and there is no further reference in the journal to the matter. If any deaths had resulted, Taylor, whose mission area included the Wanganui River, would certainly have heard about it' (p. 189).

Butterworth's second example of the distortion of historical facts demonstrates the "creeping carelessness" of scholarship that is not put to the test. Just as the Eskimo snow tale entered educated lay consciousness, so too in New Zealand is there a widespread belief that the nineteenth century European government deliberately adopted 'strategies to ensure the decline of the Maori population', enabling 'detribalisation and land alienation for settler ownership and development' (Butterworth, 2006, p. 186). According to Butterworth, this 'narrative' of 'military oppression, dispossession and sustained marginalisation [is] a result of government action or inaction' (p. 186).

Yet, as he shows, citing Derek Dow's 'important but non-revisionist 1999 study', 'Maori health was of considerable concern to colonial and settler governments' (p. 187). The view that 'land loss was caused by a scandalous purchase policy that gave no protection to Maori land sellers' (p. 188) is also rejected. Butterworth points out that 'in the historical and Maori minds population decline and land loss have been inextricably linked, an interpretation taught as fact in the nation's schools and universities' (p. 188). But, using population statistic and land sale figures, Butterworth found that 'clearly land loss and population decline are not as closely related as Durie [the influential Maori scholar whose statistics Butterworth criticises] claims' (p. 199).

Butterworth (2006) concludes with the observation that 'the revision of New Zealand history in regard to Maori-pakeha relations is less about the improving of that history and more about creating an ideology that advances the political and economic interests of the Maori elite' (p. 199). He argues that

> revisionist writers have ignored the steady reduction of the gross disparities between Maori and pakeha of the past, as well as ignoring the

> evidence that these disparities appear likely to continue to reduce as the Maori middle class continues to grow in size. Instead these influential writers have created and sustained a grievance mentality enabling a section of the Maori population to accept the role of historical victims,—a mindset in which 'it is always winter and never Christmas'. (p. 200)

In chapter 7, I discussed the way in which the mindset that enables this type of uncritical historical revisionism is created in the New Zealand education system. The view that knowledge is relative and constructed in the interests of the "knowers" is firmly embedded in teacher education courses and the New Zealand national curriculum. The competency for level 6 social sciences in history requiring students 'to understand how people's perspectives on past events that are of significance to New Zealand differ' (Ministry of Education, 2009, p. 37) symbolises this mindset. Its placement into the national curriculum will ensure that the next generation of children will understand history 'not as an objective recording of (alleged) facts but rather, as the shaping of "facts" and their presentation in a narrative, through the theoretical perspectives of the writer' (Simon and Massey, 1994, p. 37).

11 What Should Be Taught at School

It is the 'specialist forms of social organisation' (the knowledge disciplines) that 'remain the major social bases for guaranteeing the objectivity of knowledge' (Moore and Young, 2010, p. 30). Yet what happens when those disciplines do not reach students in schools, do not, to use Bernstein's words, become "recontextualised" as school subjects? In this final chapter I address the question with reference to the example of the New Zealand national curriculum. The constructivist approach to knowledge with its emphasis on student competency to use knowledge has affected that country's curriculum. There appears to be no consistent pattern across subjects about how much content is included. For some subjects the curriculum is the main source of guidance, in others assessment processes define examinable content, while in others prescriptive information is included in subject guidelines.

In the absence of specific detail about content in subjects such as English and History, the student is left "thinking" "understanding", "examining", "exploring", and all the other verbs that denote doing something with knowledge but without referring to the actual knowledge that is the raw material for the action. A second outcome of the absence of specified content knowledge is that what is actually taught is left to the vagaries of school choice, or to a teacher's arbitrary knowledge, or, in the worst-case scenario, to the students' "interests". In such cases the national assessment system becomes the *de facto* curriculum (McPhail, 2011), a situation that gives assessment a central place in the transfer of knowledge to succeeding generations. Instead of the value of knowledge being derived from its generative principles and concepts, its value is dependent on how it can be measured. This means that epistemic knowledge is equated with social knowledge or with skills—all commensurate on the assessment scale. Leon Benade (2011) points out that 'schools offer subjects such as Tourism and Travel and Employment Skills. Whereas before these subjects may have formed part of a "Transition to Work" programme for some students, now they are offered as stand-alone subjects in competition with regular academic subjects' (p. 114). In this way, subjects embedded in disciplines that are structured on the basis of cumulative principles, concepts, and content are in the same "market" as skills organised according to their vocational use.

My intention in this book has been to explain the shift in national curricula, particularly for subjects based in the arts, humanities and social sciences, from a focus on content knowledge to an emphasis on generic skills and concepts, and on "constructing" knowledge. I explain this shift as a consequence of the wider forces of localisation, forces that break down the democratic imaginary of the people within modern nations for pre-modern ways of categorising people. Content knowledge, that which is the best knowledge available in a subject, "best" because it expresses the subject's generative concepts and principles, serves a wider socio-political role in maintaining democracy. Providing a common curriculum to all children contributes to integrating the nation by creating a shared symbolic understanding of the world. It acts against the divisions of localisation. In a democracy that common curriculum and the content knowledge it contains must be one that the people agree is important for succeeding generations to know. The ongoing public discussion required to create such a curriculum is in itself democracy in action.

The integrity of disciplinary knowledge is crucial for both educational and political reasons. Popper's recognition in 1945 that 'the conflict between rationalism and irrationalism has become the most important intellectual, and perhaps moral issue of our time' (1945/2003, p. 248) has lost none of its saliency in the past sixty years. Indeed the speed and thoroughness with which the belief in localised "ways of knowing" has encroached into educational institutions in liberal democracies suggests that Popper's fears for the future were well-grounded.

While a retreat to a pre-modern non-democratic future is one possibility, the four identity poles of modernity theorised by Jonathan Friedman (1994) that I have used as conceptual tools in earlier chapters suggests that all is not lost. Primitivism, traditionalism, and postmodernism are, it is true, three of the four identities available to people in the modern world, but the fourth identity is a modern one. It is not prescribed that the modern world will descend into a reactionary future taking on identities that orient us to the past—a possibility suggested by the rise of racial ideologies in recent decades. Marx's insight that people make history is as true now as it was in the mid-nineteenth century. 'History is *nothing, but* the activity of man pursuing his aims (1844–45/1975, p.93) is a modern idea. We are trapped neither by the call of the ancestors nor in some sort of metaphysically determined retreat from modernity. If those aims to which we aspire are moral and aesthetic as well as economic, a progressive civilisation remains the human possibility envisaged by Enlightenment thinkers, but with the twenty-first century awareness that it must be sustainable progress.

However, the four decades of culturalism and constructivism have left their mark—no more so than in education. I have identified the shift to subjective social knowledge away from scientific objectivity in the university and the effect this has had on the social sciences. The associated rise of relativist-constructivism in education has, in turn, affected the status of epistemic knowledge in schools. Drawing on the recent research of realists in the sociology of education, I have explained how the weakening of epistemic knowledge in schools has affected the working class and minority groups in particular. For these groups the only place to acquire disciplinary knowledge is at school. Yet the approach that sees epistemic knowledge as the tool of the oppressor—whether a "Western" or capitalist oppressor closes off access to powerful knowledge for those groups.

Educationalists, including critical pedagogy writers, indigenous theorists, and other standpoint writers blame the system, whether it is the capitalist system directly, as with those Marxists who hold firm to class determinism or Western colonialism for those who see exploitation in cultural terms. It is a pessimistic view of education. Determined by class or culture, young people are seen as programmed by their origins to achieve already ascribed destinations. It is as prescriptive a view of the human condition as the status and gender ascription found in traditional societies. For class and culturalist writers, change can only come from group agency—from class revolution or cultural self-determination. This ignores the way in which the total loyalty of group adherence contains the seeds of another exploitation, as the group's leaders become elites within the act of representing their members.

Unfortunately the determinism that has anchored theories in the sociology of education since the 1970s is still a powerful force in that discipline, one that as Popper (1945/2003) explains 'must lead to irrationalism'.

> The theory that our thoughts and opinions are dependent on our class situation, or upon our national interests . . . is the view that thought is merely a somewhat superficial manifestation of what lies within these irrational depths (i.e., "deeper layers of human nature). It gives a determining power to forces outside our control. It is the belief that '"we think with our blood", or "with our national heritage", or "with our class". By thus abandoning reason, they split mankind into friends and foes; into the few who share in reason with the gods, and the many who don't (as Plato says); into the few who stand near and the many who stand afar; into those who speak the untranslatable language of our own emotions and passions and those whose tongue is not our tongue. Once we have done this, political equalitarianism becomes practically impossible. (pp. 260–261)

The argument developed in this book is that science (Kant's 'what may I know') and politics ('what ought I to do' and 'what may I hope') of modernity's progressive era are seriously compromised by the localisation of knowledge. This occurs as the intellectual resource of conceptual knowledge needed for scientific thinking and the individualised dispositions of independence and autonomy required for democratic politics become less available to localised groups. Ethnicised groups in the working class are doubly affected. Their universalised class status as workers in the global economy is now understood in localised terms, an understanding which sees socio-cultural experiences as the source of knowledge in education. As a consequence, learners tied to these localised experiences miss out on the powerful knowledge needed to develop conceptual thought. In saying this, I do not deny the importance of socio-cultural experiences in the socialisation of individuals into society. However, following Michael Young (2008, 2010a), I regard these as the source of pedagogy in schools, not the source of the curriculum.

The distinction between the curriculum and pedagogy that Michael Young, building on the work of Tim Oates (2011), develops in his article 'The Future of Education in a Knowledge Society: The Radical Case for a Subject-Based Curriculum' (Young, 2010a) provides insights into how social knowledge can serve education without subverting the epistemological character of academic knowledge. According to Young (2010a), '*curriculum* refers to the knowledge that a country agrees is important for all students to have access to. The second idea concerns *pedagogy*, which, in contrast, refers to the activities of teachers in motivating students and helping them to engage with the curriculum and make it meaningful' (p. 23). He points out that 'attempts to include the experiences of students in a "more motivational" curriculum blur the curriculum/pedagogy distinction and the very different roles of curriculum designers and teachers' (pp. 23–24).

Young and Johan Muller (2010) have developed three curriculum models that they refer to as Futures 1, 2, and 3. Young (2011) refers to Future 1 as a 'curriculum for compliance' (2011, p. 2). This is the old model of a highly prescribed and difficult to change syllabus that sets down to the last detail what children should know. It is the static knowledge approach that enabled social constructivists to claim content-based education a moribund failure. It is characterised and caricatured (most memorably by Dickens in *Hard Times*) as memorisation and rote learning.

Future 2 has been the social constructivist response to this conservative static model. The boundaries between subjects and between school and everyday knowledge are discarded for the inquiry "teacher as facilitator" approach that has dominated education in the past decades. Young's (2011) reference to the Scottish Curriculum for Excellence as an example of the teacher facilitation approach applies equally to New Zealand, where the approach has produced separate Maori education and the national curriculum based on competencies, values, and skills. In this model the emphasis is not so much on teaching content knowledge – the "what to know" but on "how to find out".

Future 3 is the curriculum model advocated by Young and Muller (2010) and the model that I believe has the potential to restore epistemic knowledge to its rightful place in the school. It expresses the social realist view that access to epistemic disciplinary knowledge 'must be the primary goal of schools' (Young, 2011, p. 5). The writers refer to *Future 3* as 'a demonstration of what a social realist theory of knowledge can offer' (Young,

2011, p. 269). In differentiating the Future 3 curriculum model from the traditional static Future 1 approach, Young and Muller (2010) deal with the problem inherent to the Future 1 model, that of moribund knowledge by insisting that the objective knowledge that should be taught in schools is conceptual. According to Young (2011) 'Future 3 implies that a curriculum must stipulate the concepts associated with different subjects. It is the interrelatedness of concepts in a subject or a discipline that distinguishes them from the everyday concepts that pupils bring to school and which offer them ways of going beyond their experience' (p. 6).

As both writers (Young and Muller, 2010) point out, and I consider this to be crucial, content is also important because concepts and content are linked. The meaning of concepts is in that connection, a point noted by Kant (1781/1993) in his succinct comment 'thoughts without content are empty' (p. 69). However, the consistency and integrity of the discipline is in the stability of concepts (for example, the metaphor as a concept basic to literature), while the content itself changes. Tim Oates (2011) refers to the 'substantial empirical and theoretical evidence for a very strong focus on concepts and principles. Transnational comparisons make clear that high-performing systems indeed focus on concepts and principles. But this focus on concepts is justified not only by the fact that high-performing systems include such a focus, it is also strongly endorsed by theory' (Oates, 2011, pp. 132–133). It was an idea suggested by Kant (1781/1993) in his recognition that 'all rational knowledge is based either on concepts, or on the construction of concepts' (p. 535). However this emphasis on concepts as the "static" backbone of a curriculum subject in no way relegates content to a secondary place. *Content is as important as concepts*. The difference is that the concepts of a disciplinary subject remain the same while the content may change. What *does* matter is that content provides the raw material for the concept—without which the concept is "empty". This makes the choice of content extremely important—it must express the generative principles and concepts of the discipline to have any worth to students.

In teaching poetry for example, one may refer to the work of the New Zealand contemporary poet, Glenn Colquhoun, or to Chaucer, or to Emily Dickinson, but without teaching metaphor as the concept integral to poetry, the images created by the poets would be understood only in the particular instance of the single poem. It is the concepts of a discipline that take one into its depths and that unites the concepts found in one poem to all poetry across time and space. It is here that teachers play a vital role. Choosing a poem to teach that contains metaphor (a central concept in literary analysis) so rich that it reveals layer upon layer of meaning is far superior than choosing something trite and superficial. To make that choice the teacher must make judgements about what is good and what is poor, what is worthwhile teaching and what should be avoided on the basis of the material's conceptual worth.

Teachers do need to know the content of the subjects they teach. This may sound so obvious that it need not be stated—not so. I have heard teachers say and on a number of occasions, that "I learn alongside my students"—that "we inquire together". The facilitation approach does work with social knowledge. However with epistemic knowledge, teachers are at the centre of the pedagogical relation. Graham McPhail's (2011) insightful study of secondary school music in New Zealand provides an illuminating example of the central importance of teachers given that in the absence of specified knowledge in the national curriculum, it is teachers who decide what knowledge should be included and what should be omitted. McPhail (2011) shows how a 'curriculum of cultural transmission centred on classical traditions has largely given way to alternative relativist conceptions centred on popular music and student rights of ownership' (p. 202). The resulting 'knowledge displacement, brought about by the move to generic curriculum documents, increasingly places the responsibility on teachers to manage and balance the epistemic and social demands of curriculum realisation' (p 202).

If epistemic knowledge is largely excluded as the teacher limits himself or herself to the role of facilitator and co-inquirer, then it is unlikely that the concepts of the subject will be acquired. As McPhail (2011) points out, explicit teacher instruction is required if students are to acquire conceptual understanding. 'Unlike the largely tacit and context bound process of learning folk music or playing in a garage band for example, the "curriculum" for formal instrument learning is most often sequential and underpinned by abstract theoretical concepts which necessitate the explicit guidance of a teacher' (p. 192).

This does not mean that students' social knowledge is not important. It is, in that experiences can provide the vehicle for increased motivation and serve as the mechanism to bring students into the world of epistemic knowledge. This requires the teacher to use a pedagogical style that engages the student by recognising their experiences but also providing the means to take them to the next step. Young (2008) argues that this next step occurs when teachers show students how knowledge can become context independent. This occurs in the concepts of the subject that 'can provide a basis for generalizations and explanations that go beyond specific cases . . . and it allows those who acquire it to develop the capacity to imagine alternatives' (p. 166).

McPhail (2011) explains how teachers can 'open up a space' between the social and the epistemic through pedagogies that validate student experiences. He refers to how 'students' informal and socially acquired knowledge then becomes a valuable pedagogic tool' (p. 195). However, with reference to Green's Musical Futures programme in the United Kingdom, McPhail draws attention to the importance of formal and theoretical knowledge (p. 196) and to how the distinction between pedagogy and curriculum is essential. This is a distinction that Young (2010a) has stressed. 'The curriculum needs to be seen as having a purpose of its own; the intellectual development of students' (p. 24). Pedagogy on the other hand 'refers to the activities of teachers in motivating students and to helping them engage with the curriculum' (p. 23). The problem for constructivists is that in turning the teacher into a facilitator, that pedagogy-curriculum distinction has been erased.

Teachers are central to education in transmitting the content knowledge a society deems valuable, but there is another reason for their importance. McPhail's research shows how, in their management of the relationship between classical and popular music, secondary school teachers are able to link the everyday knowledge of popular music with the theoretical concepts used in studying classical music. It is that link which contains within it the potential for social knowledge to become enriched by epistemic knowledge. In this way, societies can become more civilised as everyday "culture" is exposed to rational knowledge. With reference to Michael Young, McPhail mentions how 'in an ideal world' the process of linking everyday knowledge to epistemic knowledge can become reversed as 'learners draw on their newly acquired theoretical concepts to re-engage with and transform their everyday concepts' (Young, 2010b; McPhail, 2011, p. 189). In that way, education transforms individuals by providing them with the means to think about and change their everyday worlds. On a societal level the use of epistemic knowledge to inform social knowledge is the source of cultural change.

Given the pivotal role of epistemic knowledge in transforming society, while teachers have a central position, they should not be the final arbiters of what matters in the curriculum. Michael Young (2010b) has identified the curriculum as the 'knowledge that a country agrees is important for all students to have access to' (2010b, p. 23). An epistemic curriculum is a political instrument of enormous power. Emptying out the curriculum of epistemic content knowledge has profound consequences. There is no disciplinary standard by which to judge and select the "best" content which means there is no content to provide the raw material for the conversation the country must have in choosing what should be known. This is a key feature of the politics of knowledge because the ability of a nation's children to think outside their experience using higher order thinking depends upon the selection of knowledge in the curriculum. With knowledge limited to their experience, young people will be unable to contribute to the ideals of a progressive future, one characterised by innovative technology, and informed by the political, moral, and aesthetic ideas found in the arts, humanities, social sciences, and sciences. They are denied access to the type of knowledge—objective, conceptual knowledge, that 'has the capacity to transcend the social conditions under which it is produced' (Moore cited in Maton and Moore, 2010, p. 5).

A second, more confined consequence of the shift to localism is that the arbitrary curriculum is reduced it to a sea of information (often from the Internet) for co-inquirers to attempt to find and to understand. Yet information is not knowledge—without understanding, it simply remains bits of unrelated information. Concepts integrate those "bits" into meaningful ideas by revealing the underlying principles that link the material. This is how knowledge is built—by making associations, by forming patterns, by having the means to analyse, synthesise, and re-integrate to create new understandings. It is an integrity that exists because those processes of integration are what structures a subject. 'Packages' of information on a particular topic do not lead to understanding.

Tim Oates (2011) mentions how the specific information embedded in contexts can decay into mere 'noise' unless individuals have concepts and principles to organise and interpret the content of those contexts (pp. 132–133). Concepts and principles need to be taught using the content in ways that reveal the unifying patterns. By knowing the "best" content knowledge in their subject, teachers are able to instruct students into the conceptual means by which the content of a subject is integrated. Concepts and principles are critical. This is a central feature of Young and Muller's (2010) Future 3 curriculum model. 'Concepts must be linked to the contents that give them meaning and to the skills involved in acquiring them' (Young, 2011, p. 269).

Unfortunately the Future 1 and the Future 2 models tend to dominate as the only two choices recognised in educational circles. Teachers either co-inquire and "construct" knowledge in the ubiquitous groups that characterise constructivism or they stand accused of traditional elitism by concentrating on static content. The constructivist approach leads to an "empty" curriculum. The second option produces an overloaded curriculum where it becomes difficult to choose what should be taught amid the "noise" of information and why given the surfeit of contenders for inclusion in the curriculum. McPhail's (2011) study of the shift in New Zealand secondary school education from an emphasis on 'classical' music to 'everyday, self-taught music making and listening' (the garage band approach) shows the tension having these two options causes for teachers. They must decide on both knowledge content and pedagogy in a relativist world without a universal standard by which content knowledge can be judged.

In his reference to the consequences of the 'constructivist educational doctrine', McPhail (2011) points to the 'emptying out of explicit leaning content in the New Zealand curriculum', and the lack of 'consistency in what might define a music programme in one school from that in another' (p. 9). But it is not only secondary school teachers with specific subjects to teach who are affected. The situation is more difficult for primary school teachers who don't even have the remnants of subjects to guide them. Those subject outlines have transmorphed into themes. Where is the fixed point in this epistemic confusion?

The effect of the constructivist approach is most seriously felt in literacy education. Deciphering symbols on the page for their meaning—whether words, mathematical, scientific, or musical symbols—enables children to represent the world to themselves. It includes the world they know already, but symbolical representation gives access to more than that already known. It provides access to conceptualising the unknown because we can only experience a small part of what we actually know about. Knowledge not derived from experience is known by acquiring concepts and content through symbolic representation. Thinking about the unknown means being able to think symbolically—there is no other way of "knowing" the concept except in its representation as a symbol.

Children who are illiterate and semi-literate and who remain so despite attending school for many years miss out on not just the ability to read but on the ability to conceptualise. Unable to conceptualise, they are denied the type of thinking that enables us to understand the world. As Roy Nash (2001a) cogently argued: 'It is very likely that as a result of the literate socialisation they receive in early childhood, children are made intelligent—that is equipped with a set of effective and durable cognitive tools—and so enabled to learn what is taught in schools more successfully than others' (p. 16). This is a huge claim to make—it is one of Nash's most direct. He is quite clear in saying that literacy is the development of intelligence. I think that he is right. If thinking conceptually is being intelligent, and literacy is the means to think in that way, then it seems obvious that literacy is the most important skill that a child can develop at school.

Yet even here, indeed especially here in literacy education, social constructivism is enormously influential. For two decades in New Zealand, according to Bill Tunmer and Janet Prochnow (2009) the country 'has adhered to a constructivist approach to literacy education' (p. 158), and New Zealand is not alone. Tunmer and Prochnow argue that 'the comparatively high percentage of reading failures in New Zealand is triggered by a largely constructivist approach to beginning reading instruction' (2009, p. 167). Noting the high proportion of failures are children from low income, culturally diverse backgrounds, the researchers identify the additional 'obstacle' of 'cultural relativism' (p. 180). 'With regard to literacy, cultural relativism spawned the "new literacies" movement, where literacy experiences are seen as firmly embedded in social contexts that uniquely give meaning to the uses of literacy' (p. 181). Drawing on the views of Gough (1995), Tunmer and Prochnow consider that literacy is not confined by its social context, rather it 'should be conceptualised as a fundamental enabling skill, a tool by which readers can acquire the knowledge necessary for participating fully in the processes of society (2009, p. 182).

Another consequence of social constructivism's influence in education is a decline in the importance of separate discrete disciplines and the resulting shift to classify knowledge in units or themes. This tendency is aided by the ease with which such compartmentalised information can be broken down into easily measured outcomes. With reference to the writings of Johan Muller, Leesa Wheelahan argues that reducing knowledge to isolated and atomised units denies students 'access to a style of thinking represented in disciplinary knowledge that works from generative principles' (2010a, p. 107).

The consequences for working-class students and those from disadvantaged groups of the types of assessment systems that reduce conceptual knowledge to fragments of information is supported by evidence from New Zealand. Research by Madjar and colleagues (2009) investigating the subject choices of students from Maori and Pacific groups

> has shown that Maori and Pacific students, most of whom attend low-decile schools, tend to be enrolled in less academic subjects and *unit* rather than *achievement standards*, and to complete fewer *credits* from the *approved list* of subjects (required for completion of the UE [University Entrance] qualification). Such a pattern of course choices places students from these groups with the ability and potential to succeed in degree-level qualifications at risk of not achieving the UE qualification, or of achieving at a level that is likely to exclude them from limited entry university programmes (p. 4).

Achievement standards contain the epistemic knowledge that provides advantages to those exposed to this knowledge, for example McPhail (2011) notes that 'many of the current New Zealand Achievement Standards require a level of musical literacy in terms of music reading and writing that students more interested in popular styles often resist' (p. 93). While the alternative versions of core subjects and other applied subjects that make up New Zealand's unit standards do provide access to 'contextually specific applications of disciplinary knowledge', they do not provide access to the 'system of meaning in which it is embedded and made meaningful' (Wheelahan, 2010b, p. 119).

The rise in cross-disciplinary subjects also contributes to weakening epistemic knowledge. Cross-disciplinary fertilisation is not of itself a problem. The value of mathematics to music, anthropology to education, linguistics to literature, and so on has long been recognised. Disciplinary weakening occurs mainly when disciplines are used for instrumental purposes, as in courses for social work, nursing, and business and management studies that lead to professional qualifications. My own experience in teacher education has proved salutary. Teaching degree programmes draw on anthropology, sociology, political science, and education. Without the ongoing engagement with the principles and concepts of those disciplines that is required for intellectual scrutiny the theoretical ideas that were in vogue when the teacher education programmes were first developed remain fixed. There is little diving back into the intellectual well for new developments in the discipline. For example, cultural essentialism is discredited in mainstream anthropology but remains alive and well in teacher education in New Zealand.

The difference between epistemic knowledge and everyday social knowledge is one found in the difference between thinking conceptually and thinking from experience; in the difference between who is permitted to authorises knowledge, and in the difference between the methods and procedures by which knowledge is produced. What are the consequences of the shift to localising knowledge that has occurred with the dominance of the constructivist approach in education? What happens if children are not brought into the various symbolic codes at school, when they do not learn how to think using the advanced literacies of language, mathematics, science, and the arts? What happens to those young people themselves, and what happens to their society? The answers to those questions can be found in the ongoing under-achievement of children from the working class and from disadvantaged groups. Despite the importance of conceptual thinking for the inter-related development of symbolic representation and the imagination, children from the working class receive less of this intellectual resource than those in the middle class (Bernstein, 1971).

Research by Roy Nash (2001c) demonstrated the effects of limiting access to higher-order thinking. He observed that 'as they enter school, the average difference between the assessed intellectual level of children brought up by professional and unskilled working-class parents—to compare roughly the upper and lower 10% of the population—amounts to about a year in development' (p. 15). For those working-class children who also belong to re-ethnicised communities, the type of thinking required by communal cultures may be a double disadvantaging factor. This is the case because ethnic sub-groups within the working class are socialised into the subjective form of thinking that dominates working-class literacy *and* into the localisation of neotraditionalism. Children are denied the existential dialectic where one is turned to face the world but remaining linked through affective bonds of varying strengths to the family. Kant (1781,1993) described this 'strife of the dialectic (as) a necessity of reason' (p. 488). From this contradictory position, the individual is able to mediate the relationship between the world and the family through the development of his or her own identity as a separate and autonomous individual and to understand that partial loyalty in objective terms.

In contrast, where there is no separation between the local communal group and society, the world is merely that group writ large. How can a common universal humanity be acknowledged? There is the world conceptualised on the basis of kin to whom only kin can belong, and there is the world conceptualised on the basis of individuals who share a common humanity. The former is based on total loyalty, whereas in the latter, the concept of the individual is of someone who can be partially loyal. This is the person who is simultaneously attached to and separated from the kin-group, the partial loyalty that enables the concept of a common universal humanity (the subject of chapter 6). The school's role is to enable this separation, not to enlarge the experiential world of the family. It was a role that Hegel (1820,1967) described in his reference to the way 'education bears upon the child's capacity to become a member of society. In its character as the universal family. . . society's right here is paramount over the arbitrary and contingent preferences of parents' (Hegel, p. 148, paragraph 239).

The process of separating from the private world of the kin-group to the public world of the *demos* develops the dispositions of detachment, independence, and autonomy that are essential for conceptual thinking. In that act of separation, is the practice of abstraction, of thinking about one's experience in objective ways rather than always subjectively. Children who do not acquire the cognitive processes and dispositions of abstraction, that ability to separate from the subjective world of their own experience, are restricted from moving into the world of conceptual reasoning and, hence, from the world of educational achievement. Although literate socialisation is influenced by the family resources available in a given socio-economic location, it is also affected adversely by a curriculum based on social construction principles. For those children in re-ethnicised groups within the working class, those principles shut off access to the conceptual, higher-order thinking of a universal socio-political culture.

What conceptual knowledge must have that everyday knowledge does not require is symbolic thinking. When we think about ideas that have nothing to do with our own experience, ideas that come from the imagination to be expressed in idealised models, we need a way of expressing these ideas. Advanced literacy provides the symbols with which to conceptualise complex thoughts. But symbols in the form of advanced language are not enough on their own. They need to be coded in the literacy of disciplinary subjects. Each discipline has its own symbolic codes; that is, the symbols themselves and the ways of using these symbols that have been developed by generations of people in the discipline. For example, it is through immersion in historical literacy that we enter into the knowledge of that discipline. It is through immersion in the discipline of mathematics that people acquire mathematical literacy. Symbolic codes structure the content of disciplines in ways that provide the coherent integration of the under-pinning concepts and principles.

Children are brought into these disciplinary ways of thinking at school. Acquiring conceptual knowledge and receiving practice in the symbolic codes of language, mathematics, music, the arts, and the sciences doesn't happen as a result of everyday experiences. The ability to think conceptually and the symbolic tools needed to think in that way must be taught. For that reason teachers will remain at the centre of education, not as "co-inquirers", but as those who teach the concepts, content and symbolic codes of disciplinary subjects. This knowledge enables students to think about what they have not experienced, to predict what they don't yet know, and to "think about the unthinkable". It is, or should be, the purpose of schools to teach this knowledge.

References

Abaza, M., & Stauth, G. (1990). Occidental reason, Orientalism, Islamic fundamentalism: A critique. In M. Albrow & E. King (Eds.), *Globalization, knowledge and society* (pp. 209–232). London: Sage.

Alcorn, N., Bishop, A. R., Cardno, C., Crooks, T., Fairburn-Dunlop, P., Hattie, J., et al. (2004). Enhancing education research in New Zealand: Experiences and recommendations from the PBRF Education Peer Review Panel. *New Zealand Journal of Educational Studies*, 39(2), 275–289.

Alsayyad, N., & Castells, M. (2002). *Muslim Europe or Euro-Islam, politics, culture and citizenship in the age of globalization.* Lanham, MD: Lexington Books.

Althusser, L., & Balibar, E. (1970). *Reading capital.* London: NLB.

Apple, M. (Ed.). (2003). *The state and the politics of knowledge.* New York: RoutledgeFalmer.

Applicants' Manual. (2009). University of Auckland Ethics Committee. University of Auckland.

Application Form. (2009). University of Auckland Ethics Committee. University of Auckland.

Aronowitz, S. (1981). Preface to the morningside edition. In P. Willis, *Learning to labour: How working class kids get working class jobs* (pp. ix–xiii). New York: Columbia University Press.

Babadzan, A. (2000). Anthropology, nationalism and "the invention of tradition", *Anthropological Forum*, 10(2), 131–155.

Battiste, M. A. (2000). *Reclaiming indigenous voice and vision.* Vancouver: UBC Press.

Beck, J. (2010). Promoting official pedagogic discourses: The sacred and the profane. In K. Maton & R. Moore (Eds.), *Social realism, knowledge and the sociology of education* (pp. 81–92). London: Continuum.

Beck, U. (1994). The re-invention of politic: Towards a theory of reflexive modernisation. In U. Beck, A. Giddens, & S. Lash (Eds.), *Reflexive modernisation: Politics, tradition and aesthetics in the modern social order.* Cambridge, UK: Polity Press.

Benade, L. W. (2011). *From technicians to teachers? The New Zealand Curriculum in the context of post-1989 education reform, and its possibilities for the development of an ethical teaching profession.* Unpublished EdD thesis, University of Auckland, Auckland, New Zealand.

Bernstein, B. (1971). A sociological approach to socialization. In B. Bernstein (Ed.), *Class, codes and control* (Vol. 1, pp. 143–169). London: Routledge and Kegan Paul.

Bernstein, B. (2000). *Pedagogy, symbolic control and identity* (Rev. ed.). New York: Rowman and Littlefield.

Bernstein, H. (2005). Rural land and land conflicts in sub-Saharan Africa. In S. Moyo & P. Yeros (Eds.), *Reclaiming the land: The resurgence of rural movements in Africa, Asia and Latin America* (pp. 67–101). London: Zed Books.

Bhaskar, R. (1975). *A realist theory of science*. London: Verso Books.

Bhaskar, R. (1989). *Reclaiming reality*. London: Verso Books.

Bishop, R., & Berryman, M. (2006). *Culture speaks: Cultural relationships and classroom learning*. Wellington, New Zealand: Huia.

Bishop, R., & Glynn, T. (1999). *Culture counts: Changing power relations in education*. Palmerston North, New Zealand: Dunmore Press.

Booker, J. (2011, February 7). Alarm over cultural beliefs affecting wedding-fraud sentencing. *New Zealand Herald*, p. A7.

Bourdieu, P., & Eagleton, T. (1992). Doxa and common life. *New Left Review*, 191, 111–121.

Bunge, M. (2001). *Social science under debate: A philosophical perspective*. Toronto: University of Toronto Press.

Burbules, N. (2000). The limits of dialogue as a critical pedagogy. In P. P. Trifonas (Ed.), *Revolutionary pedagogies: Cultural politics, instituting education, and the discourse of theory* (pp. 251–273). New York: Routledge.

Burke, E. (1909–1914). Reflections on the revolution in France and on the proceedings in certain societies in London relative to that event in a letter intended to have been sent to a gentleman in Paris. In *The Harvard classics* (Vol. 24, para. 50–74). Pall-Mall, UK: Printed for J. Dodsley. (Originally published 1790)

Buruma, I., & Margalit, A. (2004). *Occidentalism: The West in the eyes of its enemies*. London: Atlantic.

Butterworth, G. (2006). Historical revisionism in New Zealand: Always winter, never Christmas. In E. Rata & R. Openshaw (Eds.), *Public policy and ethnicity: The politics of ethnic boundary making* (pp. 185–200). Houndmills, UK: Palgrave Macmillan.

Butterworth, G., & Mako, C. (1989). *Te hurihanga o te ao Maori: Te ahua o te iwi Maori kua whakatatautia*. Wellington, New Zealand: Department of Ministry Affairs.

Callister, P. (2003, July). *The allocation of ethnicity to children in New Zealand: Some descriptive data from the 2001 Census* (Working Paper). Population Association of New Zealand Conference, Christchurch, New Zealand.

Callister, P. (2007). *Special measures to reduce ethnic disadvantage in New Zealand*. Wellington, New Zealand: Institute of Policy Studies.

Cameron, D. (2011, February 5). Full transcript: Speech on radicalisation and Islamic extremism [Web log message]. Retrieved from http://www.newstatesman.com/blogs/the-staggers/2011/02/terrorism-islam-ideology

Cannadine, D. (2008). *Making history now and then*. Houndmills, UK: Palgrave Macmillan.

Carrier, J. (Ed.). (1995). Maussian Occidentalism: Gift and commodity systems. In *Occidentalism: Images of the West* (pp. 85–108). Oxford, UK: Clarendon Press.

Chapple, S. (2000). Maori socio-economic disparity. *Political Science, 52*, 101–115.

Clark, J. (2006). Dogmas of ethnicity. In E. Rata & R. Openshaw (Eds.), *Public policy and ethnicity: The politics of ethnic boundary making* (pp. 170–184). Houndmills, UK: Palgrave Macmillan.

Collier, A. (1994). *Critical realism: An introduction to Roy Bhaskar's philosophy*. London: Verso Books.

Collins, R. (2000). *The sociology of philosophies: A global theory of intellectual change*. Cambridge, MA: Harvard University Press.

Connell, R. (2009). *Southern theory: The global dynamics of knowledge in social science*. Cambridge, UK: Polity Press. (Originally published 2007)

Connor, S. (2010, September 25). Lower life slows ticking of clock. *New Zealand Herald*, p. B14.
Coxon, E., Marshall, J., & Massey, L. (1994). Introduction. In E. Coxon, K. Jenkins, J. Marshall, & L. Massey (Eds.), *The politics of learning and teaching in Aotearoa New Zealand* (pp. 9–31). Palmerston North, New Zealand: Dunmore Press.
Culley, L., & Demaine, J. (2006). Race and ethnicity in United Kingdom public policy: Education and health. In E. Rata & R. Openshaw (Eds.), *Public policy and ethnicity: The politics of ethnic boundary making* (pp. 128–143). Houndmills, UK: Palgrave Macmillan.
Culliver, A. (1983). Preface to the French edition of 1955. In E. Durkheim, *Pragmatism and sociology* (J. C. Whitehouse, Trans., pp. ix–xxii). Cambridge, UK: Cambridge University Press.
Cunningham, C. (2000). A framework for addressing Maori knowledge in research, science and technology. *Pacific Health Dialogue, 7*, 62–69.
Dale, R. (2001). Shaping the sociology of education over a half-a-century. In J. Demaine (Ed.), *Sociology of education today* (pp. 9–22). Basingstoke, UK: Palgrave Macmillan.
Dale, R. (2009). Renewing or rupturing the sociology of education? *British Journal of Sociology of Education, 30*(3), 379–387.
Daston, L., & Galison, P. (2010). *Objectivity*. New York: Zone Books.
Davis, S. (1995). Leaps of faith: Shifting currents in critical sociology of education. *The American Journal of Sociology*, 100(6), 1448–1478.
Deputy Secretary, Energy Safety Service. (2004). *New Zealand electrical code of practice for homeowner/occupier's electrical wiring work in domestic installations*. Wellington, New Zealand: Energy Safety Service.
Descartes, R. (1956). A discourse on method. In C. Brinton (Ed.), *The portable age of reason reader* (pp. 49–55). New York: Viking Press. (Originally published 1637)
Diderot, D. (1995). Encylopedie. In I. Kramnick (Ed.), *The portable enlightenment reader* (pp. 17–20). New York: Penguin Books. (Originally published 1759)
Durie, M. (1999). Mental health and Maori development. *Australian and New Zealand Journal of Psychiatry*, 33, 5–12.
Durie, M. (2003). *Nga kahui pou: Launching Maori futures*. Wellington, New Zealand: Huia.
Durie, M. (2009, 14 July). Pae mana: Waitangi and the evolving state. *The Paerangi Lectures, Maori Horizons 2020 and Beyond*. Massey University Te Mata O Te Tau Lecture Series 2009, Wellington, New Zealand.
Durie, M. (2011). Indigenizing mental health services: New Zealand experience. Transcultural Psychiatry, 48, 24–36.
Durkheim, E. (1956). *Education and sociology*. Toronto: Free Press.
Durkheim, E. (1983). *Pragmatism and sociology* (Trans. J. C. Whitehouse & J. B. Allcock, with an Introduction by F. Cuvillier). Cambridge, UK: Cambridge University Press.
Durkheim, E. (1995). *The elementary forms of religious life*. New York: Free Press.
Ecclestone, K. (2010). Promoting emotionally-vulnerable subjects: The educational implications of an 'epistemology of the emotions.' *Pacific-Asian Education*, 22(1), 57–76.
Education Counts. (2009a). Education report: Annual census of early childhood education services: July 2009. Wellington, New Zealand: Ministry of Education. Retrieved from http://www.educationcounts.govt.nz/__data/assets/pdf_file/0006/65868/ECE-July09-Licensed-and-Licence-exempt-report.pdf
Education Counts. (2009b). Maori medium education as at July 1 2009. School roll summary report. Wellington, New Zealand: Ministry of Education. Retrieved

from http://www.educationcounts.govt.nz/statistics/maori_education/schooling/6040/57547
Education Information and Analysis Group/Group Maori [Ministry of Education]. (2009, February). Chapter 4: Maori Language Education. *Nga Haeata Matauranga: The annual report on Maori education 2007/08*. Wellington, New Zealand: Ministry of Education. Retrieved January 13, 2010, from http://www.educationcounts.govt.nz/__data/assets/pdf_file/0020/35408/Nga_Haeata_Chap4.pdf
Eltringham, N. (2004). *Accounting for horror, post-genocide debates in Rwanda*. London: Pluto Press.
Evans-Pritchard, E. E. (1954) Introduction. In M. Mauss, *The Gift* (pp. v-x). London: Cohen & West Ltd. (Translated by Ian Cunnison)
Faulks, S. (2009). *A Week in December*. London: Hutchinson.
Fischer, C. S., Hout, M., Jankowski, M. S., Lucas, S. R., Swidler, A., & Voss, K. (1996). *Inequality by design*. Princeton, NJ: Princeton University Press.
Foucault, M. (2001). Power/knowledge. In S. Seidman & J. C. Alexander (Eds.), *The new social theory reader, contemporary debates* (pp. 69–75). London: Routledge.
Fraser, P. (1939). *Appendices to the Journal of the House of Representatives*, E–1, pp. 2–3. Wellington, New Zealand: Ministry for Culture and Heritage.
Freeman, C. (2003). *The closing of the Western mind*. New York: Alfred A. Knopf.
Friedman, J. (1994). *Cultural identity and global processes*. London: Sage.
Friedman, J. (2000). Globalisation, class and culture in global systems. *Journal of World Systems Research, 6*(3), 636–656.
Friedman, J. (2002). Champagne liberals and the new "dangerous classes": Reconfigurations of class, identity, and cultural production in the contemporary global system. *Social Analysis*, 46(2), 33–55.
Friedman, J. (2003). Globalization, dis-integration, re-organisation: The transformations of violence. In J. Friedman (Ed.), *Globalization, the state and violence* (pp. 18–34). Lanham, MD: Altamira Press.
Friedman, J. (2006). Preface. In E. Rata & R. Openshaw (Eds.), *Public policy and ethnicity: The politics of ethnic boundary making* (pp. xi–xxv). Houndmills, UK: Palgrave Macmillan.
Friedman, J. (2009). Occidentalism and the categories of hegemonic rule. *Theory, Culture and Society,* 26(7–8), 85–102.
Gill, D., Pride, S., Gilbert, H., & Norman, R. (2010). *The future state* (Working Paper No. 10/08). Victoria University of Wellington, New Zealand Institute of Policy Studies.
Giroux, H., & McLaren, P. L. (1989). *Critical pedagogy, the state and cultural struggle*. Albany: State University of New York Press.
Glavish, N. (2010, April 30). Policy and enlightened way forward for all New Zealanders. *New Zealand Herald*, p. A13.
Gough, P. B. (1995). The new literacy: Caveat emptor. Journal of Research in Reading, 18, 79–86.
Gouldner, A. (1979). *The future of intellectuals and the rise of the new class*. London: Macmillan.
Grace, G. (2010). Reflection on the university and the academic as "critic and conscience of society". *New Zealand Journal of Educational Studies,* 45(2), 89–92.
Grande, S. (2004). *Red pedagogy*. Lanham, MD: Rowman and Littlefield.
Grande, S. (2009). Red pedagogy: Indigenous theories of redistribution (a.k.a. sovereignty). In M. Apple, W. Au, & L. A. Gandin (Eds.), *The Routledge international handbook of critical education* (pp. 190–203). New York: Routledge.

Habermas, J. (2001). Contributions to a discourse theory of law and democracy. In S. Seidman & J. C. Alexander, *The new social theory reader, contemporary debates* (pp. 31–38). London: Routledge.
Harding, S. (1998). *Is science multicultural? Postcolonialisms, feminisms, and epistemologies*. Bloomington: Indiana University Press.
Hegel, G. W. F. (1967). *Philosophy of right* (T. M. Knox, Trans., p. 148, para. 239). Oxford, UK: Oxford University Press.
Herf, J. (1984). *Reactionary modernism, technology, culture, and politics in Weimar and the Third Reich*. Cambridge, UK: Cambridge University Press.
Hobsbawn, E., & Ranger, T. (Eds.). (1983). *The invention of tradition*. Cambridge, UK: Cambridge University Press.
Hook, R. (2006, September). *A future for Māori education*. Seminar to New Zealand Treasury, Victoria University of Wellington. Retrieved from http://www.treasury.govt.nz/publications/media-speeches/guestlectures/pdfs/tgls-hook.pdf
Howe, K. (2009). The politics of culture: A personal history of history in New Zealand. In R. Openshaw & E. Rata (Eds.), *The politics of conformity in New Zealand* (pp. 14–24). Auckland, New Zealand: Pearson.
Human Rights Commission. (2011). Treaty of Waitangi in review. *Tūi Tūi Tuituiā—Race Relations in 2010*. Auckland, New Zealand: Author. Retrieved from http://www.hrc.co.nz/wp-content/uploads/2011/02/RRR_Treaty_chapter_web.pdf
Irwin, R. (2008). *Heidegger, politics and climate change*. London: Continuum.
Irwin, R. (2010). Climate change and Heidegger's philosophy of science. *Essays in Philosophy,* 11(1), article 4.
Israel, J. (2001). *Radical enlightenment: Philosophy and the making of modernity 1650–1750*. Oxford, UK: Oxford University Press.
Jacoby, R. (1999). *The end of utopia, politics and culture in an age of apathy*. New York: Basic Books.
Jahnke, H., & Taiapa, J. (1999). Maori research. In C. Davidson & M. Tolich (Eds.), *Social science research in New Zealand, many paths to understanding* (pp. 39–50). Auckland: Longman.
Jones, A., & Jenkins, K. (2008). Rethinking collaboration: Working the indigene-colonizer. In N. K. Denzin, Y. S. Lincoln, & L. T. Smith (Eds.), *Handbook of critical and indigenous methodologies* (pp. 471–486). Los Angeles: Sage.
Ka'ai, T. (2005). Indigenising the academy: Indigenous scholars as agents of change. World Indigenous Peoples' Conference on Education, Hamilton, Aotearoa/New Zealand.
Kailo, K. (2008). *Sustainable cultures of life and gift circulation—A new model for the green/postcolonial restructuring of Europe? Sustainable cultures—Cultures of sustainability* (Background Paper 9). Coalition for Environment and Development, Ministry for the Foreign Affairs of Finland. Retrieved from www.gift-economy.com/backgroundpaper9.pdf
Kandall, I. L. (1970). Educational theory. In *The making of Nazis* (pp. 33–43). Westport, CT: Greenwood Press. (Originally published 1935)
Kant, I. (1990). *Foundations of the metaphysics of morals and what is enlightenment?* New York: Macmillan. (Originally published 1784)
Kant, I. (1993). *Critique of pure reason*. London: Everyman. (Originally published 1781)
Kellner, H., & Berger, P. L. (1992). Life-style engineering: Some theoretical reflections. In H. Kellner & F. W. Heuberger (Eds.), *Hidden technocrats: The new class and new capitalism* (pp. 1–22). London: Transaction.
Kincheloe, J. L. (2008). *Critical pedagogy* (2nd ed.). New York: Peter Lang.
Kolig, E. (2006). Freedom, identity construction and cultural closure: The taniwha, the hijab and the wiener schnitzel as boundary markers. In E. Rata & R.

Openshaw (Eds.), *Public policy and ethnicity: The politics of ethnic boundary making* (pp. 25–39). Houndmills, UK: Palgrave Macmillan.
Kovach, M. (2009). *Indigenous methodologies: Characteristics, conversations, and contexts*. Toronto: University of Toronto Press.
Kukutai, T. (2004). 'The problem of defining an ethnic group for public policy: Who is Maori and why does it matter?' *Social Policy Journal of New Zealand*, 23, 86–108.
Kuokkanen, R. (2007). *Reshaping the university: Responsibility, indigenous epistemes, and the logic of the gift*. Vancouver: UBC Press.
Kuper, A. (2001). *Culture: The anthropologists' account*. Cambridge, MA: Harvard University Press.
Kuper, A. (2005). *The reinvention of primitive society* (2nd ed.). London: Routledge.
Kymlicka, W. (2002). *Contemporary political philosophy: An introduction* (2nd ed.). Oxford, UK: Oxford University Press.
Lacan, J. (1977). *Ecrits: A selection* (A. Sheridan, Ed.). New York: Norton.
Lachmann, R. (2000). *Capitalists in spite of themselves: Elite conflict and economic transformations in early modern Europe*. New York: Oxford University Press.
Lakatos, I. (1980). *The methodology of scientific research programmes* (J. Worrall & G. Currie, Eds., Vol. 1). Cambridge, UK: Cambridge University Press. (Reprinted 1995)
Landes, D. (1998). *The wealth and poverty of nations*. London: Abacus.
Larson, E., & Zalanga, S. (2003). Indigenous capitalists: The development of indigenous investment companies in relations to class, ethnicity, and the state in Malaysia and Fiji. In D. E. Davis (Ed.), *Political power and social theory* (pp. 73–102). Oxford: Elsevier.
Lashley, M. E. (2000). Implementing treaty settlements via indigenous institutions: Social justice and detribalization in New Zealand. *The Contemporary Pacific*, 12(1), 1–53.
Lauder, H. (2010). Introduction: Educational policy and social inequalities in school achievement. In R. Nash, *Explaining inequalities in school achievement* (H. Lauder, Ed., pp. 1–6). Farnham, UK: Ashgate.
Li, T. (2010). Indigeneity, capitalism, and the management of dispossession, *Current Anthropology*, 51, 385–414.
Lindberg, D. C. (1992). *The beginnings of Western science*. Chicago: University of Chicago Press.
Lopez, J., & Potter, G. (2001). *After postmodernism: An introduction to critical realism*. London: Athlone.
Lovejoy, A. O., & Boas, G. (1935). *Primitivism and related ideas in antiquity*. Baltimore, MD: John Hopkins University Press.
Lukes, S. (2003). *Liberals and cannibals, the implications of diversity*. London: Verso Books.
Lyotard, J.-F. (1984). *The postmodern condition: A report on knowledge, theory and history of literature* (Vol. 10). Minneapolis: University of Minnesota Press.
Macfarlane, A. (2002). *The making of the modern world: Visions from the West and East*. Houndmills, UK: Palgrave.
Madjar, I., McKinley, E., Jensen, S., & Van der Merwe, A. (2009). *Towards university: Navigating NCEA course choices in low-mid decile schools*. Auckland, New Zealand: University of Auckland Starpath Project.
Main, S. (2009). Balanced development: A Maori model for beginning teacher support. *Asia Pacific Journal of Education*, 29(1), 101–117.
Maori Mental Health Model. (2010). Retrieved from http://www.maorihealth.govt.nz/moh.nsf/pagesma/445

Marie, D., & Haig, B. (2006). Kaupapa Maori research methodology: A critique and an alternative. *New Zealand Science Review*, 63(1), 17–21.

Marie, D., & Haig, B. (2009). The Maori renaissance and the politicisation of science in New Zealand. In R. Openshaw & E. Rata (Eds.), *The politics of conformity in New Zealand* (pp. 115–134). Auckland, New Zealand: Pearson.

Martin, L. (1986). "Eskimo words for snow": A case study in the genesis and decay of an anthropological example. *American Anthropologist, New Series*, 88(2), 418–423.

Marx, K. & Engels, F. (1844–45/1975). *The holy family or critique of critical criticism: Against Bruno Bauer and company, Karl Marx, Frederick Engels Collected Works, Volume 4* (chap. 6). London: Lawrence & Wishart.

Maton, K. (2010). Analysing knowledge claims and practices: Languages of legitimation. In K. Maton & R. Moore (Eds.), *Social realism, knowledge and the sociology of education* (pp. 35–59). London: Continuum.

Maton, K., & Moore, R. (Eds.). (2010). *Social realism, knowledge and the sociology of education, coalitions of the mind*. London: Continuum.

Matthews, M. R. (2000). *Time for science education*. New York: Kluwer Academic.

Mauss, M. (1954). The gift: forms and functions of exchange in archaic societies, trans. by Ian Cunnison. London: Cohen and West. (Originally published 1923).

McCulloch, G. (1989, December). *History, ideology and policy in New Zealand education*. Paper presented at the New Zealand Association for Research in Education Conference, Palmerston North, New Zealand.

McKenzie, D., Lee, H., & Lee, G. (1996). *Scholars or dollars? Selected historical case studies of opportunity costs in New Zealand education*. Palmerston North, New Zealand: Dunmore Press.

McLaren, P. L., & Jaramillo, N. (2007). *Pedagogy and praxis in the age of empire*. Rotterdam, Netherlands: Sense.

McPhail, G. (2011). *The canon or the kids: Teachers and the recontextualisation of classical and popular music in the secondary school curriculum*. Unpublished EdD thesis, University of Auckland, Auckland, New Zealand.

McPhail, G. (in press). From singular to over crowded region: Curriculum change in senior secondary school music in New Zealand. *British Journal of Music Education*.

Mill, J. S. (1985). *On liberty*. London: Penguin Books. (Originally published 1859)

Mill, J. S. (1999). *The subjugation of women* (J. Manis, Faculty Ed.). Retrieved from Pennsylvania State University's Electronic Classic Series Web site: http://www2.hn.psu.edu/faculty/jmanis/jsmill/sub_wom.pdf (Originally published 1869)

Mills, C. (1998). Alternative epistemologies. In L. M. Alcoff (Ed.), *Epistemology: The big questions* (pp. 392–410). Oxford, UK: Blackwell.

Ministry of Education. (2007). *The New Zealand curriculum*. Wellington, New Zealand: Learning Media Limited.

Ministry of Education. (2009). *The New Zealand curriculum guides*. Wellington, New Zealand: Learning Media Limited.

Ministry of Maori Development. (2001). *He Tirohanga ō Kawa ki te Tiriti o Waitangi: A Guide to the Principles of the Treaty of Waitangi as expressed by the Courts and the Waitangi Tribunal*. Wellington, New Zealand: Department of Justice.

Ministry of Research, Science and Technology. (2006). Vision Matauranga: Unlocking the potential of Maori people, knowledge and resources. [Brochure] Wellington, New Zealand. Retrieved from . http://www.morst.govt.nz/publications/a-z/v/vision-matauranga-brochure/

Moore, R. (2000). For knowledge: tradition, progressivism and progress in education—Reconstructing the curriculum debate. *Cambridge Journal of Education*, 30(1), 17–36.

Moore, R. (2007a). Going critical: The problem of problematizing knowledge in education studies. *Critical Studies in Education*, 48(1), 25–41.

Moore, R. (2007b). *Sociology of knowledge and education.* London: Continuum.

Moore, R. (2010). Knowledge structures and the canon: A preference for judgements. In K. Maton & R. Moore (Eds.), *Social realism, knowledge and the sociology of education* (pp. 131–153). London: Continuum.

Moore, R., Arnot, M., Beck, J., & Daniels, H. (Eds.). (2006). *Knowledge, power and educational reform: Applying the sociology of Basil Bernstein* (pp. 1–8). New York: Routledge.

Moore, R., & Maton, K. (2001). Founding the sociology of knowledge: Basil Bernstein, intellectual fields and the epistemic device. In A. Morais, I. Neves, B. Davies, & H. Daniels (Eds.), *Towards a sociology of pedagogy: The contribution of Basil Bernstein to research.* New York: Peter Lang.

Moore, R., & Muller, J. (1999). The discourse of "voice" and the problem of knowledge and identity in the sociology of education. *British Journal of Sociology of Education*, 20(2), 189–206.

Moore, R., & Muller, J. (2010). "Voice discourse" and the problem of knowledge and identity. In K. Maton & R. Moore (Eds.), *Social realism, knowledge and the sociology of education* (pp. 60–80). London: Continuum.

Moore, R., & Young, M. (2001). Knowledge and the curriculum in the sociology of education: Towards a reconceptualisation. *British Journal of Sociology of Education*, 22(4), 445–461.

Moore, R., & Young, M. (2010). Reconceptualising knowledge and the curriculum in the sociology of education. In K. Maton & R. Moore (Eds.), *Social realism, knowledge and the sociology of education* (pp. 14–34). London: Continuum.

Morehu, T., Lolesio, V., Piper, D., & Pomare, S. (2009). Benefits of a Maori immersion programme at tertiary level. *MAI Review*, 1, 1–7.

Muller, J. (2000). *Reclaiming knowledge: Social theory, curriculum and education policy.* London: Routledge.

Muller, J. (2001). Progressivism redux: Ethos, policy, pathos. In A. Kraak & M. Young (Eds.), *Education in retrospect: Policy and implementation since 1990* (pp. 59–71). Pretoria, South Africa: Human Sciences Research Council/ Institute of Education, University of London.

Muller, J. (2009). Southern theory: The global dynamics of knowledge in social science. *Globalisation, Societies and Education*, 7(4), 505–509.

Munz, P. (1985). *Our knowledge of the growth of knowledge: Popper or Wittgenstein?* London: Routledge and Kegan Paul.

Munz, P. (1991). How the West was won, miracle or natural event? *Philosophy of the Social Sciences*, 21(2), 253–276.

Munz, P. (1992). What's postmodern anyway? *Philosophy and Literature*, 16, 333–353.

Munz, P. (1994). The two worlds of Anne Salmond in postmodern fancy-dress. *The New Zealand Journal of History*, 28(1), 60–75.

Munz, P. (1999). Open and closed research. In *New Zealand Books*, 9(5), 4–6.

Munz, P. (2000, November 13–16). Te Papa and the problem of historical truth. *History Now*, 6(1).

Murray, S. (2005). *Achievement at Maori immersion and bilingual schools 2004.* Wellington, New Zealand: Ministry of Education.

Murray, S. (2007). Achievement at Maori immersion and bilingual schools 2004 update for 2005 results. Wellington, New Zealand: Ministry of Education.

Nanda, M. (2003). *Prophets facing backwards: Postmodern critiques of science and Hindu nationalism in India*. New Brunswick, NJ: Rutgers.

Nash, R. (1983). *Schools can't make jobs*. Palmerston North, New Zealand: Dunmore Press.

Nash, R. (2001a). Cultural capital and competent children. *The first years: The New Zealand journal of infant and toddler education*, 3(1), 13–16.

Nash, R. (2001b). Class, "Ability", and attainment: A problem for the sociology of education. *British Journal of sociology of Education*, 22(2), 189–202.

Nash, R. (2001c). Models of Maori educational attainment: Beyond the "class" and "Ethnicity" debate. *Waikato Journal of Education*, 7, 23–36.

Nash, R. (2003). Social class and education in New Zealand. In J. Freeman-Moir & A. Scott (Eds.), *Yesterday's dreams: International and critical perspectives on education and social class* (pp. 60–85). Christchurch, New Zealand: Canterbury University Press in association with Christchurch College of Education.

National Ethics Advisory Committee. (2006). Ethical Guidelines for observational studies: observational research, audits and related activities. Wellington: Ministry of Health.

New Zealand Centre for Political Research. (2011). http://www.nzcpr.com

Nola, R. (1997). Constructivism in science and science education: A philosophical critique. *Science and Education*, 6, 55–83.

Nola, R. (2001). Review of Michael Matthews, time for science education, *Educational Philosophy and Theory*, 33(3&4), 427–430.

Oates, T. (2011). Could do better: Using international comparisons to refine the National Curriculum in England. *Curriculum Journal*, 22(2), 121–150.

Oliver, W. H. 2001. The Future Behind Us. In. Sharp, Andrew. and McHugh, Paul. (Eds). *Histories, Power and Loss.* (pp. 9—31). Wellington: Bridget Williams Books.

Openshaw, R. (2006). Putting ethnicity into policy: A New Zealand case study. In E. Rata & R. Openshaw (Eds.), *Public policy and ethnicity: The politics of ethnic boundary making* (pp. 113–127). Houndmills, UK: Palgrave Macmillan.

Openshaw, R. (2009a). *Reforming New Zealand secondary education*. New York: Palgrave Macmillan.

Openshaw, R. (2009b). Solution or problem? Te kotahitanga as cultural politics. In R. Openshaw & E. Rata (Eds.), *The politics of conformity in New Zealand* (pp. 135–153). Auckland, New Zealand: Pearson.

Openshaw, R., & Rata, E. (2007). The weight of inquiry: Conflicting cultures in New Zealand's tertiary institutions. *Journal of International Studies in Sociology of Education*, 17(4), 407–425.

Openshaw, R., & Rata, E. (2008). Flax rope or iron fetter: How cultural essentialism threatens intellectual freedom in the New Zealand tertiary education sector. *New Zealand Journal of Tertiary Education Policy*, 3(1). Retrieved from http://teu.ac.nz/2008/12/the-new-zealand-journal-of-tertiary-education-policy/

Parkin, F. (1968). *Middle class radicalism*. Manchester: Manchester University Press.

Perry, O., & Webster, A. (1999). *New Zealand politics at the turn of the millennium*. Auckland, New Zealand: Alpha.

Poata-Smith, E. (1996). He pokeke uenuku i tu ai: The evolution of contemporary Maori protest. In P. Spoonley, C. Macpherson, & D. Pearson (Eds.), *Nga Patai: Racism and ethnic relations in Aotearoa/New Zealand*. Auckland, New Zealand: Dunmore Press.

Politis, V. (Ed.). (1993). Introduction. In I. Kant, *Critique of pure reason* (pp. xxvii–lii). London: Everyman.

Popkewitz, T. S. (2001). Dewey and Vygotsky, ideas in historical spaces. In T. S. Popkewitz, B. M. Franklin, & M. A. Pereyra (Eds.), *Cultural history and education: Critical essays on knowledge and schooling*. New York: RoutledgeFalmer.

Popper, K. (1972). *The logic of scientific discovery.* London: Hutchinson.
Popper, K. (2003). *The open society and its enemies, vol 2: Hegel and Marx.* London: Routledge. (Originally published 1945)
Powick, K. (2002). Maori research ethics. Wilf Malcolm Institute of Educational Research, School of Education, University of Waikato.
Priestley, J. (1995). The organization of scientific research. In I. Kramnick (Ed.), *The portable enlightenment* (pp. 69–73). New York: Penguin Books. (Originally published 1769)
Ramirez, F. O., & Boli, J. (2007). The political construction of mass schooling: European origins and worldwide institutionalization. In A. R. Sadovnik (Ed.), *Sociology of education, a critical reader* (pp. 199–217). London: Routledge.
Rata, E. (1996). 'Goodness and power': The sociology of liberal guilt. *New Zealand Sociology,* 11(2), 231–274.
Rata, E. (2000). *A political economy of neotribal capitalism.* Lanham, MD: Lexington Books.
Rata, E. (2003a). Leadership ideology in neotribal capitalism. *Political Power and Social Theory,* 16, 45–73.
Rata, E. (2003b). An overview of neotribal capitalism. *Ethnologies Comparéés,* 6. Oceanie. Retrieved from http://alor.univ-montp3.fr/cerce/r6/e.r.htm
Rata, E. (2010a). Localising neoliberalism: Indigenist brokerage in the New Zealand university. *Globalisation, Societies and Education,* 8(4), 527–542.
Rata, E. (2010b). A sociology "of" or a Sociology "for" Education? The New Zealand experience of the dilemma. *Journal of International Studies in Sociology of Education,* 20(2), 109–128.
Rata, E. (2011a). Discursive strategies of the Maori tribal elite. *Critique of Anthropology,* 31(4), 359–380.
Rata, E. (2011b). Encircling the commons: Neotribal capitalism in New Zealand since 2000. *Anthropological Theory,* 11(3), 327–353.
Rata, E. (2011c). *Researching academic agency in the cultural production of indigenous ideology in New Zealand universities* (Working Papers on University Reform No. 17). Education, Policy and Organisation in the Knowledge Economy programme, Aarhus University, Copenhagen, Denmark. Retrieved from http://www.dpu.dk/forskning/forskningsprogrammer/epoke/
Rata, E. (2011d). Theoretical claims and empirical evidence in Maori education discourse. *Educational Philosophy and Theory.* doi: 10.1111/j.1469–5812-.2011.00755.x Published online 25 May.
Rata, E. (2012). The politics of knowledge in education. *British Educational Research Journal,* 38,1, 103–124.
Renwick, W. L. (1986). *Moving targets: Six essays on educational policy.* Wellington: New Zealand Council for Educational Research.
Richards, R. (2002, Summer). Mormonism and academic freedom. *New Zealand Skeptic,* 62, 3–7.
Roberts, M. R., & Wills, P. R. (1998). Understanding Maori epistemology: A scientific perspective. In H. Wautischer (Ed.), *Tribal epistemologies, essays in the philosophy of anthropology* (pp. 43–79). Aldershot, UK: Ashgate.
Robertson, R. (1992). *Globalization: Social theory and global culture.* London: Sage.
Round, D. (2011). Two futures: A reverie on constitutional reform. *Otago Law Review,* 12(3), 525–556.
Salmond, A. (1982). Theoretical landscapes, on cross-cultural conceptions of knowledge. In D. Parkin (Ed.), *Semantic anthropology* (pp. 65–87). London: Academic Press.
Salmond, A. (1985). Māori epistemologies. In J. Overing (Ed.), *Reason and morality* (pp. 240–263). London: Tavistock.

Salmond, A. (1991). *Two worlds: First meetings between Māori and Europeans 1642–1772*. Auckland, New Zealand: Viking.

Sandall, R. (1999). *Culture cults: Designer tribalism and other essays*. Boulder, CO: Westview Press.

Sayer, D. (1991). *Capitalism and modernity: An excursus on Marx and Weber*. London: Routledge.

Schroder, I. W. (2003). The political economy of tribalism in North America: neotribal capitalism? *Anthropological Theory*, 3(4), 435–455.

Semali, L. M., & Kincheloe, J. L. (Eds.). (1999). Introduction. In *What is indigenous knowledge? Voices from the academy* (pp. 5–57). New York: Falmer Press.

Shalem, Y., & Bensusan, D. (1999). Why we can't stop believing. In S. Appel (Ed.), *Psychoanalysis and pedagogy* (pp. 27–44). Westport, CT: Bergin & Garvey.

Sharp, A. (2002). Blood, custom and consent: Three kinds of Maori groups in New Zealand and the challenges they present to the governments and the constitution. *University of Toronto Law Journal*, 52, 9–37.

Shapin, S. (1994). *A social history of truth: Civility and science in seventeenth century England*. Chicago: University of Chicago Press.

Shuker, R. (1987). *The one best system? A revisionist history of state schooling in New Zealand*. Palmerston North, New Zealand: Dunmore Press.

Simon, J., & Massey, L. (1994). Historical perspectives on education in New Zealand. In E. Coxon, K. Jenkins, J. Marshall, & L. Massey (Eds.), *The politics of learning and teaching in Aotearoa New Zealand* (pp. 34–81). Palmerston North, New Zealand: Dunmore Press.

Smith, G. H. (1997). *The development of kaupapa Maori: Theory and praxis*. Unpublished doctoral thesis, School of Education, University of Auckland, Auckland, New Zealand.

Smith, G. H. (2000). Protecting and respecting indigenous knowledge. In M. Battiste (Ed.), *Reclaiming indigenous voices and vision* (pp. 209–224). Vancouver: University of British Columbia Press.

Smith, G. H. (2003, January). *Kaupapa Maori theory: Transformative praxis and new formations of colonisation from Cultural sites, Cultural theory, Cultural policy*. Paper presented at the Second International Conference on Cultural Policy Research Te Papa Museum, Wellington, New Zealand.

Smith, L. T. (1994). Kaupapa Maori research. Unpublished paper, University of Auckland.

Smith, L. T. (1999). *Decolonizing methodologies: Research and indigenous peoples*. Dunedin, New Zealand: University of Otago Press.

Smith, L. T. (2005). On tricky grounds. In N. Denzin & Y. Lincoln (Eds.), *Handbook of qualitative research* (pp. 85–108). Beverly Hills, CA: Sage.

Snook, I., & O'Neill, J. (2010). Social class and educational achievement: Beyond ideology. *New Zealand Journal of Educational Studies*, 45(2), 3–18.

Statistics New Zealand. (2005). Statistical standard for ethnicity 2005. Wellington, New Zealand: Author. Retrieved from http://www.stats.govt.nz

Statistics New Zealand. (2011). Review of the measurement of ethnicity, a question of ethnicity', executive summary. Wellington, New Zealand: Author. Retrieved from http://www.stats.govt.nz/browse_for_stats/population/census_counts/review-measurement-of-ethnicity/a-question-of-ethnicity.aspx

Steur, L. (2005). On the correct handling of contradictions: Liberal-culturalism in indigenous studies. *European Journal of Anthropology*, 46, 169–176.

Sutton, P. (2009). *The politics of suffering: Indigenous Australia and the end of the liberal consensus*. Melbourne, Australia: Melbourne University Press.

Sykes, A. (2010, October). The politics of the brown table. *Bruce Jesson Lecture*. University of Auckland, Auckland, New Zealand.

Takao, N., Grennell, D., McKegg, K., & Wehipeihana, N. (2010). *Te piko o te mahuri: The key attributes of successful kura kaupapa Maori*. Wellington, New Zealand: Ministry of Education.

Tau, T. M., Ormsby, D., Manthei, M., & Potiki, T. (2003). *Tertiary-based guidelines and protocols for tertiary education institutions*. Christchurch, New Zealand: Te Tapuae o Rehua, in association with University of Otago Press.

The Dominion, 14 July 1937.

Tobin, K. (Ed.). (1993). *The practice of constructivsm in science education*. Washington, DC: AAA Press.

Tremewan, C. (2005a). Ideological conformity: A fundamental challenge to the social sciences in New Zealand. *Sites*, 2(1), 1–27.

Tremewan, C. (2005b). It's time to answer the important questions—A response to Sissons and Ryan. *Sites*, 2(1), 34–38.

Tremewan, C. (2006). Repoliticising race: The Anglican church in New Zealand. In E. Rata & R. Openshaw (Eds.), *Public policy and ethnicity: The politics of ethnic boundary making* (pp. 95–112). London: Palgrave Macmillan.

Tunmer, W. E., & Prochnow, J. E. (2009). Cultural relativism and literacy education. In R. Openshaw E. Rata (Eds.), *The politics of conformity in New Zealand* (pp. 154–190). Auckland, New Zealand: Pearson.

Turner, T. (2003). Class projects, social consciousness, and the contradictions of "globalization". In J. Friedman (Ed.), *Globalization, the state and violence* (pp. 35–66). Lanham, MD: Altamira Press.

Turton, D. (Ed). (1997). *War and ethnicity, global connections and local violence*. Rochester, NY: University of Rochester Press, Center for Interdisciplinary Research on Social Stress.

United Nations Educational, Scientific and Cultural Organization. (2010). Education for All global monitoring report: Reaching the marginalized. Retrieved from http://www.unesco.org/new/en/education/themes/leading-the-international-agenda/efareport/reports/2010-marginalization/

University of Auckland News, April 1, 2011, p. 8. http://www.auckland.ac.nz/uoa/tm-issue-archive

Voltaire, F. (1994). *Letters concerning the English nation*. New York: Oxford University. (Originally published 1637)

Wai 11. (1988). *Report of the Waitangi Tribunal on the Te Reo Maori Claim. Waitangi Tribunal*. Section 3.5.2. Wellington, New Zealand: Ministry of Justice, New Zealand. http://www.waitangi-tribunal.govt.nz/publications/published_reports.asp

Wai 143. (1996). *The Taranaki Report*. Waitangi Tribunal. Section 12.2. Wellington, New Zealand: Ministry of Justice, New Zealand. http://www.waitangi-tribunal.govt.nz/publications/published_reports.asp

Walker, R. J. (1982, July 24). Capitalism v tangata whenua. *New Zealand Listener*, 16.

Walker, S. (1996) Kia tau te rangimarie kaupapa Māori theory as a resistance against the construction of Māori as the other, Unpublished MA in Education thesis, University of Auckland.

Webster, S. (1998). *Patrons of Maori culture*. Dunedin, New Zealand: University of Otago Press.

Weis, L., Fine, M., & Dimitriadis, G. (2009). Toward a critical theory of method in shifting times. In M. Apple, W. Au, & L. A. Gandin (Eds.), *The Routledge international handbook of critical education*. New York: Routledge.

Wheelahan, L. (2010a). Competency-based training, powerful knowledge and the working class. In K. Maton & R. Moore (Eds.), *Social realism, knowledge and the sociology of education, coalitions of the mind* (pp. 93–109). New York: Continuum.

Wheelahan, L. (2010b). *Why knowledge matters in the curriculum*. London: Routledge.
Wheen, F. (2004). *How mumbo jumbo conquered the world: A short history of modern delusions*. London: Harper Perennial.
Widdowson, F., & Howard, A. (2008). *Disrobing the Aboriginal industry*. Montreal: McGill-Queen's University Press.
Winiata, W. (1998, December 8). *Reducing the socio-economic disparities in housing, employment, health and education*. Retrieved from Traditional Weather Modification Web site: http://twm.co.nz/MSoln_Win.html
Wyeth, E. H., Derrett, S., Hokowhitu, B., Hall, C., & Langley, J. (2010). Rangatiratanga and Oritetanga: responses to the Treaty of Waitangi in a New Zealand study. *Ethn Health, 15*(3), 303–316.
Young, M. F. D. (1971). *Knowledge and control*. London: Collier MacMillan.
Young, M. F. D. (1998). *The curriculum of the future*. London: Falmer Press.
Young, M. F. D. (2008). *Bringing knowledge back in: From social constructivism to social realism in the sociology of education*. London: Routledge.
Young, M. F. D. (2010a). The future of education in a knowledge society: The radical case for a subject-based curriculum. *Pacific-Asian Education*, 22(1), 21–32. Retrieved from http://pacificcircleconsortium.org/PAEJournal.html
Young, M. F. D. (2010b). Why educators must differentiate knowledge from experience. *Pacific-Asian Education*, 22(1), 9–20. Retrieved from http://pacificcircleconsortium.org/PAEJournal.html
Young, M. F. D. (2011). The return to subjects: A sociological perspective on the UK Coalition Government's approach to the 14–19 curriculum. *The Curriculum Journal*, 22(2), 265–278.
Young, M. F. D., & Muller, J. (2010). Three scenarios for the future: Lessons from the sociology of knowledge. *European Journal of Education*, 42(1), 11–17.

Index

An environmentally friendly book printed and bound in England by www.printondemand-worldwide.com

PEFC Certified
This product is from sustainably managed forests and controlled sources
www.pefc.org
PEFC
PEFC/16-33-415

FSC
www.fsc.org
MIX
Paper from responsible sources
FSC® C004959

This book is made entirely of sustainable materials; FSC paper for the cover and PEFC paper for the text pages.

#0198 - 240615 - C0 - 229/152/10 - PB - 9780415851411